More Praise for This Book

"*Find Your Fit* has distilled some of the best career advice from expert coaches to help you land your desired job. Read this book if you want to successfully navigate the new employment landscape with confidence."

—Dan Schawbel
New York Times Bestselling Author, *Promote Yourself* and *Me 2.0*

"In the 21st century, we are *all* in career transition, all the time. That's why it's a good idea to have a guide by your side to help you demystify the process of starting, changing, or re-imagining a career and finding that perfect fit. This book is it! I predict it will serve you well, again and again, along your career journey, no matter how long you've been traversing it."

—Halelly Azulay
Author, *Employee Development on a Shoestring*
Host, The TalentGrow Show leadership podcast

"I only wish I had *Find Your Fit* when I was 35 and faced with my first big career transition. I am wowed by the thorough know-how and skill building that is easy to use. I would recommend this to anyone at any stage of their career."

—Elad Levinson
Organizational Change Master and Coach
Author, *Thriving on Change*

"Some people go, rather than grow, through their career. On Mondays, others say they can't wait until the weekend. Can you imagine working five days to live just two? *Find Your Fit* will help you avoid this conundrum. It's a coach, a career GPS, and a self-assessing tool all wrapped up into one!"

—Jim Smith Jr.
Author, Speaker, Trainer, and Coach
President and CEO, Jim Smith Jr. International

"Sharing the combined wisdom of 16 well-respected career coaches and counselors, this unique book is a treasure trove of valuable information on all things career-related. *Find Your Fit* is a great resource and lifelong guide for both job seekers and career professionals."

—Wendy S. Enelow
Executive Resume and Career Consultant
Author, *Modernize Your Resume*

"*Find Your Fit* is a must read for careerists looking for a road map to their next great job. It's the perfect blend of advice from a group of smart career coaches; you'll end up not just knowing what to do, but knowing how to do it."

—Candace Moody
Vice President, Marketing and Communications, CareerSource Northeast Florida

"A valuable new resource that will help you maximize career satisfaction and success."

—Michael Lee Stallard
Author, *Connection Culture* and *Fired Up or Burned Out*

"There is a great deal of evidence linking career satisfaction and fulfillment with health. If these areas are important to you, no matter where you are in that journey, *Find Your Fit* belongs on your shelf."

—Beverly Kaye
Founder, Career Systems International
Co-Author, *Love It Don't Leave It* and *Help Them Grow or Watch Them Go*

FIND YOUR FIT

→ A Practical Guide to ←
....
Landing a Job You'll Love
....

Sue Kaiden, Editor

Foreword by Dick Bolles

atd
PRESS

To all the volunteers at Joseph's People who continue to serve the unemployed and underemployed in the Philadelphia region with such compassion and grace, and all the members of Joseph's People whom I had the privilege to work with over the years. In particular, to Cheryl Spaulding, my steering committee (you know who you are), and the memory of my friend Phil DeMarra, who taught me what it means to never give up.

Editor's Note: The names of some of the people portrayed in this book have been changed. We cannot guarantee the accuracy of URLs for external or third-party Internet websites referred to in this publication or that any content on such websites is, or will remain, accurate or appropriate.

ATD Press is an internationally renowned source of insightful and practical information on talent development, workplace learning, and professional development.

ATD Press
1640 King Street
Alexandria, VA 22314 USA

Ordering information: Books published by ATD Press can be purchased by visiting ATD's website at www.td.org/books or by calling 800.628.2783 or 703.683.8100.

Library of Congress Control Number: 2016952582

ISBN-10: 1-56286-946-9
ISBN-13: 978-1-56286-946-5
e-ISBN: 978-1-56286-573-3

ATD Press Editorial Staff
Director: Kristine Luecker
Manager: Christian Green
Community of Practice Manager, Career Development: Sue Kaiden
Developmental Editor: Kathryn Stafford
Senior Associate Editor: Melissa Jones
Text Design: Iris Sanchez
Cover Design: Jeff Miller, Faceout Studio
Printed by United Book Press, Baltimore, MD

Contents

Foreword

What should a career coach do for you? Well, according to *The Bolles Dictionary*—a mythical book if ever there was one—a career coach is one who helps people with three basic questions: what, where, and how. That is, what do I *want* to do with my life, *where* do I want to do it, and *how* do I find such work?

And if you want help figuring out these questions on a higher level—what skills would I most *love* to use, where would I most *love* to use those skills, and how do I identify such *a dream job* and actually get hired to do it—a career coach can help you with that too.

What makes talking to a career coach a better choice than, say, simply turning to your partner or best friend for help when you are trying to solve these questions? Well, career coaches have three resources that your best friend most likely doesn't have:

- *information* about careers, the labor market, "hot jobs," and the like
- *knowledge,* such as a mastery of the job-hunting or career-changing field
- *wisdom,* gained from experience, about what to avoid, steps to take, and shortcuts that have worked for previous clients.

The use of a career coach was once optional—you could seek out one if you liked that sort of thing. But the need for one is becoming more and more essential to the art of living a productive and useful life. Why? For one simple reason: You are going to live longer than you think. A longer life means you will be working longer in a world that is changing. This will affect a lot of the decisions you will need to make.

This, of course, has been true since the dawn of history. But what is different now is the rapidness of that change. The world is beginning to reimagine itself year after year. The workplace is reimagining itself. Jobs are reimagining themselves. And this is all happening at an unprecedented speed, as Moore's Law has observed and projected with its numerous revisions and updates.

You will need a career coach's help to master a new vocabulary that includes *connections, disconnections, man and machine,* and *the endless dance.*

Connections. Things that never used to be connected are increasingly reimagined as connected, because of such technology as Wi-Fi, the Internet, centralized computer systems or hubs, digital electronics, mobile computers, smartphones, artificial intelligence, integrated circuits, and sensors. Can the world connect cars on the road so they can communicate and exchange information with one another? Yes. Can the world connect our devices—our lights, security systems, fitness trackers, appliances—so they all communicate with one another? Yes. Can we connect robots so that they communicate with other robots, either directly or through a central hub? Yes, we can. Amazon already does—try typing "Amazon and robots" into YouTube.

You are going to have to make your decisions about what, where, and how in a world dominated by *The Internet of Things*—a term first coined in 1999 by Kevin Ashton—where all things, including every physical object, are connected, intelligent, programmable, and capable of interacting with humans. Experts predict that by 2020 between 34 billion and 50 billion devices will be connected. That's only four years away.

Disconnections. Things that seemed always connected until now—at least in our imaginations—are starting to disconnect from one another. In this grand reimagining of the world, the idea of work may no longer be restricted to "a job." The idea of income may no longer be "a salary." And parts of the world will be reimagining money as disconnected from work. Think of UBI—a universal basic income—which involves an unconditional stipend to all people, regardless of whether they work or not. It already is being discussed in Ireland, Germany, Greece, Finland, Switzerland, Namibia, Brazil, Argentina, Canada, and the United States. Its most prominent U.S. advocate is Robert Reich, former secretary of labor. You'll need a career coach who is more in tune with the current state of the work world than you are.

Man and machine. As the world reimagines itself, many believe that in the not-too-distant future, robots are going to take over all our work and our jobs are going to be eliminated by technology. But when you press the experts—as I have—on what percentage of jobs they think will be completely replaced by technology, they predict that only 5 percent, or at worst 19 percent, of current U.S. jobs will be replaced by robotics, technology, or computer programs. That said, while this new technology may not eliminate jobs, it will tackle certain tasks within jobs. This means that most jobs are going to involve a new kind of partnership.

MIT scientists call this partnership "human-machine symbiosis." I prefer to call it a partnership between man and machine—a partnership between humans and our inventions. Every job will have to answer the question, "How much machine? How much man?"

The endless dance. It will be an endless dance between connected objects, sensors, computers, data capture, and redesigned user outcomes. A dance that also includes the turbulence that is created when our jobs, our workplace, and our world are all being reimagined.

There are four things you are going to need that a career coach can help you with now:

- An inventory of yourself. If you were hiking in the wilderness and found a strong running stream suddenly swirling around your feet, your first instinct would be to find something solid to stand on. In similar fashion, taking an inventory of yourself gives you that "something solid to stand on" in the midst of all the change that is swirling around you. Knowing who you are, what you like and do best, what kindles your brain, and what enables you to do your best work has never been more important than in the reimagined workplace.

- A lesser fear of machines. You will need help to start thinking of machines as your friend with certain skills that supplement yours, not as an enemy that's come to steal your job.
- Shadowing. If you did a self-inventory, you may now think you know which field you would like to pursue, or a job you would like to do. If so, get permission to "shadow" a worker for a day or two to see what that job or field actually involves. How much man? How much machine?
- Familiarity with robots and sensors. Become familiar with how robots and sensors are designed, manufactured, operated, maintained, and repaired. Maybe you will discover something that you really like to do; if so, figure out how to train for it.

All of this is assuming that the career coach you will increasingly need is a flesh-and-blood person—someone who is able to learn, grow, and keep up with the times. In the meantime, you have a book. This book. *Find Your Fit: A Practical Guide to Landing a Job You'll Love* will bring you up to speed on what you need to know *now*.

The reimagined world will be built on the foundation of the world as it is today. This book will help you master this world. Read it, ponder it, master it. The life you save will be your own.

Dick Bolles
Author, *What Color Is Your Parachute? 2017: A Practical Guide for Job-Hunters and Career Changers*

Preface

In my capacity as a career coach and a volunteer for a large job search group in the Philadelphia area, I often found myself recommending books to job seekers and career changers. Because I wasn't comfortable recommending a book I hadn't read, over the years I read *a lot* of career books. Some were good, but many were clearly self-serving attempts to get the reader to hire the author to help implement the guidance in the book. As a result, I often turned to a handful of classics, including Dick Bolles's *What Color Is Your Parachute?*, for my book recommendations.

Still, I longed for a book that gave solid advice on finding a job that truly fit the job seeker. One that answered common questions I encountered as a career coach and provided step-by-step instructions for how to implement the suggestions. In 2014, when I accepted my current role with the Association for Talent Development (ATD), I learned that ATD was thinking about publishing just such a book! ATD had in mind a book that would complement the career coaching provided to ATD members at their annual conference and be relevant across all occupations.

We gathered 16 career coaches and job search experts and asked them to provide their best advice on a topic in which they had expertise. We asked them to include:
- carefully screened advice on the most common issues encountered by job seekers and career changers
- practical, step-by-step instructions
- free and low-cost resources for readers to turn to for further information.

Find Your Fit is the culmination of the efforts of those 16 coaches to provide detailed advice on how to find a job you'll love.

What Is This Book About?

According to *The Career Counselor's Handbook*, by Howard Figler and Dick Bolles, you need to answer three questions when looking for a job or seeking to make a career change:
- What do you want to do?
- What are you doing about it?
- What is stopping you from doing it?

Find Your Fit is organized into sections that will help you to answer those three questions. In Part I, you'll create a self-inventory to help tackle the question, "What do you want to do?" We cover how to identify your personality traits, interests, and skills, and how they relate to job satisfaction. Then, we discuss how to identify a workplace environment that suits you best. Finally, we help you create a career goal and plan to find such a job.

In Part II, we cover the mechanics of job searching in the 21st century. That includes basics such as resumes, interviewing, and applying online, as well as personal branding, networking, and salary negotiation.

In Part III, we cover some of the challenges that may be keeping you from realizing your goal. It begins by helping you gauge your job satisfaction and the types of problems you may be having in your current situation. We then cover how to gain experience and move up, as well as how to decide if you need new training or a credential. We also explore the world of self-employment and even include a chapter on how to look for work overseas.

How to Use This Book

Find Your Fit was written so you can read it from cover to cover or focus on the individual topics that are most important to you. The chapters also include cross-references to beneficial material in other chapters, in case you're not reading the book in order.

If you are in transition or want to make a change, I would advise you to start with Part I to make sure you are clear about what you want to do. One of the most common mistakes made by job seekers is that they don't know what type of job they're looking for—that's akin to going on a vacation without a destination in mind! So, before you jump straight to the chapter on resumes, complete the exercises in Part I to be sure you know where you're going before setting out on your journey.

If you have a job now and are not sure if it is a good fit, I suggest starting with chapter 12, "Should I Stay or Go?" It contains a quiz that helps you to diagnose the problems you are having, and directs you to the chapters that will be most relevant to the changes you might need to make.

Who Should Read This Book?

This book is written for working professionals looking to improve their job and career satisfaction. It is not only for people who are "in transition," but also for those who are looking to advance their careers, make a career change, or find a job that is a better fit than their current situation. Our hope is that you'll use the tools and methods in *Find Your Fit* to help you increase your happiness at work and grow your career in the direction you want it to go.

Is It Realistic to Find a Job That Fits?

If you're ready to identify a job and a company that is a good fit for you, and develop a plan for how to land such a job, go to chapter 1 and get started! However, if you're skeptical about this being a realistic goal, stay with me for a moment. Based on the experience and knowledge of the 16 career coaches featured in this book, it is both realistic and imperative that you take this approach. Employees who are a good fit for their jobs and the company culture are much more likely to succeed and thrive. Staying in a situation that is a poor fit makes you not only unhappy, but also less likely to succeed. So why not try to improve your chances for success and happiness?

Summary

The advice provided in this book will not go out of style. While technology has changed the nature of the job search in many ways, it hasn't changed the fact that *people hire people*. So, while a machine may screen your resume, always remember that there are still people on the other side who want to find the right person for the job. This book will help you ferret out those companies and people who are a great match, and present yourself as a "prescreened" candidate who is an ideal choice for both the job and the company. Find them—I assure you that they will be happy to hear from you.

Acknowledgments

My deepest appreciation to all 16 authors for their hard work and dedication to making this book a reality and to Dick Bolles for being gracious enough to write the foreword. Many thanks to our gifted editors Kathryn Stafford and Melissa Jones, who worked painstakingly to bring this book to fruition. Thank you also to Jennifer Homer, who had the idea for this book, and all the career coaches who have helped us over the years and provided some of the examples contained in this book. Finally, my heartfelt thanks to my husband, Tom, and children, Andy and Claire, for supporting my efforts over the past year to make this book a reality.

Sue Kaiden
Career Development Community of Practice Manager, ATD

Part I
Self-Assessment

The first part of *Find Your Fit* will help you identify your interests, skills, personality, and values that you can use to define your job and workplace preferences. You will also begin developing a career plan to guide your next steps.

Identifying Your Personality Type and Interests

Lakeisha Mathews

One of the best strategies for ensuring career success is being true to yourself by making career decisions that result in professional and personal satisfaction. While many professionals look to mentors, labor market trends, or family to determine their best-fit career path, others have uncovered the secret weapon to career success—increasing their self-awareness by discovering their own personality and interests. Possessing a healthy sense of self-awareness equips professionals with an internal compass that helps inform career decisions, define personal branding, and empower performance on the job. This chapter will get you started on the journey of understanding your personality and interests and how they relate to your career choices and job satisfaction.

Defining Personality and Interests

Assessing personality and interests for vocational purposes can be traced back to the late 1800s as the career development profession began to emerge (Hoyt 2005). Since then a variety of assessments have been developed to help with everything from coaching professionals for high performance and identifying academic majors, to matching individuals to occupations, assessing candidates for cultural fit with a company, and helping people clarify their personality preferences. Although each assessment has a different theoretical framework or approach, the basic premise of learning more about oneself to help support career decision making and management stands true. Getting to know yourself by assessing your personality and interests is priceless and will have a lasting impact on your career.

In this chapter, personality refers to *how you go about doing things and how you act*, while interests refer to *what you like to do*. Understanding why you act the way you do and what you enjoy doing can provide greater insights into the career fields, industries, and companies that will be the best fit for you. Moreover, understanding your personality and interests can help prevent you from making poor career decisions that place you in workplace cultures that do not allow you to thrive.

It is also important to note that personality and interest types do not operate in a vacuum and are affected by external forces and influences. Life experiences, personal goals, and environmental factors all influence who you are, how you behave, and what you want to be. You should reflect upon your personality and interests regularly throughout your career, because as you grow and develop personally and professionally, their influences on your career decisions will change. This is why a career that brought you great satisfaction in your 30s may become a burden and lack fulfillment in your 40s.

As life events occur—such as marriage, children, or the death of a loved one—you may feel the need to find a new job or change careers. Having a sound understanding of your personality and interests during these life-altering moments can help ensure that any career decisions you make will not only bring fulfillment and satisfaction, but also support your personal needs.

Most important, enhancing your self-awareness can help you avoid launching into a career field that will not bring you fulfillment. Or, accepting a job at a company whose culture clashes with your personality.

Step 1: Understanding Your Interests

Your interests dictate what keeps you engaged, the kinds of people you like to be with, and even the types of hobbies you choose to pursue. In some cases, interests can better predict job satisfaction than personality traits. And pursuing occupations in areas you are interested in can also be a strong indicator of your professional success and ability to persist through challenging times (Holland 1973). Like personality assessments, there are different frameworks available to assess your career interests. Oftentimes, these assessments ask you to rank different categories of interests against others. The categories vary by assessment, but can include your interest in working outdoors versus indoors, utilizing machinery, displaying artistic expression, helping others, using language skills to persuade others, or your interest in entrepreneurial endeavors.

The most commonly used interest inventories are based on Johns Hopkins University psychologist John Holland's lifetime work—a theory of careers and vocational choice that he developed in the 1970s and has stood the test of time. His occupational theme codes, also known as Holland Codes, have been used extensively by career counselors who are assisting students and midcareer professionals choose career paths. In fact, you may have taken an interest inventory that used the Holland vocational themes. The Interest Profiler is a quick way for you to categorize your interests into Holland's theme codes (Appendix A). While this is not the official assessment, take a few minutes to complete it now.

Holland Code Descriptions

Once you have completed the Interest Profiler and identified the top two or three letters that relate to your theme codes, review the following descriptions:

- **Realistic (R):** You are probably good at fixing or repairing things, are outdoorsy or athletic, and enjoy working on your own more than with a team. You are likely to ask, "What can I do to get the job done?"
- **Investigative (I):** You probably enjoyed school and love to learn new things. You appreciate the challenge of researching and solving complex problems, strategy games, puzzles, and hobbies that require technology or mastering complex skills such as sailing. You are likely to ask, "How can we get to the bottom of the problem?"
- **Artistic (A):** You probably have a creative flair and enjoy expressing yourself through art, music, theater, or writing. You are likely to say, "How can we do this in a different way?"
- **Social (S):** You probably enjoy being around people—in your spare time, you may choose to coach or teach, offer hospitality, or do volunteer work. You are likely to ask, "How can we work together to solve this problem?"
- **Enterprising (E):** You are probably competitive, enjoy taking risks, and are persuasive and good at motivating others. You prefer being a leader rather than a follower, and probably enjoy politics, volunteering on local boards or investing in the stock market. You are likely to say, "Let's get started now!"
- **Conventional (C):** You are probably very organized and efficient. You are likely to be accurate with details, good with numbers, and more comfortable with structure than improvising on the fly. In your spare time, you might enjoy collecting things, going to a family cabin or vacation home, or playing cards and games. You are likely to ask, "Can I help get this organized?"

Take a few minutes to jot down your top two theme codes in your Personal Inventory Tool in Appendix B. Now that you know your theme codes, how can they help you?

Career decision making: Interest assessments and inventories can provide you with a list of careers or industries that may be a good fit for you. The results can often shed light on the variety of available options based on your interests. The U.S. Department of Labor manages an excellent occupational website, O*NET (www.onetonline.org), which uses Holland theme codes to assist with career choices.

Job satisfaction: Professionals engaged in work that they find interesting tend to be more productive and show initiative. Research indicates that employees who are interested in their work will remain motivated and resilient, even during challenging situations and circumstances.

Growth opportunities: Understanding your interests can also help you identify growth opportunities and career progressions that will be a good fit. For example, many educators gravitate toward teaching because they have a strong interest in helping children, but overlook the amount of administrative work that comes with teaching and managing a classroom. For teachers who dislike the administrative tasks, moving into a principal's role is probably not the best career move.

Workplace Environment: Your career interests are strong indicators of the type of workplace culture or environment you prefer. This will be covered in detail in chapter 3, but the following workplace environments are best suited to each theme code:

- **Realistic:** May prefer an environment or career in which they can move around during the day. They may also prefer working on their own as opposed to frequent team work.
- **Investigative:** Tend to enjoy working in depth on one topic to get to the bottom of the problem. As a result, organizations that value depth over speed may be preferable.
- **Artistic:** May prefer to have some latitude about the way they complete their work. A company that doesn't micromanage and extends freedom to employees in how they complete tasks may be important to you.
- **Social:** If you have a strong interest in helping others, you may prefer working for a nonprofit, or a for-profit firm with a strong commitment to customer service. You may also prefer a firm that has a collaborative team environment.
- **Enterprising:** Enterprising types are often entrepreneurial, so they may enjoy start-up companies. They also prefer leadership roles, so they may prefer companies in which leadership opportunities are plentiful.
- **Conventional:** Enjoy being organized and orderly, so they may prefer to work for a company that has clear protocols and procedures, such as larger companies or well-established firms.

If you would like to explore your interests in more detail and obtain a full report of potential careers that fit your interests, a few popular interest assessment tools are listed in Appendix C.

Step 2: Understanding Your Personality

Your personality explains why you act the way you do, both personally and professionally. Many frameworks for understanding personality and describing personal preferences do so by using contrasting behaviors on a scale or dichotomy. They touch on your preferences regarding introversion and extraversion, your preference for planning or spontaneity, and your need to lead or follow. Some also address your aversion to or like of taking risks, and your preference for creativity versus big-picture thinking. By comparing opposing preferences to one another, you are able to gain a better understanding of your own behaviors.

Personality Preferences

Most personality profiles measure these preferences:

Plan or go with the flow: If you like to plan your day and have a routine, you may prefer a job that is a bit more predictable (accounting) versus one that can change at a moment's notice (emergency room nurse). Larger firms also tend to have more established procedures compared with start-ups, which require improvisation.

Details or big picture: If you are better with details than the "big picture," companies and careers that value accuracy and attention to detail (computer programming) will be more to your liking than careers that require you to deal in abstract or creative ideas (marketing). If you are an "idea person," working in a company that values innovation will allow you to utilize your creativity.

Variety or in-depth: If you like working on many different tasks rather than being able to concentrate on one thing in depth, you may enjoy a smaller company that allows you to wear many hats, or a position that has different challenges every day.

Teams or alone: If you prefer working with a team, you will be happier working in a field that requires people contact versus one that requires you to work on your own for long periods. Most people prefer a little bit of both, so think about where you fall on the spectrum when considering different types of positions.

Lead or follow: If you prefer to lead, a company with many leadership opportunities will be more to your liking. Smaller firms can sometimes offer leadership opportunities earlier in one's career, but larger firms have more positions and often provide structured leadership development programs.

Head or heart: If you tend to rely more on logic than feelings when making a decision, jobs that require the ability to analyze data and solve problems with logic will be more comfortable for you than those that require you to read others' emotions or be diplomatic.

Questions to Ask Yourself

Use this list of basic questions to home in on aspects of your personality that affect your career and work environment choices. While not a formal assessment, it can help you think through your preferences. Go to a quiet place and take a moment to work through the list. For each question, avoid answering with a simple *yes* or *no*. Try to think of examples and experiences that affirm your responses.

- Do you prefer to plan your day ahead of time or go with the flow?
- Do you like to follow the rules or make up your own?
- Do you enjoy being creative and seeing the big picture?

- Do you like variety or working on something in-depth?
- Do you prefer working alone or on a team?
- Are you better with details and facts or theories and ideas?
- Do you prefer to lead or follow? Or a little of both?
- What types of people do you like to hang around? What types would you rather avoid?
- Do you tend to make decisions with your head or your heart?
- When are you most productive? Least productive?

The answers to these questions can help you assess the types of tasks and work environments you prefer. Make note of these on the Personal Inventory Tool in Appendix B.

You may have taken a personality assessment, such as the Myers-Briggs Type Indicator or DiSC, at work or school. If you still have the results, take a few minutes to review them and enter your results in your Personal Inventory Tool. If you haven't taken a personality assessment in the past, take a look at the free and low-cost resources in Appendix C. However, if you're not comfortable "going it alone" or have been struggling with career issues for a while, you may want to consider consulting a career coach.

Using Your Personality Assessment

One of the most common purposes of personality assessments is helping professionals discover careers that will make them happy, because your personality has a great bearing on the tasks that fulfill you. Possessing a clear understanding of the type of work you enjoy and ensuring that it is present in the career path or job you choose is imperative to your work satisfaction. Simply relying on what you are good at (your skills) does not always guarantee satisfaction in a certain occupation.

For example, your preference for introversion or extroversion can affect your ability to complete your job duties. Introverts may thrive when completing tasks that provide time alone for reflection and internal processing. However, if introverts take on job duties that require a lot of public speaking, group interaction, or networking, they may begin to feel overwhelmed. Likewise, extroverts gain their energy from being around others and may thrive when working on tasks that are group centered or require high interaction with others. When extroverts take on job duties that require a lot of time alone or in solitude, they may struggle to stay motivated.

One of the best ways to ensure high performance is to consider the types of careers and company cultures that are the best fit to your personality. Even if you are a high-achieving professional with the right job, your performance may be negatively influenced if you are working for the wrong company. For example, a person who prefers a high level of interaction with others may not fare well in a company that does not value relationships. Likewise, someone who prefers working alone but works at a company that requires a high level of teamwork, collaborative projects, and socializing, will find that her productivity and stress levels are negatively affected from trying to perform in an environment that is not a fit for her personality.

If you prefer spontaneity, fluid systems, and creativity, then working in a highly bureaucratic organization may stifle your ability to innovate and create. Likewise, if you prefer structure and processes, working in a highly structured industry or organization (such as healthcare or higher education) may help you to thrive, whereas a company with less structure may frustrate you.

When to Hire a Professional

Consult a professional when you:
- do not agree with your personality assessment results
- are unsure how to move forward or what your next steps should be
- feel an internal conflict between your results and personal or family obligations
- experience difficulty narrowing down your options based on your results.

Skills and Strengths

Understanding your personality type and interests often helps point you toward your natural strengths and skills. Chapter 2 explores skills assessment in more depth, but jot down in your Personal Inventory any skills or strengths that you've identified while doing the exercises in this chapter.

Many professionals are now encouraged to identify and assess their strengths and character traits for building personal and professional self-awareness. This strengths-based approach is rooted in the positive psychology movement that has emerged over the last few decades. In a nutshell, assessments that focus on strengths draw your attention to the innate traits and characteristics that direct your behaviors and help you perform well. Some popular strengths-based assessments are *StrengthsFinder 2.0*, the VIA Survey of Character Strengths, and Dependable Strengths created by Bernard Haldane.

Understand Yourself So That You Can Better Understand Others

Personality and interest assessments should not be considered in vacuum. You can also take the information you learn from your own self-awareness building and apply it to your business relationships. Your bosses, co-workers, business partners, and employees all have unique personalities and interests. Becoming aware of your personality and interests can help you build relationships by increasing your awareness and understanding of others' preferences. Increasing self-awareness can positively affect your work relationships by helping you:

- Avoid conflict with others.
- Find points of connection and similarity.
- Identify strategies for dealing with difficult co-workers.
- Perceive how your personality affects others.
- Assign the right tasks and projects to employees you supervise.
- Hire the right employees to compliment your team.

A Word of Caution

Increasing self-awareness has many benefits and can lead to high levels of career performance and satisfaction. However, it is important to remember that personality and career interests are just one aspect of your research. You still should take skills (chapter 2), values (chapter 3), job market (chapter 4), entry points into an occupation (chapter 14), experiences, and financial needs into consideration.

Before taking any personality or interest assessments, you should make sure to:

- **Research the tool's reliability:** Regardless of which assessment you decide to take, be sure to investigate the research behind the tool's theoretical underpinnings. At the very least, reputable companies will provide information on the tool's reliability and validity, showing that the assessment tool has been tested to ensure results are consistent and accurate.
- **Understand your results:** Many of the personality and interest assessments online provide comprehensive results that explain the theoretical framework and your results. Nevertheless, it is often helpful to seek the assistance of a career coach or counselor when interpreting your assessment results. Many career professionals receive specialized training in assessment interpretation and can help you apply the results to your personal career aspirations.

Summary

Remember that personality assessments and interest inventories are just one piece of the puzzle as you put together your career story. You should not place yourself in a box or negate a career dream just because it does not show up on your personality or interest assessment report. Use all the tools in this book to help you piece together your ideal career path. If you get lost along the way, always remember it starts with knowing yourself—why you act the way you do and what holds your interest.

As you continue reading and working through the exercises in this book, it's wise to keep a job journal to track what you learn along the way. You can also use the Personal Inventory Tool in Appendix B to record key insights you learn about yourself.

Identifying Your Skills and Strengths

Dan Schwartz

This chapter will help you identify and describe your best skills and strengths. It includes some free and low to moderate cost methods you can use to assess your skills. These resources will help you determine how you can effectively use your skills assessment to choose and plan your career.

Think of your journey to uncovering your skills and strengths as similar to a television crime drama. Every experience, job, or achievement serves as a clue to finding your ultimate calling—or solving your case. Have you ever noticed that about halfway through the show, the detectives usually appear to have found the criminal and are ready to close the case? But then a new development takes place, a witness comes forward, or a piece of evidence gets discovered that throws everything into question. The storyline of a crime drama is much like a career path. It takes twists and turns. Sometimes just when you think you've found what you love, you discover a new passion. You may think you have found your calling, but it seems as though something new is always around the corner.

Discovering your skills and strengths is an important clue to cracking the mystery of what career is a perfect fit for you. During your "investigation" to find your ideal career match you will have to look back on past experiences, including jobs, education, volunteer opportunities, projects, and a host of other sources. As you reflect on your most successful past experiences, you will find a trail of similarities that will aid you in understanding what you are really good at.

Who Are You? Your Personal Inventory

One way to begin to understand yourself and what you are skilled at is to develop a personal inventory. Think of this as a full picture of you as an individual as it relates to your career preferences. A personal inventory generally includes the following areas:

- **skills and strengths:** what you are good at and what you have a knack for
- **personality traits:** who you are and how you interact with the world
- **principles or values:** the personal ethics you live by
- **logistics:** size and type of company, location, commute, salary, and experience level
- **environment:** corporate culture and preferred management style.

As suggested in chapter 1, use a job journal and the Personal Inventory Tool (Appendix B) to jot down the things you learn about yourself as you complete the exercises in this chapter, which primarily focus on completing the skills and strengths section.

Defining Your Skills

We all have a variety of skills that we've acquired throughout the years. Unlike natural strengths, skills are not something we are born with; rather, they are talents we develop over time through various experiences, sometimes through education or formal training. For example, if you are not a naturally competitive person and don't enjoy selling, but are put in a situation in which you must sell products to potential clients on various occasions, there is a good chance that you could become a skilled salesperson.

What Types of Skills Do You Have?

A crucial first step to finding a career you love is to truly understand your complete skill set. Knowing what types of skills you possess will not only help you find the right job to apply for, but also help you sell yourself through your resume and in the interview process. Understanding what you can bring to the table will make you stand out as a candidate and help boost your confidence in your ability to perform. We all have a wide variety of personal and professional skills, but most of them can be placed into four major categories:

- **Skills when working with people:** teaching, supervising, caring for others, hosting meetings or events, selling products or services, and listening or counseling.
- **Skills when working with things:** repairing things or objects, operating machinery or equipment, cooking or baking, building things, gardening, and fixing a computer.
- **Skills when working with data:** gathering and compiling information, investigating problems, computer programming, conducting research or scientific experiments, being good with numbers, and accounting or record keeping.

- **Skills when working with ideas:** writing stories or poems, composing music, creating new products or services, designing an educational program, developing a strategic plan, and playing a music instrument, singing, or acting.

One of the best ways to identify the skills that you most enjoy using is to make a list of accomplishments that you're most proud of and things you've done that gave you a sense of satisfaction. These don't have to be big accomplishments and can have occurred at any point in your life—at work, school, or home. Take a few minutes now and jot down some of these accomplishments in Table 2-1. Don't think too hard; just write what comes to mind first.

Table 2-1. Accomplishments (Big and Small) That I Enjoyed

1.
2.
3.
4.
5.

Once you've got a list of accomplishments, the next step is to write a short story describing each item on your list. Don't worry, these stories are just for you; no one will be grading them. Each story should include the following elements:

- background about the situation
- why you decided to do this particular thing
- a problem or challenge that you faced
- details about what you did step-by-step
- your results—how it all turned out.

It's also helpful to include whether or not you worked with others or on your own, what you liked most about doing it, and how it made you feel. You'll use this story format—sometimes called the CAR (challenge, action, result) or SOAR (situation, obstacle, action, result) formula—later in this book. Here's an example of a story you could tell:

> When I was a child, my family took many wonderful vacations, but my memories of the trip would fade quickly after I returned home. So after each trip, I would painstakingly record each day's events in a scrapbook using pictures and a journal entry. To preserve my memories, my mother would then take me to the local copy store to get it bound. I loved the process of recalling the events and bringing them to life with my descriptions and stories. And, I liked having a final, finished product that allowed me to go back and enjoy my vacation over and over again. I still look through them when I go home to visit.

The story is a short one, but it tells you some important things about me that are true to this day. When you read this story, what skills do you see?

- writing
- compiling information
- creating and designing a product
- record keeping and keeping a history.

Based on this story, I was able to identify a number of skills I enjoy using; in this case they were mostly related to ideas and data rather than people or things. However, this is just one story, and you need more than that to gain a full picture of your skills.

Here's another story that I've used to help identify my skills:

> In my senior year at Kansas State University, I was a tutor and also taught a study skills course called University Experience. Throughout those experiences I found that I loved helping others and teaching students how to be successful in the classroom. When I graduated, I realized that I wanted to continue sharing those insights, so I decided to write a book. About two years later, I self-published my first book, *Winning Strategies: Achieving Success in the Classroom, Career and Life.*

Once again, we see the skills:

- writing (ideas)
- compiling information (data)
- creating and designing a product (ideas).

But we also see:

- teaching (people)
- helping others (people)
- sharing information (ideas, data)
- designing an educational program (ideas).

The next section walks you through another sample story, which you can use to practice identifying skills and strengths. It includes a challenge, actions taken to solve the problem, and the end result. In addition to helping you identify certain skills, having the ability to craft stories like this that are work-related will be useful if a potential employer asks you to elaborate on skills listed on your resume during an interview.

Suzy's Story

When Suzy was in third grade, she found some broken glass in the woods where she and her friends liked to play. At first, she thought she just needed to pick up the glass, but then realized that there was so much that it would take a lot of time to clean it up. Upon closer inspection, she realized that the glass was actually old, objects from a much earlier time.

The glass objects looked antique, so Suzy wanted to see if she could find more. She got a small shovel, pail, and gloves to protect her hands. As she continued to examine the spot, she realized that the objects were in a depression in the ground. She dug carefully in that area and found many more objects and old bottles. Then she noticed that there were many other depressions in the ground where additional items could be buried. This was turning out to be a big job, so Suzy recruited several friends to help her.

The next day, they went back into the woods and dug up more than 50 objects. They were excited with their findings but wanted to know how old they were. Some of the bottles had writing on them, including the names of stores in their town that no longer existed. Suzy went to the library and found phone books going back 100 years. She found the names of an old dairy and pharmacy in the 1896-1902 phone books that matched the names on some of the bottles, so she was able to pinpoint their age.

After this expedition, Suzy began to collect old bottles and objects, learned how to date them, and even sold some of them. While she enjoyed the treasure hunting aspect, she also liked investigating the time periods from which the objects came.

* * *

What skills were used in this story? Does it present any clues as to what type of work Suzy might enjoy doing?

Basic Skills

Now select a few accomplishments from the list you created earlier and write a brief story describing what you did, using the story structure described above.

What types of skills do you possess? Next, compile an inventory list of the skills you highlighted in your stories, by referring to the Skills Checklist in Appendix D. The skills on the checklist are organized based on the four categories we discussed earlier. Highlight any skills that show up frequently in your stories—those are most likely your strengths, which are the skills that come naturally to you. Sometimes it helps to share your stories with others to see what they hear in the stories. Often, our best skills are things that feel so easy to us that we don't even realize they are valuable skills that don't come easily to others!

Defining Your Strengths

Has someone ever told you that you have a "knack" for something? If so, that person might be pointing out one of your strengths. We all have strengths that make us unique. A strength is the ability to consistently and accurately output a high level of performance within a given activity—it is something we are inherently good at doing, with little or no training. Of course, our strengths can be improved with practice and further training, but they're generally things that come easily to us.

Identifying your strengths can be one of the most challenging tasks in personal development. You may realize you are gifted in something, but it's not always easy to recognize *what* makes you so good at that activity. However, when it comes to finding a career match, understanding your strengths is equally as important as knowing your skills. You may find that your skill set is enhanced when you are put into situations that allow you to use your natural strengths, and when the two come together, it can make for a very successful career path.

Ask yourself the following questions to find out more about your strengths.

What Have You Been Successful in Without Training?

Anytime you are successful in a job or other personal experience, such as a sport or activity, there is a chance that you are using a strength. Many sports celebrities, such as Tiger Woods and Michael Jordan, realize at an early age that they have natural gifts. Sure, they receive special training and coaching, but they each have a unique athletic strength that cannot be taught or replicated. Natural strengths allow some people to come into a job with little formal training and perform at a high level.

Take some time and think about what experiences or jobs you have had that you have succeeded in with little or no training. It's likely that one or more of the stories you wrote earlier involved some of your strengths.

What Do You Have a Knack for?

Have people ever asked you how you did something and you didn't have a good answer? Maybe it was something that you know how to do well, but couldn't teach someone else how to do it. That's when you know you have a knack for something. Everyone has a special, unique strength that comes naturally with little or no effort. It could be the way you communicate with others, the way you analyze a problem, or your ability to teach someone a skill.

Pay attention to the comments you receive from others as well as the things you do yourself to uncover what sort of tasks come most naturally to you.

What Are Your Strongest Personality Characteristics?

We all have personality characteristics that make us unique. Try this self-reflection exercise: Think about a situation in which you always feel your best and completely comfortable. Once you have that situation in mind, try to pinpoint what it is about your personality that makes it so easy. It might be that you are a calming force in a conflict, or that you have the ability to be patient while teaching someone a skill. Whatever the circumstance, your personality has a dramatic influence on the way you handle things, and this is when your strengths reveal themselves in the best way. Spending some time in self-observation can go a long way in helping you discover your true strengths.

In chapter 1, you spent some time assessing your personality type. Take a look at some of the words you used to describe your personality on your Personal Inventory Tool to help you with this exercise (Appendix B).

What Do You Love to Do?

Recognizing what you love to do might be one of the best ways to uncover your strengths. We often love to do things because we excel at doing them. Whenever I have the opportunity to teach someone a new skill, I enjoy the experience because of my natural ability to connect with him and help him succeed. In turn, that feeling gives me an intrinsic level of motivation that can't be matched.

What do you love to do? And how does it make you feel? Understanding the answers to these questions might very well lead you to your natural strengths. Whether it's a sport, an activity, or a task in the workplace, we all have things we truly love to do. Did one of the stories you wrote earlier include something you love to do? If not, write an additional story or two about situations in which you were doing something you love to do.

Are You a "Go-To" Person?

A "go-to" person is someone who has a natural strength in a certain area and is often called upon to use that strength. As a trainer, I regularly count on a few different people for creative ideas when I'm developing training materials and activities in the classroom. I know someone else who is an excellent graphic designer and always has a fantastic vision for a book cover or engaging graphic.

What do people come to you for? When people frequently ask you for help with something, it is a sign that you have a natural strength in that area. Take the time to observe what people are asking you to do and then use that information to uncover your strengths.

The Link Between Skills and Strengths

Your skills and strengths represent what you have to offer—they are your core competencies and overall knowledge base, which you can use to contribute to the success of the organization. Your skill set is like a library of books. Each time you take on a new challenge or find yourself in a new role, you add a skill to your "library" and thus become a more well-rounded professional. Your strengths, however, have always existed within you and enhance your skill set.

Here's a brainstorming exercise: On a sheet of paper, list all your skills on the left and all your strengths on the right. Now, look at the two lists to see if any of the skills and strengths can work together to form unique talents you can bring to an organization. Use these as selling points on your resume and in the interview process. For example:

- As a salesperson, asking the right open-ended questions (skill) and reading the customer's emotions (strength) can work together to increase the likelihood of making a sale.

- As a doctor, reading lab reports (skill) and connecting with patients to understand their needs (strength) can work together to provide a high level of patient care.
- As a trainer, developing an activity (skill) and utilizing a creative mindset (strength) can work together to create an engaging experience for the participant.

The more you can link your skills and strengths, the better you will be able to define what type of career you would be successful in. Additionally, connecting your skills and strengths will allow you to open your mind to new possibilities and career avenues that you may not have considered before. Knowing your complete knowledge and capability set is a big first step in defining your path forward and uncovering opportunities you will thrive in.

Matching Your Skills and Strengths to a Career Field

Knowing your skills and strengths is an important component to completing your Personal Inventory, but understanding how they fit within a particular career is even more beneficial. Fortunately, there are a few free or inexpensive resources you can leverage to help get you started:

O*NET Skills Search

The O*NET Skills Search portal from O*NET OnLine (www.onetonline.org/skills) is a free tool that can help you understand which skills go together with certain careers. It provides a list of potential occupations that could be a potential fit to you, based on the skills you've selected. Once the list is populated, you can click on an occupation and view a comprehensive report for that job, including factors such as wage, work activities, education, work styles, and current employment outlook. You can also view high-level, detailed, and custom reports on this website.

MindTools

MindTools (www.mindtools.com) is a comprehensive career skills website that includes many resources about different skills and a free career skills newsletter. Its comprehensive 15-question assessment evaluates your skill set in five different areas:
- personal mastery: how you lead yourself, set goals, and understand yourself
- time management: how you manage your time and become more productive
- communication skills: how you communicate with others and listen
- problem solving and decision making: how you solve problems and choose the best option
- leadership and management: how you lead others and manage people.

MAPP Career Assessment

The MAPP Career Assessment is a 15-minute test that matches you with careers that fit your skills and strengths profile. In addition, the MAPP website (www.assessment.com) also features a variety of resources to help get you started on your career planning journey using your results from the assessment.

StrengthsFinder 2.0

StrengthsFinder 2.0 is the new version of the original book, *Now, Discover Your Strengths*. This book is a comprehensive guide to hundreds of different strengths that an individual can possess. Learn more at http://strengths.gallup.com.

Occupational Outlook Handbook

The *Occupational Outlook Handbook* (*OOH*) is a resource that includes a large quantity of information on a variety of different industries and career fields, including work environment, education, pay, and job outlook information. Once you know the type of career path you might want to take, you can use the *OOH* to see if a career fits within your skill set. Visit the website at www.bls.gov/ooh.

Summary

The tools and resources outlined in this chapter should help you flesh out your personal inventory by adding a list of skills to the earlier clues you uncovered about your personality type and interests.

Your completed inventory should help you better understand what you bring to the table that will help potential employers reach their organizational goals. If you take the time to understand your talents, you will be much more likely to find a career you love and are truly passionate about.

Identifying Your Best Work Environment

Sheila L. Margolis

The culture of a workplace can be a hard thing to describe. So how do you decide if a company's culture is a fit for you? Luckily, there is a process for understanding culture and deciding if a workplace is the right place for you. Companies screen applicants for culture fit. Now you can do the same to guide you in your job search.

When selecting a workplace, applicants typically assess their strengths, abilities, and interests to find the job that will be a fit and move them along a desired career path. But achieving job fit is only part of the formula for finding fulfilling work. Job seekers must also find the best workplace in which to do that job. That's where the additional focus on culture fit comes into play.

Understanding Yourself: Your Purpose and Your Principles

Deciding whether a company culture is a fit begins with reflecting first on the things that matter to you. To flourish, you want to find an organization whose work feels meaningful. You should also seek a work environment that operates by principles and values that are consistent with who you are. Therefore, your first step in determining culture fit is to clarify what is important to you: your purpose and your principles.

Understanding Your Purpose

Think for a moment about the things you are passionate about:
- What do you care about?

- What causes have a particular link with your life?
- What type of work would make you feel fulfilled?

When you are able to identify the things that matter to you, you gain vital information for deciding if an organization is a fit.

To understand how purpose applies to you, consider those who work in the nonprofit sector. Many people who work for a nonprofit have a genuine interest in its cause. It's not unusual for them to have a relative or friend who has been affected by the issue the nonprofit is seeking to remedy. Often, the passion of nonprofit workers is an output of their closeness to the cause on a personal level. Working for that organization is more than a job—it is the opportunity to make a difference in an area that deeply matters to them.

In contrast, for those in the for-profit world, making money has historically been viewed as the ultimate purpose. But that singular financial focus has proven to be a limited perspective.

Today, companies are more often seeing their work as a means for making a contribution to the global community. And having a purposeful focus not only promotes a thriving business, but also supports an employee's desire for achieving meaning through work. This broader lens generates high levels of energy and commitment from employees who care about the cause.

For example, Kellogg Company states its purpose as "nourishing families so they can flourish and thrive," while Starbucks exists "to inspire and nurture the human spirit." CVS Health describes its purpose as "helping people on their path to better health," and Nike seeks "to bring inspiration and innovation to every athlete in the world." And as they say at Nike, "If you have a body, you are an athlete."

In February 2012, Facebook founder and CEO Mark Zuckerberg wrote a letter to prospective investors in the company's initial public offering filing, stating that Facebook "was built to accomplish a social mission—to make the world more open and connected" (Zuckerberg 2012). The company wanted to "strengthen how people relate to each other." By enhancing openness and transparency, Facebook believes they are building understanding and connection.

So what causes matter to you? Think about the things that spark your energy. Is it helping people, preserving the environment, improving health, creating happiness, or something else?

There may be a number of areas in which you could make a meaningful contribution. Your aim is to determine which areas will make you feel fulfilled in your work. Identify the purposes that resonate with you. Don't focus on the products or services you feel skilled in providing; that is important for job fit but can be limiting when considering culture fit. If you limit your view, you will miss an array of potentially fulfilling opportunities.

Your life experiences can be a guide for your thinking. With the choices you have made, do you see any patterns? Are there particular areas that attract you? Use your past as a resource but not a limitation.

Defining Your Purpose

Answer these questions to help uncover the areas that feel purposeful to you.

- What are the things you love to do?
- What issues do you genuinely care about?
- What industries do you feel a personal connection to?
- In what types of activities do you lose track of time?
- What causes really matter to you?
- What topics do you often talk and read about?
- What events in your life have had a lasting impact because they touched you?
- What work excites you and makes you feel fulfilled and alive?
- What problems that worry or sadden you would you like to solve?
- What interests tend to repeat in your life?
- Knowing your strengths, is there a cause that you personally gravitate to?
- How would you like to use your talents to contribute to a better world?
- If you did not have to work, what would you do?
- If you could not fail, what impact would you like to make in your life?
- How do you want to be remembered?

Based on your responses, compile a list of your personal purpose options in your job journal. Put each purpose in a statement format, for example: I want to help people; I want to preserve the environment; I want to improve health; I want to make people happy.

Make sure each purpose is a meaningful cause that you will be willing to dedicate your energy to. With this list of potential purposes, you have taken the first step in understanding yourself so you can pick the right company culture.

Understanding Your Principles

The next step toward understanding yourself involves clarifying your beliefs and values. For a company to be a fit, you must feel a sense of harmony with the principles and values that are core to the organization's culture. To diagnose whether that harmony exists, you must think about yourself and the values that guide your life.

Many values may seem important, but the objective is to identify the ones that are most important to you. These are the values that would cause a disconnect if they were inconsistent with the workplace's values. Some workplace cultures are people focused while others are numbers focused. Some cultures take pride in being frugal while others see extravagance as core to who they are. Reflecting on the values that matter most to you will give you information you need to guide your job search. Keep in mind that clarifying values is also beneficial for many other endeavors in life, such as selecting a life partner, so understanding the values that matter most to you and any beliefs that ground your views will help you make good life choices.

Tool: Identifying Your Principles

Review the list of values in Table 3-1, and select the ones that matter most to you. If any significant values are missing from the list, add them to the Other Values section at the end. Be sure to pick values that meet these three criteria:

- The value is very important to you.
- The value guides how you live.
- You would require this value to feel comfortable in a workplace.

Table 3-1. List of Values

Achievement	Data	Fun	Peace	Selflessness
Activism	Design	Giving	People focus	Service
Adventure	Determination	Growth	Perfection	Simplicity
Aggressiveness	Discipline	Happiness	Performance	Sincerity
Agility	Diversity	Hard work	Persistence	Social responsibility
Attention to detail	Drive	Health	Power	Solutions
Autonomy	Duty	High standards	Predictability	Sophistication
Beauty	Effectiveness	Honor	Proactivity	Speed
Bend the rules	Efficiency	Humility	Professionalism	Spirituality
Boldness	Empowerment	Humor	Profitability	Spontaneity
Camaraderie	Entrepreneurial	Image	Promise	Standardization
Can-do attitude	Environment	Imagination	Punctuality	Status
Caring	Equality	Informality	Quality	Style
Celebration	Ethics	Initiative	Recognition	Sustainability
Certainty	Exceeding expectations	Innovation	Relationships	Talent
Change	Excellence	Intelligence	Reliability	Tolerance
Collaboration	Experimentation	Leadership	Resilience	Tradition
Communication	Expertise	Learning	Resourcefulness	Trust
Community	Fairness	Legacy	Respect	Uniqueness
Compassion	Faith	Logic	Responsibility	Weirdness
Competence	Family	Loyalty	Responsiveness	Well-being
Competition	Feedback	Measurement	Results	Work-life balance
Compliance	Financial focus	Mobility	Rigidity	
Consistency	Fitness	Openness	Rigor	Other Values:
Control	Flexibility	Ownership	Risk	
Courage	Formality	Participation	Safety	
Creativity	Freedom	Partnership	Secrecy	
Curiosity	Friendliness	Passion	Security	
Customer satisfaction	Frugality	Patriotism	Self-reliance	

Now list your top values in the left column of Table 3-2. Include no more than 10. Next, in the middle column, write a principle that explains the value so you are clear on what matters to you. For example, if you selected the value "can-do attitude," the principle might be, "I do what it takes to get the job done." Or if you selected "change," you might write, "I thrive on change and see changes as opportunities." Finally, in the far right column, add an example of each principle.

Table 3-2. List of Top Values

Top Values	Principle	Example

If these principles and values guide your life, then they must also be important at the company where you work. Otherwise, you will not be in harmony with the culture, and the tension will reduce your ability to flourish.

Once you are clear on the purposes and principles that matter to you, the next step is to assess the workplace culture to ensure you understand the organization's contribution and character.

Understanding the Organization: Purpose, Philosophy, and Priorities

Once you have clarified your purpose and principles, you'll need to compare them with the purpose, philosophy, and priorities of your prospective organizations. This is not always easy to do, but there are ways for you to gather clues about a company's culture, even from the "outside."

To evaluate your fit with a particular company, you will need to become familiar with the organization's core culture, which includes the reason why the organization exists and the beliefs and values that guide how employees do their work. The components of a company's core culture include its purpose, philosophy, and priorities (Figure 3-1).

Figure 3-1. Core Culture

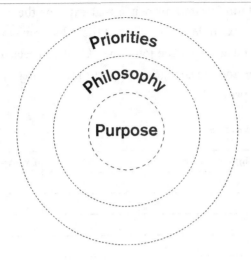

Source: Margolis (2010).

Understanding the Organization's Purpose

Most organizations have a purpose statement that answers these questions:

- What is the purpose of this organization?
- Why is the work of this organization important?
- What is this organization's contribution to society?

An organization's purpose is a statement clarifying its reason for existence. For example, many of the companies led by Elon Musk seek to improve our planet and positively affect the future of humanity. The purpose is a heartfelt contribution and a cause that serves as a source of meaning for the organization's employees.

Think of the purpose of the organization as something that is rarely completed. If it is accomplished, then the organization no longer needs to exist. Products and services change over time, but the ultimate reason for the organization's existence typically endures. The company may modify the wording of the purpose, but the essential contribution continues. The purpose serves as a filter for action and a stimulus for desired behavior. Some companies have the purpose to make people happy, while others may view their contribution as saving lives or helping people achieve their dreams. A broadly stated but genuine purpose widens the focus of a company, opening up a number of possibilities of products or services to offer. This broad perspective allows a company to thrive in a changing world.

So how do you determine a company's purpose?

- Begin by looking at the messages the company delivers through its website, its marketing, and even speeches given by its top leadership. The purpose may also be included in a mission statement.

- Network with employees, if you can, to see how they describe the company's contribution. Do they talk about the purposefulness of their work? Do they share a passion for a cause that is the foundation for their work? Do they describe why their work is important?

Evaluating a company's purpose is an important step in determining if it matters to you. Compare your list of personal purpose statements with the purpose of each company you consider for employment. Decide if the work of the company is meaningful to you. Without a personal connection to the company's purpose, you won't feel as strong of a commitment to the company. And work may not feel as meaningful.

Understanding the Organization's Philosophy

Where purpose is the *why* of the organization—why it exists—the philosophy is its distinctive and enduring *how*. Think of the philosophy as the personality or character of the company. It is what employees believe sets the organization apart from other companies—especially its competitors. Philosophy is a value or small set of principles or values that guide how employees do their work. It is usually derived from the company's founder or the principles and ideals that drove the organization's creation.

Uncovering a company's philosophy can require researching the company to discover what principles and values guide employees' decisions and actions. Often these values are posted on company walls, incorporated in employee communications, and shared on the company website. The values listed are not always the values practiced, however, so be careful in evaluating the authenticity of the stated values.

Tool: Practical Steps to Uncover a Company's Philosophy

Use the following resources to gain more insights into each company you are evaluating:

- Research the company's history on the company website. Search the Internet to find information on its founder. Read as much as you can about the founder and the principles and ideals that were important to that individual. A founder's personality and character often influence the company's philosophy.
- Identify the company's core values, which are often listed on the company website. Often, they are included in the About Us or Careers section.
- Look at websites such as Glassdoor (www.glassdoor.com) and read employee reviews about the company culture. You can uncover themes in the comments that indicate what is most important at the company. Also search the site for interview questions the company has used. These interview questions may indicate what the company values.
- Check out company pages on LinkedIn and Facebook, the tweets they post on Twitter, and the photos and videos they share on Instagram. Company values may be revealed through such entries and images.

- *Fortune's* Best Companies to Work For, Glassdoor's list of Best Places to Work, LinkedIn's North America's 100 Most InDemand Employers, and the website www.GreatPlacetoWork.net are good resources. Review the companies you find on these lists by reading company descriptions and employee interviews. These sites can reveal what life is like working in the company. Blog posts on the sites often dive deeper into exposing the company culture.

- SlideShare (www.slideshare.net) posts an array of presentations on company culture. You can search by the company name or "culture code" with the company name to find a presentation on the company you are interested in.

- The Muse, an online career website (www.themuse.com), offers behind-the-scenes looks inside companies, including employee videos. This site provides a colorful picture of hundreds of companies that can deliver added insight for your decision making.

- CareerBliss (www.careerbliss.com) is an online career community that offers data on job satisfaction, pay, and employee happiness, as well as a national job board. You can read company comments, reviews, and culture ratings.

- Vault (www.vault.com) is a website that ranks companies, provides extensive information, and offers ratings and reviews clustered as "uppers," "downers," and "the bottom line."

- Another way to uncover the company philosophy is by observing the behaviors of its employees. If a company has a lobby or restaurant where employees tend to congregate, you may be able to observe their behaviors. If you have an interview, arrive early enough to observe employee behavior.

- Current or former employees can be a good resource. If you don't know anyone who has worked at the company, consider attending a professional association meeting that company representatives would attend. Strike up conversations to discover what it's like working for that organization.

- In the interview process, observe how you are treated—before, during, and after the interview. Also, the physical environment of the workplace and even the setting where the interview takes place can reveal clues about the company's character and the things that are valued.

- During the interview process, ask employees questions that reveal the principles that are most important. Some examples include:
  - What words would you use to describe this company?
  - What principles or values are core to this organization? Ask for examples of any principles or values they discuss.
  - How would you describe the founder (or leader) of this organization?
  - If you could change one thing about this culture, what would it be?

- What qualities do your star performers exhibit? What behaviors are rewarded? What actions are celebrated?
- What traits does a person need to fit in well at this company?

In healthy organizations with a clearly defined core culture, the principles or values are easy to decipher because employees behave in ways that express them. For example, if heartfelt caring and respect is part of a company's philosophy, then employees would demonstrate heartfelt caring and respect when interacting with one another and with their customers. If this value is genuine, you would also be treated with heartfelt caring and respect in the interview process.

Understanding the Organization's Priorities

Another layer outside the purpose and philosophy are the organization's priorities. What separates priorities from the other components of the core culture is the fact that priorities change over time to enhance an organization's success. They are not as stable as the purpose or philosophy. Priorities are determined by what the company needs to focus on to compete in the current business environment.

Figure 3-2 shows the two types of priorities: strategic priorities and universal priorities.

Figure 3-2. Strategic and Universal Priorities

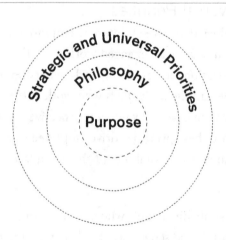

Source: Margolis (2016).

Understanding Strategic Priorities

Strategic priorities are values related to an external customer and market focus. They can be uncovered by understanding what the organization needs to focus on to achieve its business goals. If the economy is undergoing a recession, then cost control might be a strategic priority. If competition is moving quickly to take over future markets, then speed might be a strategic priority. If cybersecurity and privacy are an issue, then security might be a strategic priority.

Identifying strategic priorities can be difficult; however, you can often uncover them during the interview process by asking:

- What are the current goals of the company?
- What are the most pressing issues employees need to focus on?
- In this department, what are the priorities? What are the biggest opportunities?

Additionally, you can find priorities mentioned in the company's latest annual report, usually in the CEO's letter. Read the entire report to get a clearer picture of the company's strategy and vision. A company's website often includes sections titled Investor Relations and News or Press. These pages hold a wealth of material—including news, reports, slide presentations, and blog posts—on the company and its strategic focus. Sites like www.vault.com and www.guidestar.org offer information on strategy and financial performance for many organizations. They provide up-to-date information for a more comprehensive understanding of the company's strategy and finances.

Each industry has unique challenges. Search for industry information for the companies you are considering. The issues they face may affect their strategic priorities.

Once you understand a company's strategic priorities, you'll be able to assess how you can help the company achieve its goals. If you highlight how you can contribute to the company, you'll be able to show them that you're the right fit.

Understanding Universal Priorities

Universal priorities are values that have an internal, employee focus. They are the areas the company needs to focus on to have an engaged workforce. The universal priorities include fit, trust, caring, communication, achievement, and ownership. Practicing these universal priorities brings out the best in the individuals who work at the company.

In your job search, try to uncover how well a prospective company practices each of the universal priorities. Because these priorities drive employee engagement, their presence or absence will inform you about the desirability of the workplace.

Fit

Does the company successfully hire people who are a fit with the organization's culture and with their jobs? Companies should screen each applicant around these culture fit questions:

- Is the purpose of the organization meaningful to the applicant?
- Are the values of the organization in harmony with the applicant's values?

Companies should also screen applicants around these job fit questions:

- Will the job to which the applicant is applying feel meaningful?
- Does the job fit the applicant's strengths, abilities, and interests?

Based on the questions asked during the interview process and the information provided to you as an applicant, you can determine whether the company screens for culture fit, job fit, or both. Be clear on what the organization is looking for in the person who will be filling the position. How does the organization describe the ideal candidate? Are they seeking applicants who will find meaningfulness and harmony in their jobs at the organization? To have an engaged workforce, the organization must effectively screen for both culture fit and job fit.

Trust

Is this a workplace where employees trust their leaders? A lack of trust generates fear and disengagement. Try to understand the nature and style of the leader and the direction the leader seeks for the company. Character, consistency, competence, connection, and fairness promote trust. Employees who trust top leadership and their immediate supervisors are more engaged. It may be difficult to evaluate trust from the outside. However, if you can network with past or current employees, you may be able to uncover employee views. Listen to how employees describe the following areas that affect trust:

- Do they describe leaders as competent?
- Do they describe leaders as honest?
- Are leaders' actions consistent with their words?
- Do leaders inspire employees?
- Do leaders communicate effectively with employees?
- Do leaders show that they care about employees?

Caring

Employees are more engaged when the workplace supports a sense of belonging, where leaders and supervisors care about employees, and where employees have friends at work.

If you can observe employees at the company, note how they behave with one another. Their interactions will provide clues to the presence or absence of teamwork and friendships at work. Do you see family photos in offices or on desks? Do you see pictures of employees on walls? A caring workplace wants to bring the total person to work. When you go for an interview, consider asking a few of these questions:

- How does the organization treat its employees?
- How do managers interact with those they supervise?
- How do employees treat one another?
- Do employees socialize with one another?
- Do employees have the support they need to do their jobs well?
- How effectively do departments work together?

Communication

Communication is a key driver of engagement. Employees seek an open workplace as exhibited by honest dialogue and the ongoing flow of information. Effective communication is essential for increasing employee satisfaction and engagement.

When you go for an interview, try to collect employee newsletters or other forms of communication to discover the types of information people share in the organization. Ask to view the employee portal of the company website to get a sense of the company's openness with employees. Consider asking some of these questions in your interview:

- In what ways does the organization share information with employees?
- How do employees get the information they need to do their jobs well?
- How often does the staff meet? Ask about the variety of meetings held and how information cascades throughout the organization.
- What types of information are shared with employees? Are they kept up-to-date on the company's strategy, goals, and metrics?
- How does the company solicit information and ideas from employees? How frequently does the organization act on employee suggestions that will benefit the company?
- Are systems in place that encourage departments to communicate with one another?

Achievement

How does the organization support employee growth and development? Helping employees feel they are achieving and growing through their jobs promotes a greater connection with work, and thus increases engagement. During the interview process, try to uncover the organization's views on developing its employees. Consider asking some of these questions:

- What position did you have when you were hired at this company? What positions have you held?
- Does the organization have an onboarding process?
- What is the company's attitude about employee development? What training and development opportunities are provided to employees?
- Do employees have a development plan? What does it look like in the first year of employment? Do employees have someone in the company who supports them in their development?
- What opportunities for growth exist within the company? Are stretch assignments offered?
- Do employees receive frequent feedback on their work?
- How is employee performance evaluated?
- How does the company recognize employee achievements?

Ownership

A workplace that encourages autonomy, participation, flexibility, and accountability supports the engagement of its employees. During the interview process, try to determine how well these values are practiced. Seek to understand the areas in which you will have control and responsibility, and look for company policies that support flexibility and enable employees to balance their work and personal needs. Consider asking:

- Does the company encourage a degree of autonomy for employees at work?
- Are employees making decisions that affect them? Give some examples.
- Is there flexibility in how or where employees do their work?

Companies are typically strong in practicing some of the universal priorities, but there are always some areas the company needs to focus on and pay attention to. Ask whether employee engagement is measured at the company. Uncover the strengths of each company and the efforts they are making to improve the workplace.

By learning all you can about the organization's priorities—strategic and universal—particularly in the area where you would be working, you will be able to gauge whether the workplace is a good match for you.

Summary

To evaluate for culture fit, job seekers must have a clear picture of their own purpose and principles, as well as a picture of each prospective company's core culture—its purpose, philosophy, and priorities. This understanding will guide you in determining if a workplace will provide meaning and harmony and promote engagement:

- Is the company's purpose something you care about?
- Is the company's philosophy in harmony with your principles and values?
- Can you contribute to the company's strategic priorities?
- Does the company practice the universal priorities that promote employee engagement?

Not every organization will be a perfect fit. The aim of this process is to determine how aligned you are with each organization that could be a future workplace. The greater the alignment, the greater the culture fit.

Using the process outlined here will help you gain a better understanding of what you are choosing when you accept a position. For additional tools and information on culture fit, refer to my book, *Job Seeker Manual: A Step-by-Step Guide for Using Culture Fit to Find the Right Workplace for You*.

Once you have evaluated your fit with the culture of an organization, it is your responsibility to close the deal by showing the company how you can contribute to its purpose, philosophy, and priorities. By understanding these details of the company, you will be able to sell yourself and show how you can support the culture and goals of the organization.

Developing Your Career Plan

Alisa Cohn

You've spent a lot of time in introspection and exploration. In the last three chapters, you were a detective, uncovering the clues of who you are and what would be a good fit for you. Now you get to be a navigator—taking all the data and creating a map to guide you on your next steps on the career journey.

You will synthesize the data to form one (or two) pretty good targets of where you might want to go. Then you will begin to narrow down the options to home in on what companies and roles you are going to target.

You may want to leave your existing workplace or find something else within your current environment. You may be a first-time job entrant, midcareer, or even in the later stages of your career. Whatever your situation, this process will help you figure out where you should point yourself and what your next steps should be.

Tools for Getting Started

As with anything, the hardest part of the journey is getting started, so let's begin! The best way to get started is to collect what you've already discovered about yourself. So far, you identified your strengths and skills, learned something about your interests and personality type, and identified your core values.

Now let's explore how these areas come together to help you decide what actual roles you want to target. You will find it extremely helpful to keep your notes, documents, and tools all in one place: Keep everything in a folder on your computer, use a notebook if that works better for you, or use one of the many websites that are designed to help you stay organized. Spending a little time up front getting organized will pay enormous dividends as you go forward.

Keep a Job Journal

Another useful tool that was mentioned in earlier chapters is a job journal, which is an electronic document or a paper notebook that gives you space to jot down ideas and keep track of insights, words and phrases, contacts, and anything else that comes to mind as you move forward in your process. Depending on your preferences, you can set it up in a loose-leaf or spiral-bound notebook or use a free tool like Evernote (www.evernote.com) or JibberJobber (www.jibberjobber.com) to keep track of your insights on each topic. You can set up your job journal using the following eight sections, or create your own:

- **Personal inventory tool:** Consolidate your insights and ideas using the Personal Inventory Tool (Appendix B). This will help you keep track of the most important things you are learning.
- **Learning:** Write down what you learn through informational interviewing, as well as initial inclinations about what kind of job you want to target and what else you want to explore.
- **Workplace environments:** Note your thoughts on workplace environments, especially if you are still trying to decide what you want to target: large companies or small, established companies or startups, or nonprofit or for profit. As you visit or learn about different environments, keep your reflections here.
- **Exercises:** Keep track of your self-observation exercises and introspection.
- **Networking:** Organize your networking and contacts.
- **Job search strategy:** Write down the big picture of your goals and how you plan to organize yourself to reach them.
- **Daily schedule:** Keep your daily and weekly schedule here to stay organized.
- **Goals and lists:** Keep track of your progress. List your daily and weekly to-dos so you can check them off. Write down your areas of focus for the day or the week. This helps you continue your learning process, keep track of your insights, and organize how you use your time.

Identifying Your Preferences

In chapters 1 and 2, you took an inventory of your personality traits, interests, and skills to determine what you have to offer. In chapter 3, you identified your values and what was important to you in a work environment. Now it's time to decide which skills you most like to use and where you'd most like to focus your efforts in looking for a job. This will help you describe the attributes of an ideal job, as well as the types of jobs you would like to avoid.

Complete a preference grid (Table 4-1) to help you clarify the skills you most enjoy using and the type of environment in which you do your best work. This tool will also remind you what areas to avoid, which is helpful for finding a job that is a good fit.

Table 4-1. Preference Grid

Categories	No	Maybe	Yes
Skills *Example: Teaching or training on specific topic(s)*	Skills you have but don't want to use:	Skills you wouldn't mind using:	Skills you would most like to use:
Industry or Sector *Example: Healthcare, finance, nonprofit*	Industry or sector you'd like to avoid:	Industry or sector you'd consider:	Industry or sector you're most interested in:
Environmental Factors *Example: Commuting time, corporate culture, salary, benefits, or size of company*	Environmental factors you definitely want to avoid:	Environmental factors that you can live with but are not ideal:	Environmental factors you most desire:

Skills

For the skills section of the preference grid, take a look at the skills you've listed in your personal inventory. For each skill, ask yourself if you'd like to use it every day. Write down the skills that you love in the yes column. Most people also possess skills they don't enjoy using—identify the skills you truly dislike in the no column. Skills that you don't mind using, but wouldn't want to do all day, should receive a maybe. In your ideal job, you would use your preferred skills 100 percent of the time. However, because most jobs include some work that is less appealing to you, aim for a job that allows you to use your favorite skills 70 to 80 percent of the time and your maybe skills the rest of the time.

Industry or Sector

The next section of the preference grid relates to the industries or sectors in which you would most like to ply your trade. If you believe you can work in any industry, think about whether you would enjoy manufacturing, service, government, or nonprofit environments. In chapter 1, you uncovered some clues about the types of companies and industries you may enjoy based on your personality type and interests. Think about the types of people you like being with, the subjects that fascinate you most, and what you like and don't like about where you've worked so far. Your interests and preferences are clues to the type of industry and environment that best suits you.

Environmental Factors

The last area of your preference grid is the environment: company size, corporate culture, physical location, length of commute, type of manager, salary level, and so forth. You should include all the work environment factors that are important to you and categorize them based on your true preferences. You also unearthed some clues about the type of work environment that suits you best in chapters 1 and 3. Be honest with yourself about what you can and cannot tolerate in a workplace. For some, a commute longer than 30 minutes is intolerable, while others use the travel time as a way to unwind and separate from their workday.

Once you've completed your preference grid, the items in your yes column should describe your ideal job. Share your preference grid with trusted friends and colleagues who will help you vet, reinforce, and challenge your ideas to give you more clarity and confidence to move forward.

Determining the Right Job for You

Determining the right job is an iterative process. You learn about yourself, explore various environments and opportunities, talk to people, read, and repeat. Over time you begin to get a picture of areas you want to explore and target.

Start by creating a mission statement for your job search. This is a way to incorporate what you know about yourself and apply it to what you'd like to do. In chapter 3, you created personal purpose statements that you could identify with. Choose one or two now and see if you can craft a mission statement by adding some of your key skills, strengths, and the workplace values that are important to you. Try drafting a mission statement now. Your mission statement should be inspirational and something to which you aspire.

For example, one of my clients, Dan, wanted to transition to something completely new. He wrote this mission statement:

> "I am an uplifter. I can make any group of people work better together. I am a creative problem solver and the one person everyone comes to when they don't know what to do. I am a synthesizer of multiple points of view. I want to contribute in an environment that is driven and exciting, and where we all work together. I want to work with people who help me learn and grow. I want the work to be meaningful."

Granted, this does not point him to a specific job, like marketing or finance; rather, it is a bigger picture statement that can serve as a filter for what he is seeking.

After reflecting on your strengths and values and the kind of culture you want to be a part of, you probably have some inkling of where to point yourself to find your next position. Try drafting a mission statement now and place it at the top of the Personal Inventory Tool in Appendix B. Still not sure what you want? Try some of these exercises to gain further insights.

Interview Yourself

Ask yourself the following questions to learn more about yourself. Don't edit as you go; feel free to answer them out loud and record the interview. If you feel silly, ask a friend to do it. After you're done, take time to reflect on what you learned about yourself. Jot your insights down into your job journal and take another look at your preference grid.

- What have you accomplished that you are most proud of?
  - Chapter 2 suggested making a list of accomplishments and writing brief stories about some of them; if you haven't already, jot down a list of accomplishments now.
- What kind of challenges do you most enjoy overcoming?
- Describe the colleagues you have enjoyed working with the most.
- What kinds of environments do you thrive in? What environments have not worked well for you?
  - Chapters 1 and 3 provided some guidance on the types of environments that most appeal to various personality types. If you found any clues there, jot them down in your job journal.
- Look at the following related workplaces. Which environments speak more to you?
  - large company or small company
  - for profit or nonprofit
  - established company or startup
  - fast paced or moderate paced
  - "execution culture" or "family culture"
- How important are your physical surroundings?
- Do you want to go to the same place and office every time, or do you want to be more mobile, remote, or flexible?

Jot down any new insights you gained from this exercise in your job journal.

Creating an Advisory Board

If you're struggling to do this alone, another exercise that can be helpful involves asking a few of your friends and colleagues to become members of your advisory board. Find a trusted, insightful friend or mentor, or invite a small set of close friends or colleagues to dinner to be a part of your personal advisory board. Share with the group what you found out about yourself in your information gathering phase, and show them your personal inventory or your preference grid. Then ask them what type of job or environment comes to mind and what suggestions they have for you about where to point yourself. Ask probing questions about how they view you and encourage them to talk among themselves about you as if you were not in the room. Take notes. (Pro tip about advisory boards: When you serve pizza they stay longer.)

Here's an example of how a personal advisory board can help:

> Lori was a vice president of marketing in a large public company, but she wasn't happy. After some reflection, she realized that one of her core values was "to make a difference." She loved marketing and she loved building a team, but she missed having the ability to contribute in a meaningful way to a cause or a mission that was important to her. She was also tired of all the hoops she had to jump through to get anything done at her company.
>
> Lori assumed this meant finding her next position at a nonprofit that meant something to her, so that's where she started to look. However, after doing an informational interview and working with an advisory board, she found herself looking in a different direction. Her advisory board, in particular, gave her the guidance that she needed to be in a fluid, fast-moving environment. It also pointed out that she could "make a difference" in a small company, perhaps a startup, where she could get hired onto the executive team, run a team, and have an impact. It would also satisfy what she called her "need for speed."
>
> Ultimately she accepted a role as the head of marketing of a small, fast-growing startup. She was on the executive team and was in a role where she knew that she made a difference. And she was still able to contribute by being on the board of a local nonprofit for a cause that was important to her.

Experiment and Research

Even after this exploration, you may still need to spend time refining what job or career you want to target. At this point, follow your curiosity and use targeted experiments, which give you an opportunity to try something in a small way without jumping in with both feet. It's usually not exactly the same, but it comes close enough to give you a sense. When you conduct a targeted experiment, it's important to have specific goals about what you want to get out of it. Be clear and specific and write your goals down to remind you why you're doing it.

Talk to people, starting with people you feel comfortable and safe with. Ask about what they do and what their day-to-day entails. Go into their office so you can see what it's like, and even shadow them for a few hours if you can. It might be weird if you showed up at a corporate meeting, but you could sit with them at their computer and have them take you on a tour. Find out what documents they're working on and what they are for. Whom do they interact with all day? Does that appeal to you? Write your insights and key takeaways in your job journal.

Another way to experiment is to find short versions of things you want to do. Take Jill, for example. She was a classically trained musician, a brilliant violinist, and professor of music, but wanted to transition her career. After talking to a lot of people, she thought that consulting would be a great next step. Because it would be a stretch to get hired into a consulting firm from where she was, Jill thought she should find consulting firms focused on academia and sell her music skills as "creative thinking." She was also contemplating going to business school to formally learn business skills.

These are good ideas, but does she even know what consulting is? Jill wanted to find a way to explore consulting before diving in. After some searching, she found that her alumni organization had a group that formed small teams of volunteer consultants for nonprofits, so she joined a team that was working on developing a strategic plan. She wanted to try out consulting and gain one or two specific skills that would help her in her transition away from music and academia and into the business world. She pushed herself out of her comfort zone to work with a team member on the financial projections. It wasn't easy, but she learned a lot and found that she had an aptitude for strategy and numbers. Ultimately, after a few more volunteer engagements, Jill decided to go to business school feeling very confident in her abilities and the path it would lead her down.

To summarize so far: A starting point for career success is what you enjoy and what you're good at. It's also finding a match for your values and a cultural fit. When you think about this, you can brainstorm and use an advisory board to get an outside view of how the world sees you. You can start experimenting to test if you will like certain fields or not.

But this is still not sufficient. Career success is not just about what you enjoy and what you're good at; it's also important to consider workforce trends. Wise decision makers think about "picking a good wave"—a field or industry that is going to grow with you. As you think about the industry you want to target, take into account external waves.

Watch for Waves

Waves can be economic, demographic (the baby boom), technological (the rapid changes wrought by information technology), or environmental (climate change). They influence both what choices are available and the rewards people get from choosing them.

For example, a current wave is that the U.S. population is aging. Getting involved in services for the elderly may very well be a good "wave choice." Alternatively, print journalism is dying. Starting a career in print journalism means choosing a soft wave that may not make it to shore.

Scan the environment around you to identify good waves that won't leave you behind. Here are some ways to determine key trends:

- Pull out three to five news sources (magazines, blogs, or newspapers) you've never read before. Read them for a month and see what resources you gain.

- Review occupational data on the projected growth and salaries in existing and emerging occupations and fields. The Bureau of Labor Statistics (www.bls.gov/ooh) and the Department of Labor (www.dol.gov) are two good resources.
- Ask people in different fields what they think the key future trends are.
- Ask people in your own field to name important future trends.

Create a Career Plan

Now it's time to articulate your career plan. This plan should evolve over time, so don't worry if you don't get it right the first time. Appendix E is a career plan template you can use to articulate the target for your next position. Include the types of skills you want to use, as well as the location, industry, and type of environment you'd most enjoy working in. Use your Personal Inventory Tool (Appendix B) and preference grid (Table 4-1) to help remind you of the key factors. Include the:

- common title for the type of position you are targeting
- top skills you'd like to use
- industry preference(s)
- preferred location
- important key environmental factors
- target salary.

Now when you're asked what type of position you are looking for, you should be able to articulate a career objective or target. A career objective could sound like this:

> "I'd like to use my training and instructional design skills in a medium to large organization in the healthcare industry in the Boston area that truly values and supports employee development."

Or it could sound like this:

> "I'd like to use my analytic skills in a consulting environment that allows me to work with a small team to improve efficiency, increase revenue, or reduce costs for my clients. I'm good with numbers and with people, so I'd like to spend some of my time in client-facing activities. My ideal company will be located in the D.C. area and will be a small but growing firm with a reputation as a good place to work."

Now it's your turn. Create a career objective from the information in your career plan. Make it specific enough that it paints a clear picture of type of position you are looking for.

Once you have drafted your career target, jot down a few next steps that will get you closer to that goal and give yourself a deadline to accomplish them. Next steps could include revising your resume, setting up networking meetings, or researching target companies.

Target Companies

Before we move on to developing a search strategy, a few words about identifying target companies. A key part of your search process will include targeting companies you believe are a good fit. Use what you determined about yourself in chapters 1-3 as parameters to narrow down the types of companies that suit you best. Then start creating a list of companies that meet your criteria.

You can find target companies in a number of ways, including ZoomInfo (www.zoom info.com; sign up for the community edition), the ReferenceUSA database, LinkedIn company pages, and Glassdoor (www.glassdoor.com). Chapters 3 and 10 contain additional guidance on how to do company research. Appendix E contains a table that will help you get started with your target company list.

Create Your Search Strategy

Congratulations, now that you have drafted a career plan and identified some next steps, it's time to act! So, what should you do next?

If you are in an active job search, lay out your strategy, on paper or online, whatever works best for you. A search strategy will help you make the best use of your time, pace yourself, and bolster your spirits when you're down. Use the career plan in Appendix E or your job journal to identify your next steps and the timelines by which you want to achieve those goals.

Now think about the various activities that you will do to achieve that goal:
- research
- working with recruiters
- informational interviews
- networking
- looking for open listings on company websites
- attending industry events
- job fairs
- building your skills and knowledge
- building your brand as an expert
- honing your resume.

Everyone has a different amount of time to devote to a job search. If you don't have a full-time job that means you have more time to job search than if you do. Everyone has various outside commitments—family, community, volunteering, school—so it's important to set a realistic plan for yourself based on your own situation. It's also important to emphasize this process and devote time to it if it's important to you.

Looking Without a Full-Time Job

If you are job searching without a current job full time, your day could look like this:

9:00–Contact people: Use the first 90 minutes of the morning to respond to key people and follow up with things you committed to do (send an article, make an introduction). This is also a good time to network with new contacts and to update old contacts on what you've been up to.

10:30–Morning meetings: This is a good time to schedule morning coffee meetings. You probably got a few things done in the morning, so you'll feel productive, which will help you come across as more confident. Coffee meetings give you time to recharge with caffeine and interact with other people. They're also a reason to get dressed (some people need that!) and get you outside so you don't feel cooped up all day in front of your computer and phone. You can also use this time to do some online research, work on social media, or do other activities to build your brand as an expert. Note: This is *not* an excuse to waste time on Facebook or Twitter!

11:30–Personal errands or break: Don't forget to do your personal errands. Just because you're looking for a job full time doesn't mean life stops—you still need to go to the dry cleaner or pick up aspirin and milk. If you are married, use this time to get spouse points for taking care of household chores.

12:30–Lunch meetings: Schedule a lunch with someone if you can. Meet up with former colleagues, people from industry associations you want to get to know better, or new introductions from people in your network. In addition to being a great way to meet, having lunch with someone on a regular basis reinforces your being out in the world rather than cooped up inside. This will give you fresh perspective and help keep your spirits up.

2:00–Research and applications: Afternoons tend to be a bit lower energy, so use this time for quiet research and applying for positions that fit the criteria you identified on your preference grid. Be selective and only apply to well-targeted positions (see chapter 8 for more guidance on this topic). Research industry trends, learn something that you think is important, or write a few blog posts or do something else to set yourself up as an industry expert. This is also great time to research specific companies and to look through LinkedIn for new contacts to network with.

4:00–Strong finish: End the day with something you know will give you a high. This may be having a final networking call or meeting, reading a set of blogs in your industry you know you'll enjoy, or anything else you know will give you a sense of accomplishment.

4:30–Prepare for tomorrow: Make a detailed plan for tomorrow. This helps you think through the specifics of your highest-value activities and ensures that you can have a fast start in the morning.

New to the Workforce

If you are just out of school and this is your first job, it's especially important that you make sure you have a clear schedule to structure yourself. You should add to your activities list specific networking meetings with older successful people to cultivate as mentors. You should also add extra time for research, especially if you don't know much about workplace environments. Another option is spending one day each week interning or volunteering somewhere to help you gain more skills, test if you like something or not, demonstrate value, and build your network. This is the easiest time in your life to do this, so it's a great investment of your time if you are able to.

Parent Re-Entering the Job Market

If you are a parent who is re-entering the job market, a structured schedule will help you feel more in control and support your progress. You also should add more time to research current conditions in the job market. For example, in the past 10 years, work environments have become more mobile, with people working remotely from all over the world. And, open-plan workspaces have also become much common.

Make room in your day for filling in knowledge and experience gaps. This is especially important if you are transitioning to a new industry. Knowledge gaps can be easy to fill by reading, self-study, online courses, or short courses (see chapter 14 for resources on professional development). Experience gaps are harder to fill, so consider getting a mini internship or volunteering. Those are two quick ways to gain experience, keep your resume fresh, and signal motivation to potential employers (see chapters 12 and 13 for more suggestions on gaining experience or preparing for a career change).

Working While You Look for Work

If you have a job, you have to be strategic about how to use your time to make sure you are having the highest impact. You may be able to do some but not all of the activities laid out here. Pick or create the ones that work best for you and execute them consistently.

- **Early morning:** Use this time to network—email responses and follow-ups to your contacts.
- **Breakfast or coffee meeting:** If you can squeeze in coffee or breakfast before work, that can be the easiest time for everyone to meet.
- **Lunch:** Meeting someone for lunch is a great use of your time.
- **Two 15-minute activities a day:** Plan in advance various 15-minute activities you can do throughout the day. These can include creating a list of companies you want to target or discreetly researching a company or industry you are interested in.

- **After work:** Pick one or two evenings a week to work on your job search and apply to positions online. You might use this time for dinner and drinks networking or industry events, which often happen in the evening. If you are trying to transition to a new industry, you could use this time to take a "short-course" education program. Only go to general networking events if they are very targeted or you can use them to meet up with people you already know. Most people find these events hard to navigate and, often, a bit demoralizing. You need to keep your spirits up.

Pitfalls to Avoid

Avoid falling prey to these common job search pitfalls:

- **Not knowing what to do:** By far the biggest time waster is simply procrastinating because you don't know what to do. Having a detailed plan with specific action steps is the key.
- **Not feeling like doing it:** Who feels like doing anything? Monitor your self-talk and use it to motivate yourself. Remind yourself that you don't have to finish, you just have to start. Give yourself 20 minutes to work on a tough task before you throw in the towel. Do the hard stuff first thing in the morning when you have the most energy. Keep the bigger picture in mind: While it's true that writing cover letters is tedious and even meeting someone for coffee can be stressful if you don't enjoy networking, remember that you will have a satisfying and interesting career if you just keep going (and if you need to support yourself financially then you better get going).
- **Time wasters:** Stop rationalizing using all your time to go to a movie or watch television. Again, a plan helps here. Use these kinds of treats as a reward: If I get my work done on Monday and Tuesday, I'll treat myself by working for a half day on Wednesday. Then I'll spend the rest of the day having lunch with a friend and going to a movie or some other activity that I enjoy for its own sake.

Tracking Your Progress

Tracking your progress can be hard because the job-seeking process is not a linear one. You can't control the outcome, but you can absolutely control your behavior—the things you do to lead you to your goal. Keeping track of those elements and consistently executing your process day to day and week by week will help you stay on track, lead you to your goals, and make you feel better.

Each week you should have a combination of activities that will help you get to where you're going. Your specific goals will change based on which stage of the job search process you are in. For example:

- **If you are still figuring out what you want**, plan to spend five to eight hours a week in reflective exercises or reading books that help you think about yourself.
- **If you are narrowing down options**, plan to spend two to three hours a week researching various industries.
- **If you are networking and doing informational interviews**, keep track of the number of contacts you meet and referrals you get to expand your network. Pick a number of contacts per week that feels comfortable for you. As a starting point, try to meet five to 10 contacts and get three to five referrals a week.

Keep track of your online applications and record which ones resulted in a phone call or interview. What is your response rate? Many people have response rates in the single digits. If you are only applying to positions that are a good fit (and following the advice in chapter 8), you should have a better response rate (20 percent or higher).

Building Resilience

Job searches are circuitous and can be long slogs, with plenty of detours and no shortcuts. Just when you think you are making progress, you have a big setback. You need to find ways to keep your spirits up and keep going even when the going gets tough. Building resilience takes some effort, but it's worth it. There are a few ways to build resilience.

First, get your mindset right. Some people get upset when they have lulls in their job search simply because they didn't expect them—expect them. This is not pessimistic; it is realistic. There will always be times when someone won't get back to you, networking meetings won't go well, your resume looks terrible, and you don't know what to do next. You will get rejected from jobs, you won't get the interview, and it will take longer than it should. Make peace with all this by recognizing in advance that setbacks are normal. Strategize and plan for ways to remember this and comfort yourself when you are in the middle of a setback. You can write down your top ideas in your job journal to remind yourself of them.

The second important tool is to have a support group around you. This can be a formal or informal group of other job seekers. It should also include your friends and family. People are much more resilient when they have support from others.

Reframing setbacks is another important tool. When you are disappointed by something, instead of getting upset (which is natural), ask yourself, "What can I learn from this?" You can also experiment with challenging yourself with the question, "Why is this actually the best thing for me?"

Set up small wins. Are you better at research than writing cover letters? Do some research before starting your cover letter to prime your mind for success. Then do some research after spending time on the cover letter to reward yourself. Prefer networking? Schedule one to three networking meetings a day. Fill your time with valuable activities that you actually enjoy—there are many activities to choose from. Emphasize the ones you like more and use them strategically to help you feel successful. The momentum you gain from that will help carry you forward.

Of course, there are some things you simply have to do whether or not you like them. Some people don't like reaching out to others and networking. Others enjoy meeting people, but find research tedious. Some people find that doing the tasks they don't like first thing in the morning is helpful. "Time bounding" undesirable tasks—doing them for only a prescribed amount of time—is also a good strategy. This helps you recognize that you only have to do the task for a finite amount of time, and then you can reward yourself after that.

Even when you are down—especially when you are down—having a strong plan guides you to take specific actions and steps forward. Action leads to progress and progress is what makes you feel better.

Your Long-Term Career Plan

Now, imagine for a moment that you're done. You've landed a great new position, had your first day, and all is well. You have knowledge and information, a sense of strategy, and a very active network. Make sure you remember to maintain and nourish this asset that you have spent months building to ensure long-term career success.

Your career is a long-term journey. Every six months or so it's helpful to step back and take stock with some reflection questions:

- Am I on the right track? Why or why not?
- What is the next step (or two) in my career? What skills and experiences do I need to build to get there? Whom do I need to support me?
- What is the state of my network? Are there some people I haven't connected with in a while? What's the best way to reconnect with them?
- What are some trends in my industry that are going to influence my role?
- What workforce trends do I see coming up that I need to recognize and possibly plan for?

Summary

Keeping up with your self-reflection and industry insights will help you notice very quickly if you need to make a course correction. Maintaining this outlook will help you keep your eye out for and pursue new opportunities in your current workplace that you may have missed in the past.

Your career journey is a lifelong process. Use the tools in this chapter and the rest of the book to help you make good choices now and open up great opportunities in the future.

Part II
Putting Your Plan Into Action

In Part I, you focused on identifying what you want in a job and work environment. Now it's time to make your vision a reality. The focus turns to what employers want and how your skills and talents meet their needs. This section covers creating a resume and personal brand and how to network and interview effectively, as well as tips for applying to jobs online, handling pre-employment assessments, and negotiating your salary. At every step along the way, use your preference grid and career plan to guide you.

Crafting an Effective Resume

Michelle Riklan

Today's challenging job market demands that you are well equipped with stellar marketing tools. Did you know that your resume is one of the most crucial components in your marketing campaign? Most people think that it is simply a document that explains what you want to do and what you have done. That is a mistake. In this chapter, you'll learn how to craft an effective resume, but first let's start by defining what a resume is and its purpose.

What Is a Resume?

A resume is a personal marketing tool. Its purpose is to communicate the value that an individual has to a potential employer in such a way that the employer is compelled to call the individual for an interview. When written effectively, this strategic and powerful document will entice a hiring manager, search firm, HR professional, or another decision maker to take the next step and request a conversation. It sells the employer on the idea that the individual could be a good fit for an organization, company, or specific open position. A resume can be the difference between getting an interview and not getting an interview—it is a conduit for getting in the door. But when we say your resume is a marketing tool, what exactly does that mean?

The Applicant as "Product"

As a job applicant, you are a product that needs branding, marketing, and selling. To accomplish this, you need to construct your marketing tools. Your resume should be one a top priority.

We often hear in the job market that individuals need to clearly communicate their personal brand to potential employers. As they get ready to start creating their resumes, this is often the point where individuals panic a bit: "What is my personal brand?" "What does branding myself on my resume mean?" It does not need to be very complicated. Your brand is your promise to the consumer, who is your potential employer. Your brand lets a potential employer know what to expect from you; it differentiates you from the competition. It is a combination of who you are, who you want to be, and how others perceive you.

With this in mind, when I design a powerful and effective resume, I like to start by "labeling" the individual. I use this terminology to keep people in the "product and consumer" state of mind. After all, if we are shopping at a supermarket for soup, we need to be able to tell if we are buying chicken noodle or minestrone by looking at the packaging. Both types of soup may be Campbell's, but they are very different, so the Campbell's brand must quickly communicate to the consumer what is being sold.

Now picture this: You are in the soup aisle at the supermarket, and you decide that you want Campbell's chicken noodle soup. There are rows of Campbell's soup cans on the shelf, but instead of clear packaging listing the name of the product and a picture to show what you are buying, all the labels simply say "soup." Perhaps ingredients are listed in tiny print and you can use that to figure out what kind of soup is in the can, but what a waste of time for the consumer! It would be enough to make you say, "Hey, I'm going to look at Progresso." This is how potential employers feel when they pick up a resume and cannot immediately see who the person is, how she potentially fits into the organization, and what she has to offer. They will not go digging to find this information. Instead, they will move on to the next resume.

To avoid being passed over because the reader cannot quickly figure out who you are and therefore moves on to check out the next resume, begin your resume with a header and a subheader. For example:

Header: General Manager / Chief Operating Officer
Subheader: Private Country Clubs and Luxury Resort Hotels

Notice how the header defines the applicant, just as the word *Campbell's* defines the brand of soup. The subheader gets more specific; it's equivalent to *chicken noodle* or *minestrone*, telling readers what kind of general manager or chief operating officer they will get. This way, employers looking for an executive for a manufacturing plant will know immediately to move on and you have not wasted their time. Another example:

Header: Vice President of Sales
Subheader: Digital & Traditional Media Advertising | Organization Building

This applicant quickly communicated to readers who he is and how he could fit into an organization. Readers greatly appreciate this strategy because then they can continue reading and find out what value the person may bring.

Value Proposition Statements vs. Objective Statements

After creating a strong header and subheader, you need a captivating and engaging profile summary (also known as the value proposition statement).

I'm often asked, "I thought a resume should have an objective statement. Is this true?" While some career experts are divided on this matter, I don't use them because they are applicant-centric and only talk about the candidate's wishes or career target. Typical objective statements read like these:

> "Seeking a challenging position as a financial executive where I can utilize my management skills."

> "Looking for a rewarding career in the retail industry with opportunities for advancement."

What do you notice about these statements? It's all "I want this and I want that." There is nothing there to pique the interest of an employer.

While you need a career objective to help guide your search, recruiters or hiring managers are not particularly interested in what you want in life. The question they want answered is, "Who are you, and what can you do for me?" A career objective does not set you apart from the competition, because everyone wants a challenging and rewarding career with career advancement opportunities. It is a waste of prime real estate on your resume!

Instead, create a compelling profile section that displays your unique value. This is your value proposition statement. Use it to grab recruiters' attention right off the bat by developing a hook to persuade them to continue reading. Keep in mind that because a recruiter will most likely start reading at the top of your resume, the top third of the page is crucial. Make it easy on the reader: Create a hard-hitting paragraph that gets her excited and wanting to know more. Take a look at these three options for an opening paragraph or profile:

> Global executive with 30+ years of experience seeking a position where I can use my skills in business transformation, executive vision and execution, and team building and executive leadership.

> Visionary global executive; hardworking leader, builds strong teams and grows revenue. Excellent communication, presentation, technology, and business skills.

> The "go-to" global executive with a reputation for energizing stagnant and declining business units, connecting the dots between technology and business issues, driving client satisfaction through win-win scenarios, and turning negative margins into profit. Noted for driving rapid and long-term ROI through business transformation, executive vision and execution, and team building and executive leadership.

Clearly, the first option is an objective statement. Did it make you want to find out more about what the applicant was seeking and keep reading? If not, then it is ineffective.

The second version is moving in the right direction, but still misses the mark. The language is weak and generic. Did it make you curious about the applicant?

The third option is a value proposition statement. You clearly know what the individual has to offer and how he is perceived. The applicant has also differentiated himself by offering more than just generic information.

Core Competencies, Areas of Expertise, and Professional Skills

Including a section on core competencies, areas of expertise, and professional skills is expected in resumes today. This section helps your resume get through applicant-tracking systems. But does it help the employer? Yes! Keep the employer in mind at all times, because she is your gatekeeper. With many resumes to sift through, she wants a quick and easy way to scan your resume to see if you have the desired skills. The core competencies, areas of expertise, or professional skills section provides that checklist.

Picture a hiring manager with a stack of resumes on her desk. She pulls your resume from the pile and holds it in her left hand. In her right hand is the job description. If the resume has a professional skills section (or one of the other section headers listed here), then she can quickly eyeball both documents to see if you have some of the more crucial requirements. She will appreciate that you were considerate of her time by frontloading your resume with these keywords; now she won't have to dig for this information. When creating this section on your resume, ask yourself, "What keywords will be searched when an employer is looking for someone like me?" Make sure those keywords are included in this section, but be sure to back up them up with relevant experience and accomplishments throughout your resume.

For example, an employer is looking for someone with the following skills to fill a position: event planning, food and beverage operations, customer satisfaction, menu creation, food safety, workforce planning, recruiting, training large teams, catering, mentoring, upselling services, and vendor relations. The areas of expertise or core competencies section of an applicant's resume may look like this:

Areas of Expertise			
• Banquets	• Hiring	• Sales	• Training
• Coaching	• Large Events	• Scheduling	• Vendor

How else can you find the right keywords? One way to find the best keywords to include is to see what words are used in job descriptions and postings that look interesting to you. The *Occupational Outlook Handbook* (www.bls.gov/ooh) is another great resource. You'll read more about keywords in chapter 8.

Professional Experience

Hiring managers don't want to read dense blocks of text, and nobody wants to read a long list of bullets. Often, a person's resume becomes a laundry list of what he has done, instead of an engaging story about what he has achieved throughout his career. Remember to keep the "product-consumer" mindset. Let's compare two fictional ads. As you're reading them, think about which ad is more compelling and which one appeals to the wants or needs of the consumer.

The "CAR"—Ad #1

Come to Tony's Auto Barn and check out this great automobile for only $15,699 that comes with:
- 30 hp @ 6,300 rpm
- Gasoline direct injection (GDI)
- 4-doors
- Projector beam highlights
- Gray leather interior
- 4-wheel drive
- Heated outside mirrors

The "CAR"—Ad #2

Tony's Auto Barn would like to introduce you to our new luxury sedan. This is no ordinary sedan; it is a sports sedan in its truest form. We are not just referring to its incredible speed (0-60 in six seconds), its antilock brakes, or modern design. This sedan was designed with you in mind! We know how important it is to feel comfortable and safe, but still stylish.

Up to five passengers will experience a roomy and smooth ride, enjoying a soft leather interior with seat warmers for those cold winter days. There is no need to worry about tough road conditions because optimum weight distribution ensures excellent handling characteristics. No wonder this car has received five-star safety ratings from safercar.gov for five years in a row.

When creating your professional experience section, keep CAR in mind:
- Challenge: What were you challenged to do?
- Action: What did you do and how did you do it?
- Results: What were the positive end results and the impact on the global enterprise?

Next include numbers, percentages, or anything that will quantify and support the results. For example, is this an effective statement?

Added program management and revenue responsibility for XYZ business units (annual revenues $200M+) to existing portfolio.

We do not know *how* the individual did this, if she was successful, or the results. In other words, we need to know the quantifiable accomplishments.

Here is another example:

> Captured three business opportunities for the business unit and increased net profits.

We have no idea how the individual did this. He claims he increased net profits, but we don't know by how much. Was it $1? $1,000? $10K? Was it an achievement? Even if he stated "increased net profits by 20 percent," we still wouldn't know if that was actually an accomplishment. What if the goal was 35 percent? Then this would have been an under-achievement.

Using the CAR format, develop a challenge, action, and result story. Once you've collected all the pieces of that story, write it up in an interesting but concise manner. This will then be a strong bullet.

Remember, we want to make everything easy on the reader. Too often, people blend their job descriptions with their achievements. Instead, include a brief overview of the job description in paragraph form before you list your achievement bullet. It is much easier on the reader when your experience section is written with a combination of paragraphs and bullet points. This formatting makes it easier to navigate your resume. The following is an example of using bullets and paragraphs to describe a professional experience.

Vice President—Information Technology

Promoted into VP position; hand selected for new position by CIO. Turned around IT support operations and built an agile, customer-responsive organization. Oversaw global IT support; developed and executed strategic initiatives that aligned business and support functions, increased enterprise performance, improved customer relations, and reduced operating costs. Identified and integrated new technology into daily operations while continuously assessing internal development versus outsourcing ROI. Administered an $8M budget.

- Elevated IT support to the number 1 department in customer service surveys by revamping support policies and culture; improved client responsiveness by 85 percent while simultaneously streamlining global operations and improving financial transparency.
- Enhanced overall workforce performance by establishing a conference services department; improved support response time by 95 percent while simultaneously increasing service quality.

Note how the job description is separated from the achievements. Contextual information is also included so the reader can understand how the individual's career has progressed.

It is also important to ensure that your language is active, not passive, by using "action verbs" for each bullet point. List achievements for a current job in the present tense; for past work experiences, write them in the past tense. Table 5-1 lists action verbs you can use to start each bullet point.

Table 5-1. Action Verbs for Resume Bullet Points

Accomplished	Doubled	Maintained	Researched	Traced
Achieved	Earned	Managed	Resolved	Tracked
Approved	Edited	Narrowed	Revised	Traded
Arbitrated	Eliminated	Negotiated	Scheduled	Trained
Bolstered	Established	Operated	Serviced	Transferred
Built	Expanded	Organized	Set up	Transformed
Completed	Founded	Originated	Simplified	Translated
Conducted	Generated	Performed	Sold	Trimmed
Consolidated	Headed	Planned	Solved	Tripled
Constructed	Implemented	Prevented	Sparked	Uncovered
Controlled	Improved	Processed	Started	Unified
Converted	Improvised	Produced	Streamlined	Unraveled
Created	Increased	Promoted	Strengthened	Utilized
Decreased	Innovated	Proposed	Stressed	Vacated
Delivered	Installed	Provided	Stretched	Verified
Demonstrated	Instituted	Purchased	Structured	Withdrew
Designed	Introduced	Recommended	Succeeded	Won
Developed	Invented	Redesigned	Superseded	Worked
Devised	Launched	Reduced	Supervised	
Directed	Led	Reorganized	Terminated	

You can also incorporate a description of the company, particularly if the company doesn't have name recognition. This gives the reader an understanding of the type of environment you have worked in—small or large, public or private, national or international.

For example:

Burt & Ernie LLP, Washington, D.C.
Global accounting firm with 1,800 certified public accountants in 44 offices; among the largest accounting firms in New York City and one of the largest U.S. firms in Brazil.

Additional Sections

Once you've developed the professional experience section, start to wrap up your resume. If your experience goes back more than 15 years, consider including an earlier career section. Your earlier career is important and you don't want to lose it. After all, that makes up the building blocks of your career. However, the details of those positions may no longer be relevant, or they may simply not be as important as your more recent experience, and therefore, you don't want to waste the space. Here's an example of what this section might look like:

Earlier Career	
Assistant General Manager | Houlihan's Restaurant, New York, NY	1996 to 2000
Executive Chef | Osteria, Charlotte, NC	1994 to 1996
Food & Beverage Director | The Riviera Country Club, Charlotte, NC	1992 to 1994

Then conclude with the education section. If it includes professional training, course work, or certifications, call it education and professional development. Here is an example:

Education and Professional Development
Johnson & Wales University, Charlotte, NC Bachelor of Science in Food and Beverage Management
The Leader's Institute, San Antonio, TX Fearless Presentations | Team Building
Southern Hospitality Association, Richmond, VA Wine Pairing | Management 101 | Customer Service Excellence

Other sections people often put in their resumes include associations, affiliations, speaking engagements, patents, publications, and certifications. Whether it is appropriate to include these sections will vary. Consider developing a separate document called "Resume Addendum" for these sections. The addendum can be provided as requested either at an interview or afterward, but it also may not be necessary. Remember, the resume is the tool that procures the interview, and the employer will appreciate that you did not provide a novel.

Resume Length

Have you been told that resumes should only be one page? Wrong! Yes, a resume needs to be written clearly and concisely. However, if you are a professional with substantial experience and have tried to communicate that in one page, then your reader is probably scratching her head, wondering what you've been doing for the past XX years. One page is usually not sufficient unless you are straight out of school.

I write two-page resumes 90 percent of the time; sometimes I write three pages, which is acceptable when warranted. Beyond that is unnecessary unless you are creating a CV for an academic position. When a resume spills into four pages, the reader will not only get bored, but also wonder whether you can communicate clearly and concisely.

Format and Design

How important is the formatting and design? Extremely! Think about the formatting and design of your resume as product packaging design. You should have two types of resumes: a nicely formatted one you use when emailing or supplying a hard copy to someone, and a plain text version to use when applying to positions online. This chapter is primarily concerned with the first type, and chapter 8 covers formatting for online applications.

For a product, great packaging improves professional image and influences the company brand. Packaging can be the deciding factor for a consumer making a buying decision, and at a minimum it helps the product get off the shelf. For example, a shopper takes a child to the store to buy a new cereal. The child points to the rows of cereals exclaiming, "I want that one!" Most likely, he is pointing to a colorful box with fun cartoon characters; the company has created a design that stimulates his senses and encourages his mom to take the product off the shelf. Granted, the mom may review the ingredients, determine it is too full of sugar and preservatives, and put it back on the shelf. But the point is it got off the shelf and in the hands of the consumer. When customers see a packaging design that appeals to their senses, they are more likely to review and possibly buy a product.

According to the writer, painter, and art critic John Berger in his seminal book *Ways of Seeing* (1972), people think in pictures: "Seeing comes before words." Your first thought may be that this is an obstacle when writing a resume, because a resume is mostly words. But understanding this can work to your advantage. The entire packaging or design of your resume becomes essential for inspiring and motivating a potential employer to "take your resume off the shelf," pull it out of the pile, and pay attention to the "ingredients."

The key to selling any product is presentation and evoking a sensory response for the consumer. Here are some tips on how you can accomplish this:

- **Choose a font that is easy to read and an appropriate size.** If your reader needs to whip out reading glasses to see what you have to say, not only have you aggravated her because you've called attention to her age, but you also wasted her time because she had to find or use tools to read through your document. And then she might not even bother; after all, she has a whole stack of resumes and another one might be easier to read. A few recommended fonts include Arial Narrow, Bookman, Calibri, Cambria, Garamond, Georgia, Tahoma, and Verdana. The appropriate font size varies based on the specific typeface, but a good rule of thumb is to go no smaller than 10 points.
- **Separate your sections with clear dividers.** Segment information so that the reader can easily navigate through the document.
- **Write succinctly.** Resumes that are dense cannot be "eyeballed." The hiring manager is scanning for information and needs to find it quickly. If your resume looks like a newspaper article without white space and tons of content, then it needs reworking.
- **Pay attention to details.** Misspellings, incorrect grammar, and inconsistencies in tense, voice, punctuation, and spacing alert the reader that you do not pay close attention to details. This document is a representation of you; if you want the reader to know that you are detail oriented, prove it here.

- **Add embellishments.** Adding a graph, table, image, box, border, or some color to a resume can help support the content and draw attention to important aspects of the information. As you design your resume, keep in mind the industry and position for which you are applying. Some industries may be conservative, whereas others are more freely creative.

So, what resume style should you use? That depends on whether you have career challenges that need addressing. The three most commonly used styles are reverse chronological, functional, and targeted or hybrid.

Reverse Chronological

The traditional resume is reverse chronological, with a focus on the experience section and describing each job in detail. This style resume is often used when a person is staying in the same profession.

Pro: It appeals to the more conventional reader and can be very effective if the candidate wants to highlight some prestigious employers.

Con: Core skills are not brought to the forefront and the reader has a linear view of the candidate.

Functional

A functional resume highlights major skills and accomplishments at the top. The important skill sets and qualifications are presented under functional headings, so the reader does not need to scan through entries for several employers to see what you've done.

Pro: This type of resume format is effective for people who are changing careers, have gaps in their resumes, are returning to work, or are students or graduates just entering the workforce. It de-emphasizes or even omits employment history, dates, and so forth.

Con: This format may raise a red flag with employers, because they may wonder what you are trying to hide. Search firms do not prefer this format.

Targeted or Hybrid

The hybrid resume gives the best of both worlds because it presents work history in reverse chronological order after a strong introduction that highlights skills and key selling points.

Resume Challenges

You can address challenges in your resume several ways. Consider these tips.

Employment Gaps

Your skills and experience may be marketable, but how do you present a gap or gaps in your employment history? Yes, your reader will most likely question an employment gap, but it does not mean that you will be perceived as unemployable or a poor candidate.

Short employment gaps are not necessarily worrisome, as long as they are not frequent. Neither is an employment of one year or less. Unemployment that lasts more than a year will require a strategy. By camouflaging and explaining gaps in your resume, you're taking a pre-emptive measure to put the tides back in your favor.

Just be ready to answer the obvious question: Interviewers will always want to know the cause of your employment gap, so don't get caught without an honest, valid answer.

Hide Gaps in Plain Sight

Were you let go? If yes, say so. Were you laid off because of a downsizing or company restructuring? Explain this in your cover letter or provide a short explanation in your resume under the company description. State why it happened, such as poor company performance, obsolete jobs, outsourcing, or whatever reasons your previous employer provided.

Camouflage the Gaps

Employment gaps in your resume can be camouflaged by simply showing ranges of years. It is not important to include months in your employment history, especially if most of your jobs span years. Compare the two below. Doesn't the second one look better?

Human Resources Director, XYZ, Inc. | July 2009 to March 2016

Human Resources Director, XYZ, Inc. | 2009 to 2016

Include "Nonwork" Work in Your Employment History

If you took a class, pursued an MBA, consulted, worked in a startup, or volunteered, then put it in your employment history. This is an authentic way to account for the time, instead of having a glaring gap in your resume.

Convert Unpaid Duties Into Profitable Work-Related Skills

If you are a parent returning to work and some of your common duties include preparing meals, driving kids, organizing car pools, budgeting, and making sure that homework is completed, these are acquired skills and should not go to waste. Reframe those skills to match the target employer's vocabulary; for example:
- arranging play dates or organizing car pools = organizing or coordinating events
- budgeting and paying the bills = bookkeeping
- helping the kids with their homework= mentoring or supervising people
- selling tickets for a fundraiser or raffle = sales and customer service skills.

Emphasize Continued Learning

Many individuals who have been out of the workforce stay up-to-date with the latest in their industry by reading professional magazines and participating in LinkedIn groups. List professional memberships you've maintained, workshops you've attended, and any active licenses or certifications by creating a "Professional Organizations and Licenses" section in your resume. List any recent training programs you've attended to brush up on your skills in the "Education" section. These accomplishments will show prospective employers that you're not a dinosaur.

Ageism

If you are concerned that your age is a detriment as a job seeker, here are a few quick and easy tips:

- **Eliminate graduation dates.** Unless you are a recent graduate, the reader does not need to know that you graduated in 1979. If he went straight to that section to find out how old you are, then you have just forced him to actually read your resume so he can figure it out.

- **List your personalized LinkedIn URL** in your contact information (and make sure your profile is well crafted; see chapter 6). Providing the URL helps the reader find your profile quickly. She is going to look for it anyway. This also demonstrates that you live in the 21st century and understand both the value and application of social media.

- **Stay current on skills and certifications** and list them in your resume.

- **Truncate or eliminate older positions.** Use the "Earlier Career" section for truncating, and eliminate any positions from a long time ago that are truly irrelevant.

- **Don't be old fashioned.** Simple things on a resume can indicate your age. Resumes constructed with a wide left-side margin, objective statement, or phrases such as "references available upon request" shout "outdated individual."

Addressing a Career Change

It is not impossible to change careers and market yourself for something entirely new. The trick is perception. How a potential employer perceives you is what matters most, and your job is to positively influence that perception.

Investigate your target employers so you truly understand what they are looking for. Review the keywords and make sure that you include and emphasize any skills you have that match your prospective employer's. Highlight any success stories you have and translate them into language that the reader will understand.

Consider using the functional format when structuring your resume so that the reader is drawn to your transferable skills, which you will include in the first third of page one.

Summary

A resume is a personal marketing tool. Its purpose is to communicate an individual's value to a potential employer in such a way that the employer is compelled to call the person for an interview. There are many components of an effective resume, including the value proposition statements, keywords, skills, professional experience, and education. It is also important to choose the right format, design, and strategy when crafting your resume. Choose the one that makes the most sense for the job you're applying for and the experience you've amassed thus far. See Appendix F for sample resumes and the Additional Resources section for further information on resume writing.

SHOULD I HIRE A PROFESSIONAL RESUME WRITER?

Quite a bit goes into the process to create that compelling, personal marketing tool. Many people opt to work with a professional resume writer to help them put their best foot forward. Professional resume writers brings their own style, training, and education to the project. If you work in a specialized field, you may want someone with experience in your industry. Ask to see some samples of resumes they have written for others and request references from past clients. If you do decide to hire a writer to work with you, make sure that you select someone who is certified and has an excellent reputation. The person should be a good fit for you.

6

Managing Your Personal Brand and Digital Footprint

Marie Zimenoff

Personal branding has roots in a 1997 front-page article that business management expert Tom Peters wrote for *Fast Company*, titled "The Brand Called You." The idea has taken hold and become a commonly used term when people talk about career management. Simply put, a personal brand is how you want to be known and to whom. Just like when a company creates a branded product, the process of creating a personal brand takes into account internal strengths and how these add value for a potential target audience.

For example, think about cell phone service providers. They all offer similar services and products, much like public accountants all do similar work for organizations. However, each company has made an effort to establish its brand. Verizon created a brand focused on having the best cell phone coverage in the nation. Do you remember its series of television commercials where the spokesperson moved around the country asking, "Can you hear me now?" T-Mobile focused on value, offering similar services and products for less. Its target market was younger Americans, and its commercials featuring the girl on a pink motorcycle demonstrated the speed of their service while appealing to this audience. Both companies created a brand that advertised how their differences added value, not that one was "better" than the other.

Borrowing from this corporate example, a public accounting firm would want to sit down and figure out two things: What do they offer that is different from their peers? How does this add value for their target audience? This, of course, assumes that they have identified their target audience—a key factor in having an effective brand. For career management purposes, the target audience might be internal decision makers for earning promotions, customers of your current company, target industries, or target companies for future positions.

If you have done the exercises in the first section, you should now have ample material recorded in your Personal Inventory or job journal that you can use to develop your personal brand. When determining your strengths and how you differ from peers, brainstorm freely—ask your friends and colleagues what makes you stand out. Find out what makes you their go-to person. Then go back and filter. Years of experience, for instance, is often top-of-mind for people, but it's rarely differentiating in today's market. However, experience with specific types of problems or customers might be differentiating. Your brand also includes your values, goals, and interests, which typically affect how you work and are what make you unique. Simply put, your "personal brand" is who you are, what you bring to the world that is different from your peers, and how this added value contributes to your working life and career.

Consider the case of Frank, a software development manager. Although software developers are in high demand in today's market, there are more candidates in the manager pool. Having a generic brand will hurt him, because he won't stand out in this crowded market. So, Frank sits down to figure out his brand. He knows that the experience that differentiates him from his peers is the work he has done creating offshore development teams. This adds value for his target audience, which is midsized companies trying to achieve that same goal to cut development costs. As discussed in chapter 5, Frank would want to build a resume that highlights this experience and brands himself as a manager who can build offshore teams that maintain and improve systems for companies while decreasing development costs. That foundational brand would guide the content on his resume and across all the media he decides to use to promote his brand.

Frank might start formulating his brand by gathering three kinds of information: strengths and differences from peers, target audience, and the value of his strengths to that audience. His thoughts are outlined in Table 6-1.

Table 6-1. Identifying Personal Brand Differences

Strengths and Differences From Peers	Target Audience	Value of Strengths to Audience
• Extensive experience building outsourced teams • Technical expertise in SAAS and ERP systems • Success interacting with teams in Asia, including launching three teams in India • Multiple success stories saving money for organizations while improving software quality	• CIOs in companies who are looking to create outsourced teams • His manager and his manager's manager, who may have internal opportunities • Former partners, vendors, and contractors who can assist with his career advancement	• Saves money • Improves quality when most offshoring efforts struggle • Can jump into this type of role or project quickly and succeed • Enables international expansion

When Frank starts communicating his brand in his resume, LinkedIn profile, and daily work, he will want to highlight any experiences and accomplishments that align with these strengths. When he meets with his boss for a performance review, he should share stories that communicate this value. He should also seek out projects that can highlight these elements of his brand, and perhaps help to build his career in the direction he wants to go in the future.

How Do You Define Your Brand?

Although the idea of a brand is simple—who you are, what you want to be known as, and how that connects with your audience—defining your brand is a lifelong process.

The first step is to start with the easy part—you. If you've worked on the exercises in chapter 2, you should already have a lot of material to work with. If not, answer the following questions:

- What are your natural strengths?
- What do people in your life (work, home, volunteer) come to you for?
- When you look back at the successes in your career, what themes do you see?
- Do you offer a unique experience or skill set that your peers don't usually have?
- What do you want to do more of? What skills do you need to build or demonstrate more to move forward in your career?

Next, define your audience. How would you answer the following questions?

- Whom do you want to recognize that you have these strengths to help you advance your career (such as your boss, customers, peers, future hiring managers)?
- What is important to them?
- Are they in a certain industry? What are the trends and needs in that industry, especially related to the strengths you have identified?
- What are their demographics (gender, age, location)? How does this influence how they see you or how you communicate your brand to them?
- What opportunities do you have to communicate with them (in person, online, at industry conferences)?

The last step is to connect the dots. Answer the following:

- What does your audience value (for example, saving money, making money, or customer service)?
- What strengths, qualifications, experiences, and accomplishments demonstrate your ability to deliver that value?

The foundational work for building your own brand starts with brainstorming your unique attributes and value. Use Table 6-2 to gather your strengths and differences from peers, the target audience, and the value of your strengths to that audience.

Table 6-2. Identifying Your Brand Differences

Strengths and Differences From Peers	Target Audience	Value of Strengths to Audience

How Do You Communicate Your Brand?

Once you have determined the pieces of your brand—what differentiates you from your peers and how it connects with your target audience—the next step is to proactively communicate that brand. Your resume is one medium to communicate your brand, but it serves a specific purpose in your job search that may not be relevant to your current career needs. Communicating your brand goes way beyond your resume.

In Person

Your brand is apparent in everything you do—what you wear, what you put up in the office, and how you interact with others. This could take the form of networking, but it also includes the daily conversations you have with those at work, in your industry, and in the community.

The first impression you make in each of these settings and what people remember about you after meeting you are important to your brand. If you consider yourself to be engaging in your job as a training professional, that engaging communication style should be obvious to people you meet in every setting, and something they remember after they meet you. If you talk too much at meetings or networking events, shy away from engaging with others at industry events, or never demonstrate your style by leading an informal or formal presentation at an event, others will not perceive your brand the way that you would like them to or may even form a different opinion of your brand.

From speaking up in meetings to presenting at industry conferences, there are many opportunities to build your brand in person. Consider how those you interact with daily experience your brand. Then, depending on your strengths and the nature of the work you do or want to do, it may be important to seek out more opportunities to build your brand in person, such as public speaking, strategic networking, or becoming more visible to a specific audience at work.

Select opportunities that put you in front of your target audience, demonstrate the skill sets you want to highlight moving forward, and allow you to be clear about your value. For instance our software manager, Frank, might seek out opportunities to talk specifically about his specialty in building outsourced teams, rather than just general software development management topics. This is probably the most important aspect of your brand, as those you interact with daily at work or frequently at industry events will have the largest influence on helping you achieve your career goals.

In Writing

Written communication has changed drastically in the last few years, and we often forget that what we write every day influences how we are perceived. From emails to whitepapers or other publications, what we write can make a lasting impression.

Most people think of their resume when they think of their brand, but today your resume may not be the first thing you have written that someone reads, especially if you are proactively communicating your brand. If you are job seeking, consider that a large percentage of hiring managers will search for your name on the Internet during the hiring process. They will be hoping to find written examples of your expertise, especially for certain types of professionals. These could include a whitepaper, conference proceedings, blogs, social media profiles, social media updates, and media articles.

Written communications have longevity and offer concrete examples of your work to those in your target audience. If you are a strong writer, look for opportunities to share your expertise in a context that your target audience will see as credible and aligned with future positions you seek. For example, writing a whitepaper or publishing in an industry magazine may be more impactful for our software development manager, Frank, than starting a blog would be. But a blog could be the perfect tool for someone in marketing.

Everyone—especially Millennials, who are stereotyped that they write in texting language and emoticons—can benefit from considering the professionalism of the written communications they produce on a daily basis.

In Videos

Video is probably the most intimidating form of communicating your brand, but it's quickly becoming the most effective. People prefer watching short (less than 90 seconds) videos to reading, and video provides a much more personal introduction. The best videos are personable, not overly scripted or perfect, and add value for the audience. You might share a process you use to be more effective in your work, a clip of a presentation you gave at a conference, or a slide presentation demonstrating your expertise (make sure that you narrate your slide presentation to make it more appealing).

If you are considering using a video resume, avoid just reading through your paper resume. Video, like every other communication of your brand, should tell a story and add value for the audience. Instead of telling viewers your history, focus on a success story or share your expertise in a specific area. A 90-second video is not going to give away too much information, so pay attention to any sensitive information that you do not want to share, but be careful of using the excuse that all your material belongs to your company.

Any social medium will amplify your other communication strengths, so take a few minutes to think about what will work best for you. Check off the communication approaches that best fit you and your target audience:

- in person
  - participating in meetings
  - speaking at conferences
  - in-person networking.
- in writing
  - whitepapers
  - articles
  - blogs
  - internal communication.
- in videos
  - slide presentations
  - video resume
  - other expertise demonstrations.
- other

On Social Media

Perhaps the fastest expanding way to communicate a personal brand is on social media. Building social media profiles that are aligned with your brand is an important part of this effort. When someone searches for you and pulls up your LinkedIn, Twitter, Facebook, or Instagram account, they should get a consistent picture of who you are professionally and personally, without coming across information that is harmful to your brand. Finding a good balance of sharing your personality without raising questions about your discretion and professionalism is important. But cleansing your profiles too much can make you appear boring or not approachable, which can be just as harmful as illicit material.

Communicating your brand on social media goes beyond creating your profiles on these sites. Proactively build your brand by sharing content and driving individuals to your profiles. Every update you make on social media becomes part of your brand—you can share in groups on LinkedIn, post pictures on Facebook or Instagram, or retweet posts on Twitter. This activity weaves your story—what is important to you, what do you spend time doing, and how well do you interact with others in your networks?

Social media also provides a unique opportunity to share your brand consistently and widely across your network using the methods that best fit your communication style. If you are a writer, you can share your whitepapers, articles, or blogs using social media. If you speak in front of groups, share videos of your presentations or short videos that highlight your speaking strength and expertise. You can also build connections by sharing the expertise of others—through posting articles, reposting their posts, and commenting on their activity—if writing and speaking are not your strengths.

When used consistently and in alignment with your professional brand, social media tools can greatly expand your reach. Join and share with industry and interest groups to build visibility within your current organization and across your industry or the industry into which you would like to transition. Our software development manager, Frank, might join LinkedIn groups that focus on development and perhaps even find those that focus on outsourced development. He can post within these groups, answer questions, and share information from others to start building relationships.

Social media offers you a great opportunity to build your brand, but it can be overwhelming. Before you dive in, consider what channels or media will be the best for you, based on your knowledge, interest, and the target audience and media it uses. To determine what social media outlets make the most sense, consider the data around who is on each and the main purpose of the medium in general. Also, find out if your target audience is using a medium by searching for the company, industry, or individuals you are targeting on the specific medium you are targeting. For example, if your target company isn't using Instagram but is using Facebook, consider focusing more of your efforts on Facebook than Instagram.

LinkedIn

LinkedIn is the social medium most recruiters use to proactively source talent for their companies. It is also where most professionals are building their online networks. With 433 million members (25 percent of online users), LinkedIn has become more than just a job search platform (Statista 2016). Members are highly educated, mainly in the United States (111 million), and concentrated in urban areas (WeRSM 2015).

Companies are encouraging their employees to be on LinkedIn, have complete profiles, and be active in their industry; this is considered a powerful tool for employer branding to help attract the best talent. This opens the door for employed professionals to use LinkedIn as a medium to build their brand. When deciding if this is the best medium for you, consider this: It is the go-to resource for 80 percent of recruiters in the United States, more than 33,000 companies are using LinkedIn's talent solutions, and more than 3 million companies have created company profiles on LinkedIn (Smith 2016). Search for the company names you are interested in using the company search and see how many of their employees are on LinkedIn. You can also search for groups of individuals in your industry, target industry, or geography.

Facebook

Perhaps surprisingly, Facebook is the second-most used social medium for finding potential employees, with 50 percent of recruiters using the medium. Facebook is also a powerful employer brand tool, and companies are increasing the marketing spent on Facebook to highlight specific positions and company news that will attract top talent. Although the average age on Facebook is still under 30, more than 40 percent of users are 35 or older. Facebook users also tend to be college educated; although, given the younger demographic, their average salaries are about half that of the average LinkedIn member (WeRSM 2015).

Similar to LinkedIn, some companies are encouraging their employees to share company news on Facebook, gaining free social media marketing while making more sincere connections through their employees' networks. If you watch, you'll probably see sponsored posts from companies to like their products and pages, as well as ads from companies you are affiliated with on Facebook. Many companies also create Facebook landing pages for positions that are challenging to fill.

If you have a profile on Facebook, remember that many companies will pull up your profile at some point during the hiring process. Even if you do not use Facebook proactively for building your brand or job seeking, make sure your profile positively represents you. This does not mean taking down all personal pictures—having a personality is important for your brand—but you want to make sure your photos and posts are an accurate reflection of your brand, whether it's the content in your photos or the language you use.

Twitter

Twitter is the third choice for recruiters, with more than 40 percent using it in the hiring process. Twitter is most popular among people ages 18 to 29, with highest per capita use outside the United States (WeRSM 2015; Lipman 2014). Interaction is important for building and maintaining a network on Twitter, and this can be challenging with the large volume of information posted to the site every minute. Similar to Facebook, employers use Twitter by setting up handles for hiring managers to post jobs and interact with potential candidates.

Twitter has perhaps the lowest barrier to entry, because anyone can follow any handle. You can connect with employers without having to wait for them to accept your request (like LinkedIn) and you can interact with them directly. If you are job seeking, consider searching for job titles and companies of interest to see if there is activity on Twitter. Employers often use hashtags (#engineer #job) to make job postings easier to find.

Twitter is also a potential medium for communicating your brand and interacting with a professional community: Follow the top minds in your field, interact with them to form relationships, and share thought leadership in whatever format works best for your communication style (video, articles, and so forth). Twitter is traditionally considered to be for marketing and sales professionals, and for those looking to build a presence as a thought leader, which makes it a wonderful option if you are looking to do just that.

Pinterest

A growing number of recruiters are using Pinterest because users spend more time on the site than many other social media outlets. Some companies are using Pinterest in a similar fashion as Facebook by creating career boards that demonstrate the company's culture or boards highlighting specific job opportunities.

Pinterest is a great place for creative professionals to post their artwork, cooks to post their meals, and so forth. If you have a visual portfolio of your work, you may want to consider building a Pinterest board that shows your work and your inspirations, in addition to having a personal website. Like Facebook and Twitter, you want to engage with pages aligned with your professional brand and those that go beyond the professional and share your other interests.

YouTube

Recruiters may search for you directly on YouTube, and it will likely come up high in their search results due to YouTube's relationship with Google. Use this relationship to your advantage by sharing videos on YouTube that demonstrate your expertise. Once you've posted your videos, connect them to your LinkedIn profile, share the links in other social media updates, and, if appropriate, share the links directly with recruiters or hiring managers.

How Can You Stand Out on LinkedIn?

With LinkedIn being by far the most used social medium for networking and recruiting, it is a good place to start when you are building your brand. The first step is building a complete profile that will increase your visibility by incorporating key terms people use. Next encourage readers to stay on your page by including storied content written in the first person.

Follow these tips to improve each section of your LinkedIn profile. (Note: All character limitations include punctuation and spaces.)

Picture

You must have a picture. If you don't, readers will assume the worst. Think of it as going to a meeting, but instead of meeting a recruiter or hiring manager face-to-face, you stand behind the wall the entire meeting. That would be off-putting, right? So is not including a picture on LinkedIn.

Quick tips:

- Your face should be 80 percent of the picture (not 10 feet away). Be aligned with your brand, which should be more professional on LinkedIn than other mediums.

- Avoid pictures with your spouse or pet; a nice picture of you outside works well if this aligns with your brand.
- Your picture should represent how you would actually look if we met on the street today.

Name

Keep it simple! Including degrees (MBA, PhD) can work in your favor in recruiter searches, and you want to make sure that degree aligns with your brand. However, including titles or keywords in your name field is against LinkedIn's user policy, so tread carefully.

Quick tips:

- Put your first and last name in the correct spot. If adding a degree, put it in the last name field, after your last name.
- Getting too creative with degrees and titles will make it difficult for people to find you if they search by your name.

Headline

This is the first content on your profile that anyone sees. Combine relevant titles (which are the most searched terms by recruiters) with content that highlights your specific brand. For instance, our software developer could write "Software Development (SDLC) Manager— Building Outsourced Teams to Improve Function & Profit" and still have characters left to add in more relevant key terms or titles.

Quick tips:

- You have 120 characters to write your headline.
- Stay positive and future-focused. Use relevant terms and branding for your career goal and avoid using phrases like "seeking new position" or "currently looking."
- Recruiters want stars in the positions and industries they recruit for, so tell them who you are, what you do, and how you are different from the rest.

Summary

Like a summary or qualifications section on a resume, this section of your LinkedIn profile is your opportunity to communicate your brand. It is most effective when it reads like a conversation and tells a story.

Quick tips:

- You have 2,000 characters to write your summary.
- Use first person and tell readers who you are, what you do, and why you do what you do. This is a great place to incorporate your brand; just consider your target audience and how you want them to see you.

- If appropriate, consider adding a call to action with your contact information. This can be something simple, such as inviting readers to connect with you. However, be careful about sounding desperate for a job.

Experience

Similar to your summary, each experience entry should tell a story about your success in that job while aligning with your brand. This section of your profile is the most similar to a resume, so you want to avoid copying and pasting the information from your resume.

Quick tips:

- Each experience entry can have up to 1,500 characters.
- Tell the story of why you joined an organization, share problems that you solved, or expand on a story you were not able to fully tell in your resume.
- Split long tenures into multiple experience entries based on title changes or other changes in the job. This creates more space for telling your story.
- Use the job title field to include not only your formal titles, but other keywords and titles that are appropriate for that position and building your brand. You have 120 characters available in this field.
- Connect each experience to the company profile if possible (the company logo will appear after you complete the entry).
- Go back far enough in your job history to capture companies your target audience might find important. Just make sure you don't date yourself (in general, 20 to 25 years is plenty).

Education

Like your experience sections, you want to connect your education to the school profile if available (the school logo will show up if you have done this correctly).

Quick tips:

- You can use up to 1,000 characters to fill out your education history.
- You do not have to include a completion date! If you are avoiding aging yourself on paper, you can do the same on LinkedIn.
- Include descriptions of projects, classes, and other activities to bring more keywords to your profile. This is particularly helpful for a recent graduate or someone transitioning to a new career.

Skills

Add up to 50 skills that align with what you want to be known for and what you think a hiring manager or recruiter will use to search for you.

Quick tips:
- Remove skills you don't want to be known for, even if they have endorsements.
- Ask colleagues to endorse you for the skills you want to be most prominent. Although endorsements can seem superfluous, they may factor into search results in the future.

Media

You have the option to add media to your summary and each experience entry. This could be a LinkedIn SlideShare presentation, a video, or a PDF of a tool or dashboard you created.

Quick tips:
- Use media throughout your profile to provide proof of your expertise. Even if you have an external website or portfolio, making some of that content readily available on LinkedIn will make it easier for others to access and will also create a rich profile.

Recommendations

Ask colleagues, former colleagues, vendors, and others you interact with on a regular basis to provide meaningful recommendations for you.

Quick tips:
- Do not use the function in LinkedIn to ask everyone you are connected with to recommend you. Instead, reach out to individuals, preferably in person, over the phone, or through email first, and then send a request to that individual through LinkedIn.
- Give those who will recommend you some talking points that align with your brand.

URL

The default URL that LinkedIn gives you has a string of numbers and letters at the end (www.linkedin.com/in/first-last-1ba4b0a2).

Quick tip:
- Edit your profile link and personalize it to remove those letters and numbers. This makes your link more search engine friendly and makes you appear more LinkedIn savvy. LinkedIn has instructions on how to customize your public URL on its website.

Other Content

There are many opportunities in LinkedIn to add other content, such as projects, publications, certifications you may have completed or languages you speak. If there are aspects of your professional brand that you want to share, there is probably a forum to do it! LinkedIn is a great place to put a lot of content, and just like your resume, you want to make sure that what you share is engaging and relevant to your brand.

How Do You Manage Your Online Brand?

More than 75 percent of employers will search for your name on the Internet before hiring you. If you are working with vendors or being hired as one yourself, a similar percentage of your clients or contracting agencies will do the same thing. Do you know what they'll find?

The best way to find out is to search for yourself. When you do this, make sure the search engine is set to give you the "global" results, rather than results personalized to you. The easiest way to do this is to use the incognito window in your browser. If you don't, your results will come back with links you most commonly visit that are related to the search listed at the top. You can also set up a Google Alert to track information posted about you.

When searching in specific search engines, the links that come to the top will be those sites favored by the search engine. For Google, these sites will include LinkedIn, YouTube, Twitter, and your personal page (if you have one). There is also a special section in Google that highlights images related to the search term; hopefully they are of you.

If you want to measure your social prowess, start by getting your Klout score. Klout allows you to connect your social media accounts and it also measures your activity and interaction.

If you find something in the results that you wish wasn't listed, your first step is to contact that website's webmaster and ask for it to be removed. If it's not removed, you can ask Google to remove it. However, keep in mind that Google is not keen on doing this unless it involves a blatant violation of your privacy (not just that you are not fond of that picture or news story).

Your best strategy is to prevent negative content as much as possible up front. Be mindful of what you post on social media. Remember that while you can control your privacy settings—and this is especially recommended for Facebook—once something exists online, no amount of security settings can stop someone from finding it if they really want to. Be especially careful of your remarks on others' posts, especially on LinkedIn. If you are going to review a restaurant or other business, be tactful.

Security concerns should not stop you from sharing your brand online. In fact, sharing positive content through social media, blogs, online publications, and video are your best ways to raise the visibility of information you want to be found and, therefore, push down the negative links.

Start with the end in mind: What do you want to be known for? What name will people use when they search for you (include a middle name or initial if you have a popular name)? What keywords do you want them to associate with you (your professional brand)?

What interests do you want to share to give your brand and professional identity a bit of personality?

With this in mind, you can create great content online to build your brand. Choose two to three of these suggestions to start:

- **Buy a vanity URL.** Make it your name (firstnamelastname.com); include your middle name if that is how you're building your brand. Do not include keywords. You can build a simple website or use a platform like About.me or Branded.me to help you populate a quick, branded page.
- **Post articles or blog posts** (yours or from industry newsletters) on LinkedIn as updates. And then share them with the targeted groups you've joined.
- **Create a short video that demonstrates your expertise.** Post it on YouTube and add it to your LinkedIn profile. Remember to use appropriate keywords in the video description.
- **Write an article for an industry publication.** Get the URL after it is published and link it to your LinkedIn profile. (Add the publication section to your profile.)
- **Present at an industry conference.** Make sure someone takes your picture and tell the conference staff that you are happy for it to be posted online. Link to any media from LinkedIn.
- **Write blog posts or articles** using LinkedIn's platform to answer frequently asked questions in your industry or demonstrate your expertise in another way.
- **Volunteer to star in your company's career feature videos.** Most companies want to post videos on their website that talk about what their employees do—what a low-risk way to have a video produced for you that demonstrates your expertise!
- **Create a LinkedIn SlideShare that demonstrates your expertise.** Don't forget to include important keywords in the slide and presentation descriptions.
- **Tweet the links to any of your articles, videos, or presentations regularly.** Aim for around 20 percent of your tweets to be your own content; the rest should be retweets, shared content, and tweets about your other interests (sports, travel, news) you are comfortable sharing that align with your brand
- **Create a Pinterest board for your professional or personal interests.** If you travel for work, start a board with pictures of your travels. Make sure you include a few pictures (20 percent is a good rule) of you conducting training, meeting colleagues at conferences, in the office, or doing something interesting at work.

Building your brand online takes time and effort, especially if there is negative information about you from a highly credible source (a news article, for instance). Here are a few ways that you can be more efficient about creating and sharing your online brand:

- **Reuse content.** If you do a presentation for a conference, turn that into a short blog post on LinkedIn and a SlideShare presentation.
- **Put those newsletters to use.** Scan any daily or weekly email industry newsletters, click on any articles that are interesting, and use the embedded tools to share the article on your social channels.
- **Schedule time for social media.** It can be overwhelming and time consuming to manage your social media profiles. Schedule 15 minutes every day to check your LinkedIn group activity, comment where appropriate, and congratulate colleagues (LinkedIn will tell you who has news). This will help you cultivate relationships.
- **Automate where appropriate.** Set your LinkedIn account to automatically tweet every update you make to your LinkedIn profile. You can also set up Twitter to push your tweets to Facebook. This saves time, but can be overused; balance automation with engagement or you will lose followers.
- **Use a social media management tool.** If you are diving deep into social media, especially Twitter, consider using a tool like Hootsuite or TweetDeck to track topics by creating lists, schedule posts across all mediums, and have a dashboard of your social activity.

Summary

Although social media tools can be overwhelming, they can be extremely powerful in helping you proactively build your professional brand. Determine what you want to be known for, your brand, and how that adds value for your target audience. This is the foundation for all your activity.

Once you are clear on your brand, select a few activities and communication channels that work with your strengths. Note your Google search results and your Klout score before you make any changes. Then start small, with a strategy based on your brand and audience; monitor the impact you have on your Google results and Klout score. Most important, consider whether those you interact with every day will have a better understanding of who you are, what you stand for, and where you want to go with your career. That is the power of defining and communicating your personal brand.

Effective Networking

Laura Labovich

The term *networking* is defined as the process of "cultivat[ing] people who can be helpful to one professionally, especially in finding employment or moving to a higher position" (dictionary.com), as well as "the cultivation of productive relationships for employment or business" (Merriam-Webster). Not surprisingly, these are the very definitions that are the most unnatural and harmful for those who seek to engage in networking as a practice for their job search. Cultivating is for crops, not for people.

But networking *is* a necessary part of doing business, and when done correctly there's nothing manipulative about it. Effective networking is not about business; it is simply part of the human experience. We all seek to be better professionals and better people, but we cannot do that alone.

Dorie Clark, author of *Stand Out Networking*, writes that we should think of networking as "an opportunity to meet people you'll want to talk to and learn from professionally." We can all learn something from others, and learning, *not advancement*, is networking's ultimate goal. Even the most outgoing people dislike networking when the objective is getting something from others, or focusing on what they can do for you.

> But the "instrumental" view that some hold—seeing people as a means to an end—is damaging. This distorted image stops the best people from networking because they don't want to treat others that way, and it encourages the worst to act in an obnoxious manner because they think that's what they're supposed to be doing. (Clark 2015)

Networking is not something you do only when you need a favor or a job. It is about curiosity—curiosity is to networking as water is to a plant: It enables true relationships to bloom with ease. Asking questions and listening carefully to the answers is the best way to launch a networking conversation and grow a relationship. Inquiring first about the other person, and not about what's in it for you (with the sincere goal of looking for ways to help) is the key.

Networking is also about appreciation and gratitude. Do you know the fastest way to be written off as a networking contact? Forget to thank someone for his time, or take her for granted. Alternatively, the greatest gift you can give someone is the gift of genuine appreciation and gratitude.

The Hidden Job Market

What is this "hidden job market" we hear so much about today? Where are the jobs hiding, and how can we find them? Like the party last Saturday you didn't get invited to, but you know happened because you saw the pictures on Facebook, others are reaping the rewards of these opportunities. It may seem like a lot is happening elsewhere that you can't see.

Some hidden jobs are advertised, but they aren't really open because they are earmarked for someone else. But how can you get around this seemingly unfair recruitment and sourcing strategy? Let's first take a look at why applying for advertised jobs—engaging in a reactive job search and entering into an experience similar to waiting for your lottery number to be called—yields so few results.

If you learn about an opening at a company you'd like to work for, it's often already too late. Companies post job openings because, in theory, posting seems like a good idea and they've always done it this way. But the application process is broken. Advertising for help is no longer a help wanted sign in a window, a flyer tacked to a bulletin board, or an ad in the local paper. Today, you can sit at your computer and search and apply for jobs in any city or town in any country on any continent. And this is good, right? More opportunities for job seekers! More candidates for hiring managers! Theoretically, yes. But in practice, no.

Just as candidates have an endless list of opportunities at their fingertips, hiring managers often have as many as 300 candidates for each open position. When they receive so many qualified applications for each job posting, the uncertainty for HR constantly hangs in the air. For recruiters, the greatest fear is hiring the wrong person, so that fear is often avoided *by hiring someone they already know.*

Hiring managers are already predisposed to select someone they know, or have met before, because it makes the decision easier. This means that becoming the known candidate—the one who gets to the company contact person or hiring manager before the position is open—is the holy grail for job seekers.

Designing Your Ideal Target Job

A crucial first step to take before making these connections is defining your goal. If you completed the exercises in chapter 4, you should have defined an immediate career goal. If not, to get help from your network you must clarify:

- **Title:** What kind of job do you want?
- **Geographic location:** Where do you want to work?
- **Company size or industry:** What kind of company do you want to work for?

You might think that narrowing your search will pigeonhole you, but being too broad does more harm than good. Don't be so narrow that you wall yourself out of an opportunity ("I want to be assistant claims benefit control chief of the health policy development and program administration"), but being specific will help others help you more effectively.

During this preliminary investigation phase, or if you are exploring a career or industry change, it is absolutely acceptable to be unclear in your target, title, goals, and objectives. That's one of the benefits of this discovery phase! But to have the greatest impact on your job search networking success, once you start reaching out to people, clarity—about who you are and what you want—is crucial. If you can answer the question, "What job are you looking for?" with some level of detail, you are ready to begin networking in the hidden job market. This kind of direction helps you know where to go, but more important, it enables others to help you.

Using your resume to solicit help from your friends, neighbors, and former colleagues is not the most effective way to network, despite what many think. Sending your resume to your friends and asking them to "circulate it around" is often met with well-intentioned efforts that fall short of getting you to the right person. It's not because your contacts don't want to help you; it's because they don't know *how* to help you.

Your Personal Marketing Plan

There's a better way to get these high-quality leads: Create a personal marketing plan (PMP). This is a critical document in your arsenal; it has your target title, level, geographic areas of interest, a snapshot of your resume's career summary, and a list of target companies that you began to identify in chapter 4. A PMP will help your network better help you, and will enable them to do it with greater clarity than if they were relying on your resume alone. Before you start to network, complete a sample PMP and have it ready for your networking efforts (see the sample in Appendix G).

The purpose of the PMP is to help you find people with whom you can network and become a known candidate. By asking your contacts for help in getting meetings at your target companies, instead of asking them to do you a favor and pass your resume around, you can get high-quality leads, such as phone numbers, email addresses, and information to act on. This helps you bypass the waiting game.

Your Speed Networking Pitch

When you're in the thick of a networking opportunity, such as a conference or a professional association event, preparation is your friend. You want to be quick and memorable—like speed dating, only faster. If you rely on complicated, jargon-heavy pitches that exceed a minute in length, you risk losing your audience to the roving eye, and you may never get them back. You need a more nimble, crisp pitch that is tailored to these sorts of events—a speed networking pitch—that will enable you to be memorable and share your character and competence with ease.

It all starts with the accomplishment story. Sit down, grab a comfy pillow, and pull up a blank computer screen (or, old school, a notebook). If you haven't done this already (see chapter 2), consider your career successes and list seven to 10 accomplishment stories (things you did well and also enjoyed). This should stir up some pride because they're proof that you're good at what you do.

If you find this exercise challenging, you're not alone. Try to recall a time when you had to complete a task for your job that wasn't easy, and you had to come up with a creative way to get it done. Maybe your department had been remiss in implementing a diversity-training program since the head trainer left the company, leaving the program specifics and curriculum in shambles. You volunteered (initiative!) to step in, revise the curriculum, and get the program out the door.

Once you have your list, organize it in a way that's easy to understand, remember, and pitch. Use the CAR format you learned about in chapter 5. For example:

- **Challenge:** Producing a new employee handbook for a Fortune 500 company with more than 2,000 employees.
- **Action:** Revamped existing handbook and reorganized it into specific sections for employee classes. Instituted a policy of careful legal review and rolled out its implementation, requiring all employees to sign upon receiving and reading it.
- **Result:** Streamlined, better-organized product promoting greater understanding and clearer expectations, resulting in fewer disciplinary actions and lawsuits.

Now, pull it all together. Here is the formula for an effective speed networking pitch:

As a [job title], I work with [share target audience] to [share a problem you solve]. And here's the proof: [tell a memorable, specific, client-related story].

Here are a few examples:

I work with healthcare research and development companies looking for new products to bring to the home care market. For example, I helped develop a tracksuit for elders with mobility issues. The suits have Velcro closures to aid bending and dressing. I was excited when that product took off and netted my company millions in the process.

I am an HR consultant who enjoys building HR departments from scratch. I work with large companies to produce employee handbooks that are concise and easy to understand. After simplifying a client's company handbook and holding informational meetings for the staff, their employee relations issues decreased 25 percent and retention improved dramatically.

In-Person Networking

Once your pitch is finely crafted, start using it frequently to perfect it and make its delivery natural. Attend conferences and enroll in industry or professional affiliations, which often hold chapter meetings or annual or biannual meetings or conferences. An affiliation is an organization—such as religious groups, social clubs, volunteer groups, honor societies, or industry groups—you are a member of through your personal, academic, or professional life.

Attending a conference as a job seeker is a different ball game than attending as a company representative or industry honcho—to a job seeker, conferences are like Willy Wonka's golden ticket. But remember: Give 100 percent of your attention to the conference; don't get sidetracked by your son's academic woes, your dog's tendency to wreak havoc when he's uncrated, or anything else that might be going on outside the convention center.

Contact the organizers ahead of time to see if they can use volunteers. Volunteering is a great experience because it gives you an insider's view into what's happening and where. In addition, it gives you the opportunity to meet and talk with experienced professionals. Working alongside others gives you a natural inroad to conversation that doesn't shout *networking!* (This technique is brilliant for introverts or others who get cold sweats when they think of networking.) Volunteering can also save you money. Discounted tickets are frequently reserved for volunteers or committee chairs.

Professional Associations

Being a member of your profession's association helps you get better at what you love to do. There is no substitute for a professional association: You could be in the room with many professionals from your industry, which will enable you to learn best practices, find peers, or secure a mentor. Industry groups and professional associations are invaluable sources of insider information. You'll be a more complete package if you stay abreast of changes occurring within your industry, and more attractive to employers.

Attend local chapter meetings, read their literature, and time permitting, get involved with the organization in a leadership capacity (such as joining a committee or volunteering). You can also attend webinars and read trade journals, blog posts, and articles to refine what you want to do or learn how to do it better. This will help raise your professional cachet, make you more qualified for delivering your services, and enable you to uncover best-in-class processes and strategies. When it comes to deciding whether to join a professional association or an industry association, don't choose; join both: one for people who do what you do and one for people who need what you offer. If your budget is an issue because you are between positions, be sure to ask if they have a discount for those in transition.

Industry Associations

The National Marine Manufacturers Association is a group that advocates for and promotes marine manufacturing products, such as boats and yachts. If you are a digital marketing professional who has always worked with luxury boat liners, either out of passion or convenience, this industry association would be an incredibly good fit for you. You may be one of the only marketing people in the room, which would put you in an enviable networking position and enable you to become the go-to person in your field for marine manufacturers. This is where you'd go to be in the room with people who need what you do.

Email or call the president of the association to share your excitement about becoming a member and ask for the three best action items to take to get involved quickly. You likely won't have trouble finding associations to join if you know where to look, but IndustryWeek (www.industryweek.com/associations) and Directory of Associations (www.directoryofassociations.com) are two good places to start.

Online Networking

In chapter 4 you started a list of target companies you'd like to work for. Now is the time to reach out to them. Most online networking conversations originate with LinkedIn. Twitter and Facebook may have tremendous value for your search, but LinkedIn is far superior in its ability to provide data around jobs, people, industries, and companies.

To Whom Do You Reach Out?

Finding contacts at companies on LinkedIn can be overwhelming, but it all boils down to one question: If you landed your target job at your target company, who would be your boss?

Ideally, you should be seeking out people who are one to two levels above you. If you are an organizational consultant, you want to find the director of OD. If you are a human resources director, it's the vice president or senior vice president of HR that you're looking for. If you want to be a marketing manager, the director of marketing would make the decisions. This isn't a perfect science, however. If you can't find the right person at the right company, level, and position who can hire you or recommend that you be hired, you can still gain value from meeting with someone in a different role at your target company.

For example: Your dream job is to be the marketing manager of the Discovery Channel. If your neighbor, Joe, introduces you to his cousin, Mark, who works for the Discovery Channel in the engineering department, it's not a wash! Take that lead and have a meeting with Mark. You still have a lot to learn about the company culture and challenges facing the Discovery Channel, and Mark can help you understand what it might be like to work there. This is extremely valuable insider information.

How Do You Reach Out?

To get names of people within your target companies, make a list of everyone you know and start grouping them by categories: friends from college, bowling buddies, people who join you for art class on Friday nights, your book club, friends from your church, and so forth.

Instead of focusing on who's hiring, look at your target company list. Do you know anyone who works at any of these companies? Do you know anyone who might know people at your target companies? Make a list. You'll be tapping into them as a resource for advice and introductions. Then, in short emails (or when you see them in person), ask them for help.

> You: "As you know, I'm in a job search right now. Would you mind taking a peek at my personal marketing plan and telling me if you know anyone on my target company list?"

> Your bowling buddy: "Sure! No problem. Anything for you! I do know someone at company X. Would you like me to give her your resume?"

> You: "Thank you! Actually, if you could give me her name and contact info, I'd love an opportunity to set up a brief call or in-person conversation, you know, to learn more about her company and what she does. Will that work?"

Once you get the names of people who are within your target companies, it's time to start initiating meetings. If you are working the hidden job market correctly, you are getting to these companies before there is a posted open position. This is the magic hour!

Go into these meetings asking for support or counsel in the form of advice, insight, recommendations, referrals—but do not ask for a job. These types of meeting are often called informational interviews because their purpose is to gather information about companies, industries, contacts, or new career directions. You can ask about the industry: What are the current trends, competitive landscape, or industry challenges? But don't ask for a job. Or, you can ask about the person in general: How did she get there? What is the best advice she got along the way? How does she stay on top of industry trends? What conferences does she frequent? What trade journals does she read? But do not ask for a job.

The goal of these meetings is to foster rapport, establish a relationship, and make a connection. As we discussed, networking is all about mindset. If you go into it with the goal of "getting something," you have missed the boat.

The adage "it's who you know!" is only partially correct. Landing a job is about whom you know, and about who knows, likes, *and* trusts you in return. When a recruiter has a job to fill, employee referrals and recommendations from those he knows, likes, and trusts will be in short supply and high demand. You want to be one of those. These meetings will help you get in the door, before the position opens.

Focus on People, Not Openings

Sleuthing out people to contact on LinkedIn with the LinkedIn Advanced Search function is easy: Type in the company name, title, and location, and voilà! You can easily see who you know and who they know. Your second-degree connections (your connections' connections) are statistically the most powerful ones. In addition, LinkedIn Company Pages will enable you to view anyone in your network who currently works for, or used to work for, your target company.

When it's time to reach out, either by email or phone, your goal is to get an informational interview or a meeting with someone at your target company. Once you have a few names, your initial email could be as simple as:

> Dear Dr. Smith:
>
> Samantha Barrows suggested we talk! I've known Samantha since our kids' Little League days, and she shared with me your success in my target industry, hospitality. As a former event planner in the manufacturing industry, I am now looking to learn more about switching industries to hospitality, still in a project management role, and Samantha believed you'd be a great resource. Would you be willing to speak with me briefly about your experience at the company, and any industry challenges or trends you see on the horizon? I will call you at 10 a.m. on Tuesday to see if we can arrange a time to meet.

You'll want to send a lot of these emails! The more you send, the greater your chances are of gathering insider information that will make you a strong fit for a position, when it opens.

During the meeting, you may wonder what should be discussed. Here are a few things you could say:

- May I tell you a bit about my background? (If you don't know the person well.)
- How did you land your position at the company?
- What do you love about this industry?
- Would you be willing to review my personal marketing plan and give feedback?
- Would you be willing to put me in touch with someone in my target function in your company?
- Is there anything I can do to help you?

If this person is at one of your target companies and you plan to stay in touch, send an immediate thank you (by email is fine). Keep this person in the loop with occasional updates as your candidacy progresses.

Ambassadors: An Essential Job Search Contact

During these first meetings, your goal is to forge relationships with ambassadors. Ambassadors are successful professionals in your target industry who have the power to hire you or the ability to influence others to hire you. When you start hearing them say "you would be great here!" you know you have turned them from an acquaintance to an ambassador. These ambassadors are game changers to your job search because they can introduce you to people within their own organization, or help you meet decision makers in your other target companies or industries. With these meetings, your goal is to recognize when you have met an ambassador. Because they can help shepherd you through the process, you must make sure to stay in touch with them throughout your search.

It's not always easy to remember to stay in touch with key contacts, especially in the digital age, but LinkedIn's Mentions feature can help. Within LinkedIn, simply begin typing the name of the person you wish to mention in the status field, select the correct person from the drop-down menu, and that person or company will receive a notification. Use mentions to congratulate a connection on a new job or celebrate achievements in your network. This is a useful way to stay in touch between longer conversations.

Networking Over the Phone

People don't talk on the phone as often as they used to. They text. They email. They IM. So it may feel strange to you to pick up the phone and call someone—especially someone you don't even know. But eschewing this avenue in your job search is neglecting an important and powerful networking tool.

When you're networking over the phone, there are three kinds of calls you can make. You can call someone you know, someone who knows someone you know, or someone you don't know.

According to Katherine Moody, author of *How to Have a Great Networking Conversation on the Phone*, having a script makes these phone conversations a thousand times easier than winging it. In fact, in your job search alone, the people with whom you interact at various stages can be vast and unique, including hiring managers, receptionists, recruiters, headhunters, friends, family members, neighbors, or salespeople at your target company. In her informative and entertaining e-publication, Moody shares various scripts that are invaluable to job seekers. (Not to be missed: Her "hiring manager: slightly gutsier script," which is great for those days when confidence is not in short supply.)

The bottom line is that having a script takes the guesswork out of the conversation for you. You never know who will pick up the phone when you call, or if you'll get an answering machine instead, and it's refreshing to be able to leave a message rather than abruptly hang up for fear of saying the wrong thing.

Once you have crafted a script for people you could encounter in your search, design ideal outcomes for each situation. For the purposes of this chapter, the kind of networking we're focused on is for the purpose of accessing the hidden job market. Therefore, it's important to remember that *there is no job*. You are simply aiming to get meetings with people within your target companies who are one to two levels above you and ideally in a position to hire you or to recommend that you be hired. And there is only one goal: Get them to believe you have a place at the organization in the future. During these calls, your goal is to get in the door, or get on the phone, with a decision maker.

When you have a face-to-face meeting, or a successful phone conversation, ask for help with the next steps. If you are feeling bold and believe that the conversation has been productive, ask for names of others with whom you could meet. Ask if you may stay in touch with them. (And then do!) Make a note in your calendar of the date you met, what was promised, and any advice given. If this is a person at your target company with whom you wish to stay in touch (and this is important because it's not essential to stay in touch with everyone in your search), you'll want to follow up with them three times after this initial call to:

- **Within 24 hours:** Thank them for their time.
- **In two to three weeks:** Provide something of value to them that has nothing to do with you (for example, information about a conference, upcoming event, or something they would value).
- **Within six weeks:** Share successes and provide a status update on advice they offered that you took.

Summary

If you are finding that your job search efforts are getting you nowhere and your feverish attempts to apply for jobs online are coming up short, take a step back and concentrate instead on formulating your personal marketing plan. Identify your target companies and vow to infiltrate them, learning what you can and ensuring your name and face are known among the decision makers, so that when a position opens up you're the first person they think of.

Don't sit home frantically scanning the want ads, LinkedIn, and Indeed.com. Shift your focus to networking, whether it's online, over the phone, or in person. Get out of the house and meet people. Join clubs and associations, go to industry events, and spend time each week trying to schedule meetings with people in your industry and at your target companies. Practice your speed networking pitch.

Putting yourself out there can be daunting, even downright scary. But it's the only way to reach your goal, and as you practice, it will get easier. Your efforts will inevitably pay off, opening doors for you that may have previously been closed.

Applying to Positions

Lynne M. Williams

This chapter offers an overview of the many ways to apply for jobs—some traditional and typical and others more creative—as well as an in-depth examination of the applicant tracking system (ATS) and sections on best practices, tips, and tricks.

The Hidden Job Market

Remember the hidden job market you learned about in chapter 7? Why does it exist? Wouldn't employers want to hire the best employees possible? Is it preposterous to think that jobs would be hidden from job seekers, or would terms like *unadvertised, unposted,* or *unpublished* be more appropriate to use? There are many reasons why employers might not publicize an opening—perhaps they are trying to replace someone who is not performing a job well, or they don't want competitors or stockholders to be aware that they are gearing up for some big changes. Maybe there is a hiring freeze, a job is published in a nontraditional way (perhaps on social media), or there is a retained search done by a recruiter. These are some of many reasons why jobs may be considered part of the "hidden" market.

In addition, even if a job *is* published, it may not be real. Perhaps a candidate has already been identified and the company is just meeting a requirement of someone posting a job to conform to company policy, Department of Labor (DOL), or Equal Employment Opportunity Commission (EEOC) labor laws. There seem to be some mysteries in the world of hiring people that may just remain mysteries.

Thirty years ago, Dick Bolles, author of *What Color Is Your Parachute?*, told the *New York Times* that 80 percent of jobs are not advertised and suggested that one's contacts are key to a job search (Sanger 1980). In the last several years, career websites such as Live Careers estimate that the hidden job market remains sizable (Hansen 2010). More recently, thanks to the Internet and social media, online sources such as job boards, search engines, and career websites have made significant inroads in company hiring, although employee referrals still produce the top number of hires (SilkRoad Technology 2015).

A Case for Employee Referrals

While the hidden job market may not be as large as it once was, job seekers should still focus on networking while in transition. Your goal is to not only increase your local connections, but also start building relationships with people in your industry. Many companies have employee referral programs, so networking helps capitalize on "know, like, trust" in the hopes of a referral. Companies use the referral system because it's not only a cheaper way to hire, but a faster one (Jobvite 2012). When a company makes good hiring decisions, employees stay longer, and there is less turnover. Research shows that retention with a referral hire after one year is 46 percent, and at two years is 45 percent, versus 20 percent and 14 percent, respectively, with hires from job boards (Sullivan 2012). You also have a better chance of getting hired as a referral, especially if the referral comes from someone at the director level or above (Morgan 2015). Additional benefits from employee referral programs include a better fit, better quality of hire, and added diversity (Sullivan 2012).

So, it still pays to continuously go out to meet people and network to build your own sphere of influence. Many people believe relationships are more powerful than resumes, so it is always good to be prepared with a thriving network, even if you are between transitions (that is, currently employed). If your network connections mention your name in conversations, along with a positive message about you when you are not present, you have created a successful brand and have a virtual sales force. It also doesn't hurt to be in the right place at the right time, as opportunities may present themselves based on someone who recently decided to resign or retire or for a requisition that no one has yet had the opportunity to write.

If humans are doing the hiring in or out of the hidden job market, then logic would have it that having a creative, eye-catching resume would be the most important thing (especially if there is more competition for visible published jobs and less competition for unpublished jobs). But another way to beat out your competition before a job actually becomes available or is announced might be to send out a value proposition letter en masse without a resume. To determine which methods produce the best results for you, it may be wise to pursue all avenues at the beginning of your search. Send out some value proposition letters, mail some cover letters with your resume to target companies, apply to some jobs online, set up some informational meetings, and try networking. By tracking your results, you will be able to guage which avenues work best for you.

Don't Forget About Snail Mail

Consider using snail mail to gain a unique edge. Yes, don't forget about the envelope and stamp and that special high-quality resume paper you can purchase from your local office supply store. I can tell you from personal experience working in the C-suite that not many CEOs and presidents receive stamped envelopes with cover letters and resumes. Why? Good question! Many applicants assume they should be exclusively using technology to apply to jobs. However, this "old-fashioned" approach is a great way to apply to an advertised job or contact a target company that you would like to work for because it seems like no one is doing it and would make you stand out. You can share your unique value proposition or branding statement in the cover letter.

You can also use snail mail to start a direct mail campaign to send your value proposition letter to your target companies. You want the letter to be read, especially since you are taking the time and expense, so make sure to personalize each letter to a decision maker and use high-quality stationery. Information on senior leaders is often available on company websites, so start small and research your target companies. While it is usually preferable to be introduced to someone through a warm lead, this job search technique can increase your odds of getting a phone call especially if your skills are very specialized. It should be noted that while general industry standards for direct mail are low—only a 1 to 2 percent response rate—most direct mail does not include personalized value proposition letters. For more information on using a direct mail approach, refer to the website of the late career coach Mark Hovind (www.JobBait.com).

Optimize Your LinkedIn Profile

Employers or recruiters looking for people with certain skills may consult their network for referrals; however, they may also use LinkedIn's advanced search techniques to find people. Applying to jobs where someone has recruited you may be a relatively easy way to find your next position. Just know that even though you may wear many hats and have many interests, you should only have one LinkedIn profile.

Your LinkedIn profile must be strategically filled with keywords, especially your headline, summary, job titles, publications and projects, and skills and endorsements. Chapter 6 provided guidelines for optimizing your LinkedIn profile and managing your online brand. Keywords are discussed in greater detail later in this chapter.

If you click on the Jobs tab on your LinkedIn profile, you will find choices to set up job preferences, search for jobs, save jobs, and apply to jobs. Once you start searching for jobs, LinkedIn will autosuggest jobs you may be interested in. You can even set it up so LinkedIn sends you job alerts.

Sign Up for Google Alerts

Create Google Alerts for companies you are interested in. This way, you will be notified if your target company is in the news with any expansion activities, new leases, new deals, and so forth. If you see some activity that might create a job opening for you, this could be the perfect time to make yourself known. Take the initiative to start setting up informational interviews and sending your resumes to any contacts you have in the company.

Blog Your Way to a Job

Sometimes you can garner attention by blogging about a particular industry, profession, or company. Your knowledge base, combined with your enthusiasm to create engagement with others, may be a viable way to your next career step. Increase the likelihood that others in your industry will read your blog posts by linking them to your LinkedIn page or other social media outlets you have. The more people who see what expertise you have, the more opportunities you will have for a job in the hidden market to open up for you.

Could YouTube Be a Digital Interview?

YouTube videos can act as a digital interview for you, and may be a creative way to job hunt in some industries and for some positions. It's a way to promote yourself and build SEO (search engine optimization) or name recognition in a particular field and possibly catch someone's attention for your next opportunity. A video that is done right can help make a personal connection and lasting impression. And don't forget, posting YouTube videos makes it more likely that your name will be a top hit on a Google search, which further helps to promote you and your brand.

What About Social Media and Websites?

Social media can absolutely be used to your advantage if you set up professional profiles on sites such as Twitter, Facebook, and About.me. It's an opportunity to brand and promote yourself and your areas of expertise. Personal websites are also a great way to create an online presence. Your site could include an online portfolio, as well as your resume, bio, picture, videos, writing samples, links to other social media platforms, and more.

Attend Conventions and Trade Shows

When you are able to make face-to-face connections with people at a conference or trade show for your industry, you may discover unposted jobs or new company endeavors. If the cost is prohibitive to attend, you may be able to volunteer, which often means free or discounted admission to the show after your shift is complete.

Instead of a Job Search, Do a Company Search

Instead of looking for a job, shift your mindset to companies of interest. Build your target company list based on culture, growth, company size, proximity, industry, or whatever parameters are important to you (this is something you started doing in chapter 4). You can use databases such as Reference USA, which is available through a subscribing library, or you could use ZoomInfo.com. You can also look up classifications of business establishments with the U.S. Census Bureau's North American Industry Classification System (NAICS) codes or the U.S. Department of Labor's Standard Industry Classification (SIC) codes, which will be helpful when using Reference USA.

Don't Do Things That Are Too Out of the Ordinary

There are still conventions in the world of business, and you don't want to draw negative attention to yourself or seem desperate. So, don't send your resume tucked in a shoe inside a shoebox to make the point that you now have one foot in the door. While different industries might value or welcome some creativity, be sure to know what's appropriate before doing something outside the box.

Schedule Informational Interviews

Ask a few people who work in your target industry or company if they would take 30 minutes to speak to you about their company, industry, or themselves and their journey as to how they got to where they are today. It's a great networking opportunity. Once they agree to meet, send an agenda so there is a focus to the meeting, to really make you shine.

Write a Value Proposition Letter

What is a value proposition letter? It's a brief statement (100-150 words) that succinctly explains the unique qualities, skills, and accomplishments of a candidate. In other words, it states how you will add value to a company. Using persuasion, value proposition letters explain how you can solve a problem or fix a pain point in a company better than anyone else thanks to your expertise and unique offerings. It also focuses on actions you will take if hired and can be used for most positions where you can offer some technical expertise or specialty knowledge. The letter sets you apart from the competition and can also highlight your transferable skills. This is certainly not meant for an entry-level position because you need to be able to highlight your quantifiable achievements, although it might be a key tool for a high-level executive. Appendix H includes a sample value proposition letter; other examples be found online, Just Jobs Academy and About Careers are two good websites to visit (Shannon 2012 and Doyle 2016).

What About That Salary Question?

When it comes to discussing salary, many job seekers have heightened anxiety levels. They don't want to undervalue or undersell themselves, nor do they want to provide a number that will knock them out of an opportunity. First thing first: Do your homework and review typical salaries based on the scope of the job. Chapter 11 contains more details on researching your market value, but Payscale.com, Salary.com, and the Bureau of Labor Statistics are all good places to start.

Once you review industry salary information, you should also create a salary history for your personal information and also determine your personal salary expectations. For example, how much money do you need to make to continue living the lifestyle you are accustomed to? Use the worksheet in Appendix I to help gauge your expenses.

Job advertisements occasionally list the salary or range for the job, but they usually don't. If the advertisement requests that you provide salary information when you apply, you might stipulate in your cover letter that you're seeking a competitive salary or the market value of the position, but are flexible and prefer to discuss the matter in person during an interview. If you feel compelled, you could tell them you are seeking a range between $x and $y. However, it is always best for an employer to state the first number or range rather than you, so try to postpone any salary talk until there is an actual offer. You should also try to defer revealing information about your current salary because you want to be considered based on your background and experience, not your past salary.

If the "how much did you make in your last position" question comes up in a telephone screening, you can tell the screener that you have researched fair market values of similar jobs, and would imagine that you could find a common ground at the appropriate time with a competitive compensation package. It's not just about base salary, but total compensation with all the other benefits that go along with it: vacation, proximity, health coverage, bonuses, 401(k), stock options, insurance, tuition reimbursement, and other perks, not to mention the bigger picture of career path, culture, challenges, and travel.

Your past salary information is private and confidential. Previous salaries should have no bearing on a potential salary, but employers often ask for salary history on employment applications. Whenever possible, leave it blank or enter a range. If you are asked for this information during an interview, you may be able to defer with a comment such as "let's further explore how my capabilities, qualifications, background, and skills would be an asset to the company and keep an open mind on compensation at the moment." However, if strongly pressed for this information, provide a range that is consistent with your past salaries and current market value.

What if you are applying for a job online and the application has those annoying little boxes for salary information? It really irks a lot of job seekers when they cannot move on in an online application until those boxes are complete. So what can you do other than provide the truth? First, you can try to put $0 or the minimum accepted number. You can also try entering a range. If none of those options work, you may have to enter a number. If you have done your research, you will have a figure in mind that is consistent with industry standards. Then, in the first available comment box, note, "Salary is flexible and negotiable, salaries reported reflect my current salary target," or whatever comment is appropriate to the numbers you listed. If there is no comment box, then include your comment on salary in your cover letter.

Applying for Jobs Online

There are so many jobs advertised online nowadays. Decades ago, many jobs were advertised in newspapers, and while some still are, the number has dwindled. Some advertisements ask for resumes to be emailed or faxed, which is a good thing, because there's a chance your resume will actually be reviewed by a human. However, if your resume is not deemed a "stand out" in the first six to 15 seconds, it doesn't matter how qualified you are for that position. You probably won't wind up in the "A" pile, especially if there are hundreds of people applying for the same job. In chapter 5 you learned how to craft an effective resume. Make sure to take that advice to heart.

Challenges of the Applicant Tracking System

Many job applicants have had the experience of submitting their overly formatted resume to an online job posting, but despite being extremely qualified, they are not receiving a response. This is probably because the company used applicant tracking system (ATS) software to help their talent acquisition personnel or hiring managers have an easier and more efficient screening process.

When candidates submit their resumes online, the ATS scores, sorts, and stores them in a database. This may be good for the company, but it's bad for the job applicant. Why? Because your resume is being routed through an electronic gatekeeper into a black hole—in fact, research suggests that nearly 75 percent of all resumes are never even seen by human eyes (Peggs 2015, Resume Genius, Levinson 2012).

The reason for so many "lost" resumes is most likely the ATS filtering system. What goes in doesn't necessarily mean that is what comes out. This is reality check time. When was the last time you won the lottery? The odds are stacked against you—maybe 25 percent of submitted resumes will get through the online system to even be looked at by a human. However, miracles can and do happen. So, you need to be prepared with the knowledge of how to actually get your resume through the proverbial "black hole."

How the ATS Works

When you submit your resume to an ATS it is run through a parser, which assigns meaning to the content. Resumes are scanned not only for keywords, but also for key phrases. In other words, the technology has the ability to look for words in front of and following the key words. This is known as *contextualization.*

Once the content is analyzed for terms that are both related and unrelated, it is then mathematically scored for relevance. In addition, the depth of experience that a potential candidate has and how this experience falls into the candidate's career path is also reviewed. Your score is then validated and the resume either moves on to human eyes—or into the black hole.

Applying for Jobs Through an ATS With LinkedIn

Some applicant tracking systems allow you to log in with your LinkedIn account. This is great news if you have fully optimized your profile and packed it with keywords and kept it up-to-date. Refer back to chapter 6 for more information about optimizing your LinkedIn profile.

How to Avoid the Black Hole

What do you need to do to beat the ATS? You need to be a savvy job seeker and optimize your resume with strong content. Here are 18 important tips that you should consider as you review and optimize your resume for online applications.

1. Customize your resume for each position with applicable skills and experience. Quality of resume versus quantity of submissions is the preferred path. Carefully read the job description and highlight key terms, then weave those terms into your current resume. Jobscan (www.jobscan.co) compares the text in your resume to the job description and provides a percentage of how well your resume matches. Wordle (www.wordle.net) or Tagul (http://tagul.com) will create a word cloud from your resume to highlight keywords.

2. Remove all images and graphics—including logos, pictures, and photographs—from your resume because they are not readable.

3. Fonts matter! Do not use a font size smaller than 10 point, and do not use any script fonts. Arial appears to be the best font to use, although Courier, Impact, Lucinda, Tahoma, Trebuchet, Times New Roman, and Verdana are also acceptable. However, if the ATS requires a document that is .txt or .rtf, the font will most likely be Courier. Don't bold, italicize, or underline either.

4. Don't hide any text or keywords and try to cheat the system. In other words, don't type words from the job description in your resume and then change the font to white hoping it will get through the ATS. The parsers will probably catch this, and it will come out the other end in something that is black on white and readable. The end result will be a human judging you for trying to be sneaky.

5. Consider removing irrelevant positions from your resume. Remember, you're tailoring your resume to the job, so only include positions that are relevant. If, for example, you are a CPA and MBA and worked retail during a busy holiday season, you might not want to include that in your resume if it was just to help you manage to pay your bills while in transition.

6. Beware of special characters. Do not use arrows, stars, or squares. The round dark filled-in bullet points are the most appropriate to use.

7. Avoid shading, fancy borders, tables, and section breaks, as well as lines that cross the page to separate resume sections.

8. Check for spelling errors because, in addition to making you look careless, the ATS may miss keywords if they are misspelled.

9. Make sure your contact information is at the top of the document and not in the header or footer. Include your name, phone number, and email at a

minimum. It's always good to include your customized LinkedIn, too. You can also provide your Twitter handle and links to other social media sites if they are professional, rather than personal.

10. Type the dates of your employment after listing your employer, rather than before. Be consistent with how you format the dashes between the dates. Know the difference between a hyphen, en dash, and em dash, as well as the proper way to use them.

11. Send your resume through the ATS from a Word document or a rich text format rather than a PDF. Microsoft Word documents are typically used because the ATS readers seem to handle them better than a PDF. However, each software platform is different. In addition, uploading a resume is preferred over copying and pasting it into text boxes. If you have to copy and paste your content into boxes, that is a pretty good indication the ATS is not reading your resume.

12. Do not upload your resume multiple times because this may hurt, rather than help, your cause—it won't help you get noticed in a good way. If you are applying to multiple positions in a company, make sure your resume is consistent.

13. Highlight your area(s) of expertise with descriptive text rather than being a generalist (unless this is your title for HR). Companies look for experts, so focus on your specialized niche. Generic terms include *marketing, communications,* or *operations,* whereas more specific descriptions include *customer experience, multilingual global marketing communications,* and *commercial facilities management.*

14. Only include typical resume sections such as summary profile, core competencies, professional experience, education, and skills. Do not add unfamiliar headings such as affiliations, memberships, and publications (unless you are an academic). Also ditch the objective section, because it is outdated. Typical resumes may be formatted in chronological order, a functional format, or perhaps a hybrid of the two. Whatever format you use, if it copies over correctly, then you know the ATS is able to read it.

15. In lieu of listing job descriptions under your professional experience, list bullet-pointed quantifiable accomplishments and achievements. Any statistics, numbers, or percentages you can include will help describe your contributions to the position. List the bullet points most relevant to the job description first. If the bullet points are not full sentences, they should not include a period. The bullet points should begin with an accomplishment or action verb. If it's for a current job, the verb tense will be present. If it is for prior employment, the verb tense will be past tense. Examples include supervised xxx people, increased sales $xxx in an x-year period, decreased expenses by xx%. (See chapter 5 for a list of action verbs.)

16. Use industry terminology that is relevant to the position so the applicant screening tools that index and crawl submissions will pick up these key terms and phrases. It's particularly important to include specific terms that are included in the job description. If you're trying to move into a new industry, make sure you use the terminology common to that industry.

17. Keywords are one of the main ways that the ATS mathematically scores and ranks a resume. One way to determine which keywords to include is to run the job description through a keyword or text analyzer. Jobscan is an online analyzer program that lists how many skills are matched in your resume to the job description, how many skills are found in the job description, and what words you are missing in your resume. Jobscan recommends at least an 80 percent match before you attempt to apply to a job.

18. As mentioned in chapter 5, you will need two resumes: one that is visually attractive and nicely formatted for sending out through email and snail mail, and another that is totally deconstructed and unformatted for submitting to online job sites. Appendix F contains an example of a deconstructed resume that will have a much better chance of being read by the ATS. Many ATS software programs ask you to upload your resume at the beginning of the application process; this is when you would use your deconstructed resume. Other times you may be asked to upload your resume at the end of the online application; in that case, you would upload your eye-catching resume along with a cover letter, letters of reference, and so forth.

Cover Letters

Do you need a cover letter? Yes, if it is requested or if you need to sell yourself in a stronger way. Cover letters give you the opportunity to show your succinct and persuasive writing skills and demonstrate if you know how to use proper grammar, correct spelling, and correct punctuation. It also showcases your knowledge on the conventions of properly formatting a business letter. If a cover letter is not requested, it is up to you to decide whether to include one. In my experience, a third of recruiters never read cover letters, a third read them if they like the resumes, and a third read the cover letter first and will not consider anyone who doesn't send a good cover letter. As a result, it can't hurt you to send a cover letter, but it might hurt you if you don't send one.

The contact information at the top of your resume should match what you put on your cover letter exactly, including the font. The distance from the top and bottom of the cover letter should be equivalent so that the white space is balanced at the top and the bottom. Left justified is the preference of many professionals. The following is a common order for cover letter components:

- Sender's Address
- Date
- Recipient's Address
- Salutation
- Body Text Paragraph 1
  - Identify the position and how you learned about it.
  - State why you are interested in the organization or position.
- Body Text Paragraph 2
  - Summarize your strengths and why you are a good match for the position.
  - Target how your personal skills match the job requirements.
  - Highlight a few accomplishments and how they relate to the position.
  - Share your value proposition and how you can fulfill the needs of the company with your background and experiences.
- Closing Paragraph 3
  - Thank the reader for considering you for this position.
  - Offer further information.
  - State that you would like to schedule an interview and look forward to hearing back from them.
- Signature Block
  - Use a sign off such as "Sincerely" followed by four lines to place your signature before your first and last name.
- Enclosures
- cc:

Cover Letter Styles

There are different kinds of cover letters (see Appendix J for a few sample cover letters). While you can use the traditional paragraph format, cover letters can be written for different reasons and in different styles, including, but not limited to:

- response to an invitation to apply to a specific job opening: explains your qualifications for the position
- referral letter: notes the name of the referral (warm contact)
- networking information request: asks for advice on the industry or company
- pre-networking letter: notifies the recipient that you will be calling
- prospecting letter: expresses an interest in the company without applying to a specific job (cold contact)
- job match or "T" cover letter: has two columns in the middle of the letter with the job requirements on the left and your matching qualifications on the right
- bullet list cover letter: highlights key areas of proficiency or specific attributes

- recruiter cover letter: explains the type of role you are qualified to fulfill
- former employer cover letter: notes no ill feelings for the downsize
- value proposition letter: explains your uniqueness and strengths and how you can help the company, rather than focusing on past accomplishments.

Summary

There are several traditional and more creative ways to bring your skills, accomplishments, and resume to the attention of target employers, as well as tips and tricks to format your resume for the applicant tracking system. However, even though you are now armed with this knowledge, don't forget to go out and network your way to a new job. If it seems harder trying to find a job than actually having one, then you are probably being successful in your quest to network in the morning, afternoon, and evening while building your local connections on LinkedIn. Consider using value proposition letters, especially if you are looking for a senior executive-level position or have desirable industry-specific skills. Continue to be active and persistent in person and online so that you can accomplish your mission. Remember that each "no" is one step closer to a "yes."

Ace the Interview

Thea Kelley

The entire interviewing process boils down to one question, whether it is asked in so many words or not: "Why should we hire you (instead of one of our other candidates)?"

This chapter will help you answer that question clearly, credibly, and memorably—not just when it's specifically asked, but throughout your interview process, so that you stand out as "the one."

Relax and Be Confident

Almost everyone is nervous about job interviews. It's normal to have the jitters, or even to be downright scared. But it's not helpful when you're so anxious that you sweat heavily or your mind goes blank.

Relaxation exercises can help you stay calm before and during your interview. Search the Internet for "relaxation techniques Mayo Clinic" and you'll find several exercises you can use anytime, anywhere. Experiment with a few, choose the one you like best, and practice it frequently so it's ready when you need it.

As for confidence, that comes from being prepared. Put in some time and practice, and use everything you learn in this chapter to get thoroughly ready for successful job interviews. If you've been "winging it" until now, you may be amazed at how much more confident you'll feel when you're properly prepared.

Now let's think about the main messages you want to confidently communicate in your interviews.

Communicate Your Key Selling Points

There may be 50 reasons why a certain employer should hire you, but nobody can remember 50 reasons. So, narrow it down: What's the number one factor that is most likely to make them want to hire you? Now think of a few others that are almost as powerful. Those are your key selling points.

Ask yourself these questions to help you identify your key selling points:

- What qualifications do I have that are hard to find?
- What do I do better than my peers?
- What have my employers appreciated most about me?
- What are the most impressive accomplishments in my resume?

Once you have a short list, review it to make sure your key selling points are:

- **Relevant from the employer's point of view:** Although you might think the best reason to hire you is that you write very creatively, the employer may be more interested in your achievements in configuring databases.
- **Exceptional:** Presumably, all the candidates have the basic skills to do the job. What do you have that's above and beyond or hard to find?
- **Verifiable, not just an opinion:** If you have a professional certificate, that's a verifiable fact. Great communication skills are less concrete, so they may not be such a good key selling point unless you can offer some form of evidence, such as related experience in your resume, a writing sample, or a sound bite from a LinkedIn recommendation.

Prepare to communicate your key selling points memorably. Think about this: What do we remember?

- **We remember what comes first and last.** Emphasize your key selling points in your first interview answer—generally, your answer to "tell me about yourself"—and in your closing remarks.
- **We remember what is reinforced.** Make some reference to your key selling points in your follow-up messages.
- **We remember what is vivid**—what we can see in our mind's eye. Illustrate your key selling points with stories.

Tell a Story

Stories are to interviews what pictures are to a website. They illustrate the content and make it much more engaging. Stories are often required by the way an interview question is phrased. When you hear "tell me about a time when you (handled this or that)," you're being asked a behavioral interview question, which requires you to tell a story. Having plenty of stories ready is a must.

Even when a story isn't asked for, it can liven up your answer. A well-told story enables the interviewer to imagine you doing skillful work and achieving results. In her mind's eye she can actually see it—and seeing is believing.

You used stories earlier in the book to identify skills and craft accomplishment statements for your resume using the CAR format (challenge, action, result). You'll use these stories again in an interview, but you will add one more element to your story: the context or situation. We call it the SOAR technique because it includes the *situation* or context, an *obstacle* that required extra skills to overcome, the *actions* you took to solve the problem, and the *results* that benefited the organization.

So when interviewing, build your stories around SOAR: situation, obstacle, actions, and results.

Here's an example, told by a candidate for a sales manager job.

SOAR Story: Tripling Sales Leads

When I was sales manager at Terrific Technology, we had a third-party call center that was supposed to pass along leads to our inside sales team, but we were only getting about 10 leads a day. (The Situation)

So I decided to work closely with the call center reps. There was initially some resistance because they had their own methods. So I called their manager in Bangalore and got to know him, listened to his concerns, and collaborated with him to figure out how to make it work. We negotiated methods and schedules that worked for both of us. (Obstacle and Actions)

I then improved their scripts, provided a sales training webinar, and coached some of the reps one-on-one. (More Actions)

Within a month, the flow of leads went up to 30 a day, which increased revenue by at least $50,000 that year. (The Results)

How Does SOAR Help?

SOAR reminds you to organize your thoughts so that your stories are complete, compelling, and concise. SOAR also teaches you to make sure you include results. The most common mistake in interview storytelling is to shortchange the results. Many people telling this story would end with, "So I improved their scripts, provided a sales training via webinar, and coached some of the reps one-on-one."

"Hmm," thinks the interviewer, "So you spent a lot of time, but did it *work*?"

Be specific about results. Quantifying can really help: Say how fast, how much, or how many hours saved or dollars earned. If you don't have exact figures, estimate.

Develop Your Stories List

Start compiling a list of stories, especially stories that illustrate your key selling points. Having trouble remembering stories? Find lists of behavioral interview questions online, and they'll help jog your memory.

Try to build your list to at least a dozen stories, and preferably 20 or more. In today's lengthy interview processes, you may be asked dozens of questions. You don't want to have to tell the same handful of stories over and over.

Don't write your stories out as full scripts because that will make you sound over-rehearsed and result in a huge list that's hard to review quickly. Instead, for each story simply write down a title and a few points you might otherwise forget to mention.

Then list the skills and strengths the story demonstrates. Now, if an interviewer asks about a particular skill, you'll know which story to tell.

Use the template in Figure 9-1 to start your story list. This will be one of your most powerful job search tools.

Figure 9-1. SOAR Stories List Template

Title:

Be sure to mention:

Skills and strengths this story illustrates:

Tell Me About Yourself

Because it comes first, "would you tell me about yourself" may be the most important question in the whole interview. Build your answer around your key selling points, and you'll have an answer that shows you're the right person for the job.

For example, Claudia Candidate is interviewing for a job as an instructional designer. Following the instructions provided earlier in this chapter, she has identified the following as her key selling points:

- 10 years of progressively responsible training department experience leading up to her most recent role as a lead instructional designer.
- Strong accomplishments.
- Exceptional motivation to work for this company: She has been talking with people from this company and watching for openings for a year; working there is her dream.
- An MA in instructional design.
- Web design and graphic design skills above and beyond the requirements.

Her answer to "tell me about yourself" could sound something like this:

I'm really excited to be here because I use all your apps and I've been following Cool Company for a long time. I was thrilled to be referred to you by Shandra Smith.

As you can see in my resume, I've been working in training departments for 10 years, and I've progressed through various positions up to my recent role as lead instructional designer at XYZ company.

I've made a real difference there. For example, last year I led an overhaul of our sales training programs for 600 reps nationwide. Participant ratings went up from 7 to 9.5 out of 10, and the reps started performing better, which led to revenue growth.

Some of my other strengths include web design and graphic design skills and a master's in instructional design from QRS University, which gives me a solid grounding in [here she names a couple of hard-to-find skills relevant to the opening].

For me, the most motivating thing about designing training programs is finding out that people are actually doing their jobs better and enjoying them more because of what I created. That's always my goal.

Working here sounds like a perfect fit with what I'm looking for. I've talked to several people connected to the company, and I like what I've heard about the culture and where you're going.

Do you have any questions about what I've said so far?

Elements of a Good "Tell Me About Yourself" Answer

When crafting a good "tell me about yourself" answer, try to include most or all of these elements:

- an opening that gets the interviewer's interest
- focus on key selling points
- a very brief career summary
- an accomplishment example, demonstrating that you get results
- a little work-relevant insight into your motivations and personality
- a brief statement of your well-informed enthusiasm about the job
- a good question at the end (the one in the example is ideal—feel free to use it).

Then practice saying it. To make sure you don't sound robotic or over-rehearsed, don't memorize a script. Instead, create a simple outline or list of your key talking points (but don't write it out in full sentences). Talk through your answer, referring to your outline, until you can say it from memory. Then practice with a partner, asking him to tell you what he liked best about your answer and what could be better. Keep working on it until you feel confident that your answer will leave employers with a clear sense of why they should hire you—and an interest in hearing more!

Prepare for Common Interview Questions

Plan your answers to common interview questions (which you can easily find online), as well as others you know they'll ask based on your resume, such as "How did you win this award?" or "Why is there a gap in your work history?" Create a list of typical questions and jot down a few notes under each as needed. As with your "tell me about yourself" outline, keep your notes brief. When you're preparing for a specific interview, you can look up the company on Glassdoor.com to see if past interviewees posted interview questions there.

Use every answer to market yourself for the job by keeping the focus on your key selling points. Every answer should show employers why they should hire you.

Sometimes it's not obvious what an interview question is really about, so you should get in the habit of asking yourself, "What are they really trying to find out here?"

Notice when the question requires a story. If it starts with a phrase such as "tell me about a time when" or "give me a specific example of," then a general answer isn't enough. Even if specific stories and examples are not asked for, use them frequently. SOAR stories will make your answers more believable *and* memorable.

Make sure you are authentic in your answers. Lies and exaggerations will probably come back to haunt you, and answers "borrowed" from websites can sound phony. Be strategic and be real.

One important question to prepare for is, "What are your salary expectations?" This is often asked in phone screenings, which can occur unexpectedly. In general, you should try to delay answering this question until later in the interview process. However, if pressed, it's best to provide a range that is based on your research of your market value. This issue is covered in detail in chapter 11, so review it for further guidance on handling salary questions. Plan and rehearse your answer carefully, because it can affect your earnings for years to come.

Once you're in the interview, listen carefully! Make sure you understand what the interviewer is asking. If you're not sure, ask a clarifying question. Don't repeat yourself. Once you've said what you need to say, stop. Table 9-1 addresses commonly asked interview questions and what the interviewer is looking for.

Table 9-1. Common Interview Questions and What They're Really About

The Question	What They're Looking For
"What's your story?"	• Why should we hire you? • Do you have the good judgment to handle this strange question and give me an answer that's relevant?
"Tell me about your current or past job."	• How did that job prepare you for this one?
"What's your biggest weakness?"	• Is it a weakness so serious it disqualifies you? • Are you transparent about areas in which you need to improve? • Do you strive for continuous improvement?

"Tell me about a time when you failed."	• Are you open and honest? • Do you learn from your failures? • Do you do everything you can to "save the day"?
"Tell me about your best boss ever."	• Do you value a boss who makes you stretch and grow, or one who's just easy? • Have you worked well with past managers?
"Tell me about a difficult person you had to work with."	• Are you able to work well with everyone? • Are you fair and nonjudgmental, or do you get caught up in complaining? • Can you answer this sensitive question discreetly, without damaging someone else's reputation (or your own)?
"Are you having other interviews?"	• Are you about to take another job? • Are we wasting our time interviewing you?
"Where do you see yourself in five years?"	• If we hire you, will you stay a reasonable amount of time? • Will you grow and take on more responsibility? • Are you realistic and patient about seeking advancement?
"Who are our competitors?"	• Do you understand our market position and our challenges? • Are you interested enough to try to find out?
"How would you describe the color yellow to a blind person?"	• Can you show us you're comfortable with ambiguity and unexpected challenges? • Can you demonstrate certain soft skills relevant to this job (e.g., creativity, intuition, and communication skills)?

Impress by Asking Good Questions

Acing an interview is not just about giving the right answers. Asking the right questions is crucial. Good questions show that you're seriously interested in the job, and that you're already thinking ahead about how to do it well. Failing to ask questions will make you seem uninterested.

It's important to prepare 10 or 12 questions for the end of the interview. You won't actually ask that many, but you need plenty because some may have already been answered by that point.

The end of the interview isn't the only time to ask questions. Asking questions early can arm you with information that helps you sell your skills, because the more you know about the employer's needs, goals, and activities, the better you can target your message.

Think about this. A good question:

- shows good communication skills and a sense of appropriateness
- focuses on the work, not the pay: until the company has made you an offer, never ask about compensation, benefits, flextime, or perks
- shows that you've done your homework: the best questions are grounded in the research you've done on the company. For example, "I've read articles about

your company's new push for online self-service. How is that affecting this department?"

Any of the following questions could be customized and improved by referring to what you already know:

- What are the most important aspects of this role?
- Can you describe a typical day in this role?
- What are the goals and priorities for this role?
- Is this a new position?
- If not, what happened to the person who was previously in the job?
- What changes are ahead for this company in the coming year, and in the next few years?
- What are the greatest strengths and weaknesses of this company?
- What do you love about working here? Why have you stayed at this company?
- What do you find frustrating about working here?
- How would you describe the company culture, and how is it evolving?

These questions are good to ask a recruiter:

- What is the name and title of the person I would be reporting to in this role?
- What kind of person works best with him or her?
- What's the next step after our conversation today?

These questions are appropriate to ask the hiring manager (your prospective boss):

- What are your goals for this role? If I were successful, what would that look like?
- What are the top priorities for this role in the first 60 days?
- How does upper management view the role and the impact of this department?
- What training, development, and recognition have your reports received in the past year?
- What is your management style?

You could ask these questions to members of senior management:

- How does this department contribute to the growth of the company?
- How do you see this department's role changing as the company grows?
- How is this company looking to evolve so it continues to compete effectively?
- How could a person in this role support that evolution?

We've looked at how to answer questions and how to ask them, but only in terms of words. Now let's look at the important dimension beyond the verbal.

Nonverbal Communication and "Chemistry"

Employers don't make hiring decisions on a purely rational basis. A lot of it comes down to gut feelings, and nonverbal communication has a big influence. Some experts say two-thirds of communication is nonverbal. So, what do you need to do to make sure you're giving off the right vibes? Get feedback on your nonverbals.

Your first step is to look in a mirror or videotape yourself while you practice. This way you can see what you look like and gain some perspective. However you also need an outside perspective, so ask a friend or coach to do mock interviews with you. Ask for critique about not just what you said, but the overall impression you give. How was your handshake, smile and other facial expressions, eye contact, posture, movement, tone of voice, and appearance? What did you do well and what could use improvement?

Much has been written about body language—more than will fit into this chapter—so for now, let's look at some of the most important points.

First Things First

The interviewer's first in-person impression of you is likely to involve a smile, eye contact, and a handshake. When you are practicing, give special attention to these actions. Ask a friend for feedback.

Mind Your Posture

In most cases good posture means sitting up straight and leaning forward slightly, with both feet on the floor or with your legs crossed all the way; avoid resting your ankle on your knee, which looks too casual. Your hands can be in your lap, or sometimes gesturing. But don't cross your arms because it can make you seem standoffish; you want to look open and receptive.

Say the Interviewer's Name

Most people like to hear their own name, so use it when shaking hands at the beginning and end of the interview, and maybe once or twice in between.

Should you say "John" or "Mr. Jones"? The etiquette on this is changing, and not everyone agrees on it. One common view is that it's best to follow the interviewer's cues: If she calls you by your first name, reply in the same way. Other experts say it's better to address the interviewer formally until they specifically invite you to use their first name. Use the approach that seems to fit your particular situation.

Dress to Impress

What to wear depends on many factors—the role, the industry, and the company. As a general rule, dress one level higher than the way you would dress on the job.

If the workplace is casual (jeans, T-shirts, athletic shoes), come to the interview in business casual: dress slacks, a skirt or a dress, an open-collared shirt, semi-dress shoes, and maybe a blazer. If business casual is the standard workplace attire, wear a suit—preferably blue or gray, closed-toe dress shoes, and if you're a man put on a tie. If you'll be wearing a suit every day, you can't get much dressier than that. Wear a suit.

Etiquette

An interview is more formal than most day-to-day situations, so watch your manners even before you walk into the building and as you reach your car afterward. Here are some things you may not have thought of:

- Wait to be offered a seat before sitting down, or at least wait until the others have taken their seats.
- If offered a beverage other than water, it may best to politely decline. This is considerate to your host. Also, nervous people are more accident-prone, and you don't want to risk spilling coffee on yourself or your host's furniture! Water is simpler and safer.
- Don't place personal items—briefcase, water bottle, and so forth—on the interview table. Instead, put them under your chair or on an empty chair next to you. You may place a portfolio or notepad and pen on the table if you bring one.
- Don't just turn off your cell phone—put it out of sight.
- As of this writing, it is still inadvisable to take notes on an electronic device at an interview.
- When leaving the interview, if possible, stop in the outer office and thank the person who greeted you when you arrived.

Interview Formats: Know How to Ace Them All

Not every job interview is a one-on-one, question-and-answer session. There are many interview formats, and each has its own challenges and opportunities. Reduce the "surprise factor" by knowing how to succeed in any format.

Phone Screening

A phone screening can be a little like a "pop quiz"—it may arrive out of the blue. So as soon as you've sent in your resume, get ready. Keep all job announcements you've applied to readily available, along with your cover letters and resumes. When a recruiter calls and says he's calling about *X* company, you don't want to be struggling to remember, "Which job was that? What did I tell them about myself?" Having these materials handy helps keep you prepared.

The recruiter may subtly pressure you to "talk for a few minutes *right now*" even though it's not a good time for you. Asking to reschedule may put you at a disadvantage, because a busy recruiter may simply move on to other candidates. However, if it really is a bad time, it may be better to ask, "Is there another time we can talk today?" rather than do a poor interview because you're distracted.

In any phone interview, your tone of voice is crucial. Make a point of smiling, which can be heard in your voice, and stand up, which makes your voice sound more energetic.

One-on-One, Face-to-Face

This type of interview is familiar to most of us. Typically longer than a phone screening, an in-person interview may be a half hour, an hour, or longer. (A lengthy interview is often a good sign!)

Did you know that being more than 15 minutes early to an in-person interview can actually make a bad impression? It's smart to get to the interview location well in advance to ensure you won't be late, but wait in a coffee shop or in your car until 10 to 15 minutes before the scheduled time. Use this extra time to review your notes about the job, the people, and what you plan to say. You can also do your relaxation exercises and visualize a successful interview.

When you go inside, pay attention for clues about the company culture and what it's like working there. Be friendly, but not too chatty, with the receptionist and whoever else you encounter.

Panel Interview

Panel interviews are usually intended to standardize the interviewing process, so they are firmly structured. Often, several interviewers are lined up across from you, taking turns asking prepared questions. The situation may feel artificial and not very comfortable, but look at it this way: The interviewers probably don't enjoy it either. Let that thought give you a feeling of empathy toward them. Try to be gracious and put them at ease, and you may end up making yourself feel more relaxed as well.

As you answer the interview questions, include all the interviewers in your gaze and body language—not just the person who asked the question. And don't only focus on the friendly people; the grumpy one needs to be convinced, too.

If note taking is allowed, write down the name and role of each person present. Arrange the names on your notepad in the same way the people are arranged in the room—Kyle on the left, Lisa on the right—this will help you remember who is who. If possible, exchange business cards.

Group Interview

The term *group interview* can mean different things, but here we'll focus on a process in which multiple candidates interact together in a round-table discussion or small-group exercise. This format allows interviewers to observe interpersonal skills such as teamwork, leadership, and helping to facilitate the stated goals of the exercise.

It's a balancing act: Demonstrate your skills without taking over, and collaborate with people who may also be your competitors as you might do on the job if you were competing with teammates for a promotion while still working together for a common goal.

Behavioral Interview

Behavioral interview questions generally start with language such as "tell me about a time when" and require you to tell a specific story from your experience. Some interviewers rely heavily on such questions. The theory behind behavioral interviewing is that your behavior and performance in the past is the best predictor of how you'll perform if hired. So, as stated earlier in this chapter, it's important to develop a list of success stories that you can draw from to answer these questions.

Sequential or All-Day Interviews

It is increasingly common to have multiple interviews for a single position, and when they're crammed into one day it can be a bit mind-boggling. It is important to fight the fatigue! You may want to bring along a bottle of tea or a snack such as a protein bar.

In each interview, vary the stories and examples you tell because interviewers may compare notes later. If possible, take a few notes after each interview, before it all begins to blur together. This will help you write smart follow-up messages later.

Meal Interview

A meal with your prospective boss and teammates may not be called an interview, but it can have the same effect on your candidacy, so prepare. Plan your order in advance to save time. Order a very light meal so you can concentrate on communicating rather than eating. Avoid alcoholic beverages, even if the boss is drinking. Keep your phone off and out of sight. Be polite to restaurant staff.

Should you socialize or get down to business? Follow the lead of your host. One good conversation strategy is to ask the others what they enjoy most about their work and the company. Relax, but don't be caught off guard and be on your best behavior as to conversational topics and table manners—even if the boss is less correct!

Testing

Various types of tests may be given at interviews, including aptitude tests, which could involve anything from basic skills of reading, writing, or math to computer or technical skills, as well as behavioral or personality tests.

It's best to be honest in personality tests because they are designed to spot dishonesty. However, it may be helpful to take practice tests in advance. The Dummies website (www .dummies.com) is a great resource for practice personality tests. Chapter 10 covers pre-employment testing in great detail, so review it for more guidance on this topic.

Case Interview

Case interviews are a specific type of testing. In a case interview, candidates are given a situation or problem similar to one they would face on the job and asked to resolve it. Many webpages and books have been written on this type of interview, and this chapter cannot begin to cover the subject.

If invited to this type of interview, plan to spend many hours preparing for it, over a period of many days if possible. You can read more about case interviews on websites such as www.LiveCareers.com and www.Vault.com.

Presentation-Facilitation Interview

You may be asked to develop and give a presentation, either on a topic of your choice or one selected by the interviewer. If your work involves training, you may be asked to facilitate a short workshop. Others within the company may join as an audience or active participants.

Of course you need to demonstrate your knowledge, but strive to make it enjoyable for others as well. Make it interesting and encourage comments and interaction. Use appropriate humor to put people at ease.

Video Interviews

Although many employers use video interviewing, few people really enjoy the process. Even the interviewers are likely to be uncomfortable. If you can make the experience feel more natural, engaging, and enjoyable for all concerned, you will stand out and make a good impression. Video interviews may be either two-way calls or asynchronous. Two-way calls happen in real time, typically through platforms such as Skype or Google Hangouts. In an asynchronous interview, you're not interacting with an interviewer in real time; instead, you are sent a list of questions and record your responses.

You should familiarize yourself with the technology. Test it out in advance if possible, and make sure you understand what to do before you start. It is also important to make sure your face is well lit. Look at yourself through your computer's Photo Booth or Crazy Cam application, through a camera, or even in a mirror, to see how your face is lit. Then adjust the lighting in the room as necessary.

Make sure you're looking directly into the camera because this creates the effect of eye contact. If the camera isn't at eye level, adjust its position. If you're using a laptop, put a box or books under it to raise it.

To really master digital interviewing, refer to Paul Bailo's book, *The Essential Digital Interview Handbook: Lights, Camera, Interview: Tips for Skype, Google Hangout, GoToMeeting, and More.*

"Wow Factor" Extras

Whatever type of interview you're participating in, consider demonstrating that you're the kind of employee who goes above and beyond by sharing something extra, such as a portfolio, PowerPoint presentation, or a 30-60-90-day plan showing how you will create value if hired.

Your portfolio could include work samples, summaries of projects, graphs and other visual aids, letters of recommendation, copies of certificates or recognitions, transcripts, or highly favorable performance evaluations, as well as your resume and references.

If you've prepared a presentation to show on a computer, make sure it can be simply and instantly displayed on your laptop or tablet without any need for additional equipment or setup.

If you bring a 30-60-90-day plan, make sure it is customized to the specific job and company, thoroughly researched, and brief—no more than four pages.

Know that some interviewers may not want to look at these extra items, so try to find out in advance whether they're welcome. Whatever you bring, choose the right moment to use it. A good time might be when the employer has asked a question related to the items you've brought.

Closing the Interview

You've marketed your skills impressively from the first handshake to the last question and the interviewer is wrapping it up. You're done, right? Not quite. Remember, you want to be remembered as the best person for the job—and in addition to first impressions, final impressions are memorable as well. So it is important to reiterate your key selling points and your interest in the job.

Remember Claudia, the instructional designer from earlier in this chapter? Here's what her closing statement sounded like:

> Thank you again for your time today. I'm even more excited than before. Your plan for the new training portal sounds exactly like the type of project where my web design and graphic skills can be a big asset. And overall, I've got the experience and education to lead your design team credibly and be a great resource. I think it's a great fit and I'd love to join your team!

Assuming they don't hire Claudia on the spot, she should then ask about next steps, including whether it would be okay to call on such-and-such day to follow up.

Follow Up Right–Not by Rote

Most candidates send a brief thank you note after an interview. But if you want to stand out, make sure your follow-up communications reinforce the reasons why you're the right person for the job. The purposes of the follow-up thank you note are to:

- Express appreciation.
- Reiterate your strong interest in the position.
- Remind the employer of your key selling points.
- Add a bit more information—another accomplishment, for example—or to correct a misimpression.

Should you send a handwritten note, an email, or a typed letter? Each has its advantages, and the impact depends on your industry. A handwritten note could seem old-fashioned in some industries, but could be a good way to stand out in others. Whatever form it takes, make sure your message arrives soon, preferably by the next business day.

Then stay on their radar screen. Additional written messages, or possibly a phone call, can help demonstrate that you're highly motivated and assertive. Take a helpful tone—"I wanted to see whether you need any additional information"—rather than asking whether they've made a decision.

Checklist: What to Bring to the Interview

As we approach the end of this chapter, you've probably noticed that there is a lot to remember about interviewing. Use this checklist to keep track of your logistics on the big day. Add or delete items to adapt the list to your own unique situation.

- Pen and notepad
- List of questions you want to ask
- Copies of your resume and cover letter
- Copies of up to three letters of recommendation
- Notes to review beforehand (for example, SOAR stories, talking points in response to common questions)
- Job posting, names of people you'll meet, any other details you have about the interview
- Master application to copy information from
- Carrying case (folder or briefcase)
- Address, directions (including an alternate route), and a map (paper or app)
- Cash for alternate transportation, just in case
- Plan B for wardrobe malfunction (spare tie, safety pin, spare nylons, makeup)
- Cell phone, off
- Optional: Portfolio, presentation, or 30-60-90-day plan.

Summary

Acing the interview is not simple; in any type of interview—from the shortest phone screening to an all-day interview on-site—there are many opportunities to answer the unspoken question, "Why should we hire you?"

You can demonstrate you're the one to hire by:

- initiating rapport with a firm handshake, eye contact, and a smile
- memorably communicating your key selling points right from the start
- effectively telling SOAR stories so the employer can easily visualize the skillful way you do your work
- nailing every detail, from appropriate clothing to what you brought (and didn't bring) with you
- marrying authenticity with strategy to sell your skills with every answer.

Successfully interviewing takes work. Reading this chapter was a great start, and now comes the most important part: Go through it again and act on every tip that applies to you. Plan and practice like the smart, hard-working professional you are! Because most candidates don't prepare enough, you will stand out and be remembered. Get ready for a job offer!

Pre-Employment Assessment

Jean Juchnowicz

Along the path of your job hunt journey you may have to take a pre-employment assessment. Typically, this step follows a successful interview and can occur as part of an application for employment process, such as providing your resume, completing the employment application, supplying your reference information (with all contact information), passing your first interview evaluation, and perhaps providing letters of recommendation.

So, let's assume you are basking in the glow of a successful interview, and along comes an email from the company recruiter informing you that the company wants you to take a pre-employment assessment and the deadlines to observe. Now what? How much weight in the hiring decision do these assessments carry?

An assessment is a test that helps to provide a fair and consistent method of comparing job applicants and evaluating the match with the job description for the open job. While the exact weight given to these tests differs with each company, rarely would assessments be the primary decision-making tool. The goal is to hire the best candidate for the job and increase the chances of that person's success and retention, because sourcing, recruiting, testing, selecting, and hiring are expensive functions in a company. The better you understand pre-employment assessments, the better you can compete for jobs in this competitive, post-recession environment.

Types of Assessments

There are many different types of assessments: personality, cognitive, honesty, genetics, U.S. employment eligibility (E-Verify), Internet name search, social media screen, skills, job knowledge, job aptitude, drug (including urine, blood, saliva, or hair), physical fitness (must be correlated to the physical job duties), medical exam (done by a physician or a registered nurse), work references, verified letters of recommendation, background screens (including identity and criminal record), fingerprint check, credit checks (only if allowed by the Fair Credit Reporting Act), language fluency, assessment centers, and realistic job previews.

Assessments such as reference checks, medical exams, and pencil-and-paper honesty tests and simple knowledge tests have been in regular use since the 1970s. The newer tools have been growing in popularity over the past 15 years, spurred by wider access to the Internet. However, every test an employer uses must be validated, reliable, and nondiscriminatory. For more information, refer to the Equal Employment Opportunity Commission (EEOC) fact sheet on this topic, which you can find on the EEOC website.

Keeping It Simple . . . and Legal

Employers should keep their choice of testing assessments simple, taking care to ensure that their tests are directly related to the job. In 2015, the discount retailer Target agreed to pay $2.8 million, settling a claim with the EEOC that employment assessments the company had used "had disproportionately screened out applicants for exempt-level professional positions based on race and sex." Additionally, "the EEOC found that one of the assessments violated the Americans With Disabilities Act. This assessment—performed by psychologists on behalf of Target—was a prohibited pre-employment medical exam" (Smith 2015).

Typically, an employer performs the assessments that it believes will yield the best information for acquiring talent, whether it is a new, external hire or a current employee seeking a transfer or promotion. From 2001 to 2013, the number of large U.S. employers that used pre-employment assessments grew from 26 percent to 57 percent (Weber 2015). In 2015, about 76 percent of organizations with more than 100 employees used aptitude and personality tests when hiring, a statistic that is expected to rise (Chamorro-Premuzic 2015).

It is important to recognize the significance of testing in today's employment recruiting and hiring. Try to find out what kinds of tests will be administered, show interest in each test, prepare as best you can, and calmly complete each test in a timely fashion. If at all possible take all assessments on a computer, rather than a mobile device. Although some tests have been rewritten for mobile-enabled platforms, many will not work properly on a smartphone or a tablet. After completing the test, follow up in two to four days to ask for the test results.

Social Media and Internet Screenings

Are you concerned about a social media search on you? You should be. You have two choices: make the content on all your sites private or do not post personal content that could be interpreted in a negative manner. For example, avoid posting about religion, politics, ethnic jokes, partying, illegal activities, negative reviews, job dissatisfaction, or similar things. What happens on the Internet, stays on the Internet!

Do you have a criminal record? This need not be a barrier to employment, except in certain industries and jobs, and depending upon the nature of your conviction. Employers conduct background screening for many reasons in addition to a criminal check:

- Negligent hiring lawsuits are on the rise. If an employee's actions hurt someone, the employer may be liable.
- To avoid negligent retention lawsuits if the employer knew or should have known about the employee's record.
- Terrorist acts, both domestic and abroad, that had their roots with the terrorist being an employee in a company.
- Corporate senior executives, officers, and board directors face a degree of scrutiny in both their professional and private lives when corporate scandals occur.
- False or embellished information supplied by some job applicants makes employers wary of blindly accepting what is put on an application.

Checking Further

You can use an online service that dips into databases to check, for a fee, whether you have a criminal record. The National Crime Information Center (NCIC) is a collection of databases that the federal government uses; however, access to it is primarily limited to law enforcement or other very specialized approved organizations. At the local level, you can check with your county sheriff's department or court clerk's office. Additionally, the Department of Public Safety, State Police Department, and State Bureau of Investigation have records you can check for state-level crimes. At the national level, the FBI has those records. Be careful if you pay a service for a report on yourself or anyone else, as many of these companies over promise and under deliver because they simply do not have access to all the databases. Applicants may believe, incorrectly, that after a certain period of time convictions are dropped or "expunged" from their record; know that errors do occur. If you can, determine if you have a criminal record, what is on it, and if it is correct. If it is not correct, contact the agency and provide the correct documentation.

Criminal Checks

Because employers decide how deep of a criminal records check is required for their company, these can vary. International checks can also be performed, but the accuracy of those can vary from country to country.

Genetic Testing

There is much debate about genetic testing's use as a pre-employment assessment. These tests can detect the presence of genetic abnormalities in healthy individuals that may place them at increased risk for developing certain diseases. In the workplace, such tests can be used to screen job applicants and employees who, because of their genetic makeup, may be more likely to develop diseases if exposed to certain worksite substances, such as chemicals or radiation. The Genetic Information Nondiscrimination Act of 2008 is a federal law that protects individuals from genetic discrimination—which is the misuse of genetic information—in health insurance and employment.

E-Verify

E-verify is an optional Internet-based system that allows businesses to determine the eligibility of their employees to work in the United States. U.S. law requires companies to employ only individuals who may legally work in the United States—either U.S. citizens or foreign citizens who have the necessary authorization. E-Verify is fast, free, and easy to use—and it's currently the best way employers can ensure a legal workforce. It is used after an employee is hired and has presented his documents. Like any federal database program, it has its supporters and its detractors.

E-Verify has a self-check process, which lets you confirm that your employment eligibility information is in order by checking it against the same databases E-Verify uses when employers enter your information. The website is www.uscis.gov/mye-verify/self-check. Go ahead, check yourself now!

Realistic Job Previews (RJP)

RJPs are useful for both the employer and the applicant. It is a chance for the employer to observe you interacting with the staff, asking intelligent questions, shadowing a worker, and talking about what you know. For the applicant, it is a chance to learn more about the job, your co-workers, and the good and the bad about the company—it provides a view into the company and its culture.

Personality Tests

Let's do some time traveling. It's Han dynasty, third-century China, and employment tests are done to assess the mental capacity of civil servants. Jump forward to the 20th century. In 1921, Thomas Alva Edison invented a pre-employment test because he was challenged to find technical help. The test was denounced as exceedingly hard; that only a walking encyclopedia could have passed. Notably Henry Ford and Nikola Tesla passed his test and were hired; both went on to achieve success with him and later on their own.

Now fast forward to the 21st century. Personality tests are given to determine if you will be a fit with the company culture and your work style. Many, but not all, are based on "the Big Five" personality traits—openness to experience, conscientiousness, extraversion, agreeableness, and neuroticism—also known as the five factor model (FFM). This model originated in the 1920s, and was clarified in 1980, with additional research conducted in the 1990s.

Cognitive tests, such as Wonderlic and CCAT, assess IQ and a person's ability to learn. The most popular standardized personality tests (in no particular order) include Myers-Briggs Type Indicator (should not be used for hiring), Minnesota Multiphasic Personality Inventory (should not be used for hiring), Predictive Index, Kolbe A Index, the four Hogan Assessments, DiSC, *StengthsFinder 2.0*, Caliper Profile, and the 16 Personality Factors.

Once you know which test you will be taking, research it and try out some sample questions for practice. Ask the recruiter if you are not sure which test or type of test is used. The more information you have, the better you will be able to prepare. Each test has redundancy built in so you cannot "game" the test.

Who Uses What? And Does Size Matter?

Employers using pre-employment assessments range from Fortune 500 companies to small, "mom and pop" businesses. Google says that the number one thing they look for in a prospective employee is cognitive ability and an ability to learn quickly. Facebook uses StrengthsFinder for career development, but not to hire. Walmart uses a custom assessment test after the application process, but before the first interview. The government at all levels uses a variety of branded assessments.

References and Recommendations: The Good, the Bad, and the Ugly

Reference checking is a process that proves past performance is a predictor of future performance. However, because of threats of litigation, many employers have become reluctant to provide information about former employees beyond employment dates, salary, job description, and title. As a consequence, many states have passed "immunity" laws that provide protection from civil liability for employers who provide good-faith references for former employees; employers who knowingly relay false or misleading information are not protected by their state's immunity laws.

Who writes references? The best references are current and former managers, coworkers, and subordinates; however, references also can be provided by human resources or an outsourced service, such as www.theworknumber.com. Vendors and clients can also be good references. When asking if people will serve as a reference for you, let them know you are job hunting and would appreciate their help. Ask them to let you know if they are contacted.

Be sure you include their complete contact information on the employment application you fill out: supervisor name, supervisor title, work phone number, and dates of employment. You can also provide a professional reference page with your resume. Include your identifying information at the top (name, email, phone number), with the column headers reference name, company, relationship, cell phone, work phone, and email.

Providing complete, timely, and accurate information will help facilitate the reference process. How many references you list is your choice, but typically six to eight is appropriate. Every few years, update your reference list to ensure all the information is still accurate: People change names, jobs, titles, phone numbers, and email addresses. Your reference page is always a work in progress and should be ready to be submitted at an interview, if requested. There are services that offer to check your references to confirm if they are good, for a fee. However, the reliability of these services is not certain, so you have to evaluate them carefully. Do not have a friend call to check on your references because this may raise suspicion.

Once your references tell you they have been contacted, follow up with the company to make sure they don't need any additional references. Sometimes your contact will let you know if your references have been positive.

The two most important questions a hiring company will ask your reference are "what is the reason for your leaving?" and "what is your eligibility for rehire?" If you are not confident that a current or former supervisor or co-worker will provide a good work reference, take steps to mitigate this. If you don't have to provide a potentially negative reference to your prospective employer, don't provide it.

If you do need to provide a person with whom you are not confident as a reference, first, ask yourself why you think you will get a poor review from that person. Then, talk with co-workers with whom you had a good relationship and seek to understand what concerns could be relayed to a future employer. Did you walk off the job? Were you discharged? Was your attitude less than stellar? Did your attendance record reflect tardiness or absences? How were your performance appraisals?

Whether you are blindsided by a bad reference you did not expect or you knew to expect one, it is important to explain up front, prior to the work reference checks, any situation out of the ordinary from your perspective. Never blame or deflect a negative situation. Explain without emotion and be factual. Take accountability if it was a situation in which you made a bad decision, had a personal situation, suffered a health issue, or were not serious enough in your job. If you are questioned about this, offer to provide other references from people who can attest to your good work.

Employers are not interested in work references from places where you worked or people you worked with more than seven years ago. If you have not been working recently and are now ready to work and are in the process of being hired, provide reference information that is current from professionals who may know you in a business capacity: perhaps your banker, the president of an association you belong to, your religious leader, or a long-time neighbor. Don't dredge up people from your far past. Keep it current. If you have been volunteering, the head of volunteers is an excellent prospect to ask to serve as a reference. Do not provide family members, in-laws, or friends as references, unless you are asked for character or personal references. If you have been rearing children or taking care of an ill family member, whom have you been interacting with who could describe your virtues in a professional manner?

There are two ways employers obtain your permission to check your references: the statement you signed on the employment application or a specific reference form you signed and authorized. If an employer uses a service, the information provided may be limited. If only job title and dates of employment are given, that is not a reference but a verification of past employment. Employers who are interested in you want strong references from people in authority who are able to provide accurate information.

Letters of recommendation, presented at the time of the first in-person interview, are extremely valuable. Just as your resume should always be up-to-date, the same applies to your letters of recommendation. Have current letters of recommendation in electronic form so that you can print them out quickly—you may be scheduled for an in-person interview two days after a phone interview. Think of your letters of recommendation as an insurance policy. Be polite and gracious when you ask people to write them. Remind them of any specific information that you think is pertinent to your skills, job hunt, and the prospective position. Make sure that they include the following three things in their recommendation letter:

- An introductory paragraph explaining how the writer knows the applicant.
- An honest description of the applicant's knowledge, skills, abilities, and accomplishments, with an example or two.
- A summary paragraph that explains why the writer is recommending the applicant for future employment.

If you are asked for a letter of recommendation from someone you respect, feel honored and write a good letter.

Do You *Want* to Work for This Company?

Prior to receiving a job offer and any related negotiations, decide whether you actually want this opportunity. Determining if this is your future company and job involves not only researching the company as thoroughly as you can, but also researching an appropriate salary and asking yourself if you see yourself working for this company. It is both an objective and a subjective exercise that involves your brain and gut instincts. Take the time and effort to do your homework and you will have your answer.

As Lou Adler, bestselling author, consultant, and trainer of recruiters and hiring managers, has written in *The Essential Guide for Hiring & Getting Hired* (2013): "Before you ever accept another job, ask yourself this question: 'Forget the money. Is this a job I want?' If not, you'll be disappointed no matter how much you get paid."

According to Dick Bolles (2016), bestselling author, speaker, and career development expert for job hunters, "In today's world, he or she who gets hired is not necessarily the one who can do that job best; but, the one who knows the most about how to get hired," as stated in *What Color Is Your Parachute?*

Start by asking yourself some questions. Did you obtain the results from your assessments? What did that process teach you? Are you clearer on your strengths and weaknesses? Why do you think you want this job? Is the timing right? Is the location right? Do you think the company culture will be a fit with your values? Job searching is like dating—you want a match. Review chapter 3 for additional information on how to assess a company's culture for fit.

Next, research the company. Did you get a good feeling from HR? Did the employees you met look happy? Do you know anyone who works there? Review the company's website. What does the company mission statement say? Can you find the vision statement or current goals? Search for the company on the Internet and see what you find in the way of reviews and company profiles. How do they score as a "best place to work"? Were you given any benefits summary information?

While the process of conducting research may seem overwhelming, the final opinion you form will be very valuable and lead you to your final decision. Use the checklist in Table 10-1 to aid you.

Table 10-1. Employer Evaluation Worksheet

Assign points to each question. Give zero points if you disagree, one point if you're neutral, and two points if you agree. The higher your total points, the more likely you will be a good fit with the company.

1. Has the company been professional to deal with from initial contact to now? ____
2. Did you feel welcome when you engaged in the interview by phone or on-site? ____
3. Is the location convenient to balance your personal life with your work life? ____
4. Were you told more about the company and the job to add to your knowledge? ____
5. Read the mission and vision statements. Can you identify with them? ____
6. Were you asked legal questions that were directly related to your qualifications and based on the job description for the open position? ____
7. High vacancy rates in a company are a red flag. Has this job been open for a long time? ____
8. Did you like the person who will be your boss? Trust your gut. ____
9. Did the employees you saw smile at you and seem happy? ____
10. Employee referral is a strong recruitment source; do you know anyone at the company? ____
11. High turnover in a company is a red flag. How long have people been with the company? Unless it is a young company, many employees with short tenures can be a concern. ____

12. Many job openings can be a red flag, unless it is due to growth. Are there many openings? ___

13. Were you asked what questions you had and were they answered to your satisfaction? ___

14. Can you see yourself being a part of the company and appreciated as a contributor? ___

15. Did the job offer present a clear picture of the total compensation components, including salary, benefits, commission, incentive pay, bonus, and so on? ___

16. Explore the company website and all company social media sites; do you think you now know much more about the company? ___

17. Read reviews from popular sites such as GlassDoor, Vault, LinkedIn, Facebook, Yelp, Yahoo!, and Indeed. Formulate an opinion. ___

18. Does the company have a positive rating from the Better Business Bureau? ___

19. Search for the company on Forbes; are there good articles and ratings? ___

20. Search for the company on Fortune; are there good articles and ratings? ___

21. Has the company won awards for being a best place to work or similar honor? ___

Total Points: ___

Should You Take the Job?

Now you are ready to wait for "the call." What did you decide? Is this the job opportunity for you? In chapter 11, you will learn more about job offers, negotiation strategies, and counteroffers, but here are a few tips to keep in mind:

- When you receive an offer, evaluate it and determine if a counter offer is needed.
- Be sure to respond to the job offer by the requested timeframe (usually no more than 48 hours). Ask if you will be receiving an offer letter to sign and return.
- Understand if an employment contract is needed for the job and be sure to read it critically before signing it.
- Clarify all pay and benefits offered to determine the true financial value of the job offer.

If you decide against the offer, be gracious, explain why, and don't burn the bridge. That offer may not be right for you, or maybe you just received another job offer that you have accepted; whatever the reason, that company may, in the future, have the perfect job for you.

Summary

A pre-employment assessment helps employers compare job applicants in a fair and consistent way and evaluate the match with the job description for the open job. Assessments are simply one tool used to determine a job applicant's suitability for the job. Such assessments include reference checks and credit checks, as well as personality and intelligence testing. Job seekers should take care to evaluate their prospective employers by analyzing a variety of factors.

Negotiating Your Job Offer

Alan De Back

Early in my adult life I needed to buy a new car. My first car, which my dad had helped me purchase several years before, was soon to be headed to the junkyard. I went to the dealership filled with confidence that I would negotiate the best deal possible. Several hours later I left with a new car, but feeling as if I had "lost the fight." I was convinced I had paid far more than I should have, but somehow still ended up paying the price and driving away. I chastised myself every time I drove that car until the day I sold it. What had happened?

Now let's fast forward to the time I found and accepted my first corporate sector job. My previous professional experience had been in the nonprofit and government sectors, but they were both undergoing a recession and my ability to negotiate had been limited. When I received the corporate job offer, the recruiter's comment to me was "don't even think about negotiating." I took him at his word and accepted the salary offered. Only a few weeks into the new job, I learned that a couple of my direct reports were earning a higher salary than I was. Once again, I was frustrated and chastised myself. What had happened?

Many of us have had similar experiences with negotiating, both in our personal and professional lives. Because we believe that we have somehow "lost" a negotiation, the experience sours us on the whole concept. We think that a winner and a loser must come out of the experience, and we are feeling the remorse of being the loser. The savvy job seeker understands that most 21st-century employers expect to go through a negotiation process with you. In addition, most employers expect to end up with a win-win solution—they want you to feel as if you have negotiated a fair deal, and they want to feel the same on their end.

In this chapter, we'll look at negotiating from the job seeker's perspective. What are some strategies that you can use to make sure both you and your new employer negotiate to a win-win final job offer?

Why Should I Negotiate?

Because many of us have such a negative connotation about negotiating, we have a real resistance to the idea of negotiating the details of a job offer. Why not just take what you are offered and avoid the whole unpleasant scenario? In many situations, you may be walking away from an opportunity to best meet your needs while also filling the employer's requirements. Will you suffer from "buyer's remorse" later?

Above all else, you are your own best advocate. No one else will represent you in the way that you will. If you do have specific priorities that need to be met, you are the best person to articulate those priorities and negotiate to ensure that they are filled. This is a challenge that only you can meet.

Secondly, you must be absolutely sure that your bottom-line needs are met. Whether the issue is a salary level necessary to maintain your standard of living, or a flexible work schedule to coordinate care for your children, you have requirements that must be met for you to be successful in a new job. Your new employer will not get the best performance you can provide if your bottom-line needs are not met. In that scenario, you are both set up to fail.

Finally, your long-range financial future could be affected—particularly if you are in the early stages of your career. The salary you accept now will affect future raises and long-term earning potential. Don't you owe it to yourself to negotiate the best and fairest salary that you can? Your decision now could make a difference of thousands of dollars down the road.

When Should I Negotiate?

Many situations merit negotiating your job offer—and some almost demand that you make the effort. Let's take a look at some scenarios in which negotiating will be to your benefit.

You should almost always try to negotiate if the salary does not meet your expectations. Perhaps, based on your research, you believe that the salary offered does not reflect your market value. Or maybe you've done the math, and the salary simply does not meet your needs to maintain your standard of living. Both scenarios can be good ones to try negotiating a higher salary. You may need to be prepared to walk away from the offer if you cannot successfully agree on a higher pay level, but at least you have the satisfaction of having tried. Your new employer wants you to come into your position with enthusiasm and energy, and feeling that you are underpaid will affect the passion with which you tackle your new job.

Recognizing that no job is ideal, a potential new employer may make you an offer contingent on responsibilities that are different or at a higher level than you originally discussed. In that scenario, you will probably believe that your value for the position just went up. This could be another good reason to negotiate salary. Because something about the job is different than you were originally led to expect, you are perfectly justified in going back and negotiating a pay rate that reflects the responsibilities now being given to you.

Finally, you may be in a scenario in which the salary offer is acceptable, but you need some sort of additional benefit because of your personal situation. Perhaps you have a child, and you need a flexible work schedule to accommodate your childcare provider. Or maybe you are willing to accept a lower salary in exchange for the ability to telecommute. These are both examples of situations in which you might want to negotiate aspects of the job beyond the salary.

When Should I Not Negotiate?

We hear so much about the concept of negotiating a job offer that some people believe they should always attempt to negotiate. However, in some scenarios negotiation is neither necessary nor wise. Why take the risk if all aspects of the offer meet your expectations?

A client of mine, Jack, was involved in a long and frustrating job search. The market in his geographic area was not good, and his skills were not in high demand. One day, he called to report that he had received an excellent offer at a salary well above what we had identified as his market value. He wanted to know if he should try to negotiate, because he had read in several job search books that you should "always" try to negotiate an offer. After a short discussion we jointly agreed that he had no real reason to make a counteroffer. The job was a great fit and the salary above expectations. He accepted the position exactly as offered.

Although I encourage my clients not to be the first to raise the issue of salary (best to leave that to the employer), the question can come up quite early in the interview process. If you indicated early on that a salary or range is acceptable, trying to negotiate something higher after receiving an offer is not a good idea. The employer took it in good faith that you were content with the salary or range—going back now could make you look less than ethical and endanger the offer you received.

Some employers (nonprofit or government organizations) simply have no flexibility in the salary that they can offer. You will probably know this up front, based on the published salary and your conversations with them. To attempt to negotiate when they have no flexibility will only frustrate you both.

It is important to determine whether or not you should negotiate, and how assertively you should negotiate (Figure 11-1). The two factors to consider are how much your skills are in demand, and how much you need the job:

- Low demand for skills and high need for job: Unless something is way out of line with the offer, you should probably not negotiate.
- Moderate demand for skills and moderate need for job: You might consider minor salary negotiation or negotiating benefits.
- High demand for skills and low need for job: You can negotiate assertively.

Figure 11-1. Should I Negotiate My Offer?

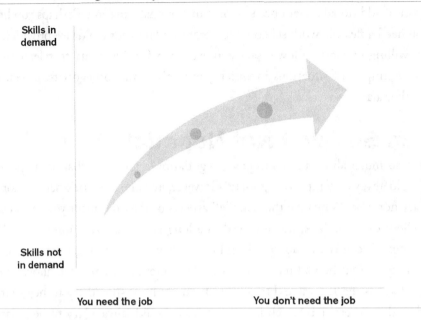

Skills in demand

Skills not in demand

You need the job　　　　**You don't need the job**

What Can I Negotiate?

When you think about negotiating a job offer, you most frequently think about negotiating salary. Salary negotiation is appropriate in many situations, as long as you are realistic. A client of mine, Pat, worked for a high-tech consulting firm. He was extremely well paid, and was aware of that fact. When his firm suddenly went bankrupt and he found himself looking for a new opportunity, he had to assess what a realistic salary range was. Although he would have loved to maintain his high salary, he knew it wasn't likely. When he accepted a new job offer it was at a salary he considered reasonable, but it was also several thousand dollars less than he had been making.

In the event that salary is not negotiable, what else could make up for a salary that is less than what you wanted? You might consider trying to negotiate the timing of your first performance appraisal and your first opportunity for a raise. Typically, this step doesn't happen until you have been with your new employer for a year. But you might be able to negotiate the opportunity for it to happen six months after your hire instead. That gives you six months to really demonstrate your value and show that you are worthy of a raise.

Many individuals use the negotiation process to discuss their benefits package. Perhaps you can get another week or two of vacation in lieu of a higher salary. Or maybe your new employer would be willing to pick up a larger portion of the cost of your health insurance. You may also find opportunities around funding your 401(k).

Because we're all balancing so many responsibilities outside work, many individuals see this process as an opportunity to negotiate flexible work options. For instance, you might ask for a flexible schedule to accommodate the needs of an elderly parent. Or you may want to telecommute a few days a week because of traffic issues. Some organizations are willing to consider variations of a 4-10 work schedule (four days a week, 10 hours a day), which would give you a long weekend, every weekend.

In short, really think about your bottom line and your lifestyle. Appendix I is a monthly expenses worksheet to help you figure things out. What options would you want to negotiate that would work best for you?

Negotiating Salary

Most people find negotiating a salary to be the most intimidating process, especially because the subject of salary is often taboo to start with. Think about the many organizations that strictly forbid employees from discussing their salaries with one another. However, if you are prepared when you start negotiating, you'll feel more comfortable.

A colleague of mine is the recruiting director for a major consulting firm, and he says that whichever party (applicant or employer) raises the salary issue first is at a disadvantage. However, some research suggests that the person who names their price first gets *closer* to their stated number (Chapman 2011).

Either way, it is very important to know your market value. Despite your previous salary or your expectations for a new salary, you need the reality check of knowing what you are worth out on the open market. If you don't do this, you could undersell yourself or price yourself out of the market.

If asked about salary expectations, try to provide a range rather than a specific figure. You could say, "Based on the research I have done, I believe that this position is worth this range in this geographic area." Then state a range of perhaps $10,000 (for example, $80,000-$90,000). Using this strategy, you show that you have done your homework to determine your market value, rather than simply stating a salary figure that you personally expect.

Finally, be realistic. Yes, that salary in the upper six-figure range would be just wonderful, but is it realistic for your market value, the type of employer, and the work that you will be doing? Remember my client Pat? He knew that it was unrealistic to expect an offer at his previous salary. If you are not realistic in your negotiation, you are not negotiating in good faith and you are risking the whole offer falling apart.

How Do I Know My Market Value?

To be realistic in your salary negotiations, know your actual market value. It will be based primarily on the job title, type of work, and your geographic region. The same job title will probably have a very different market value in rural Idaho than it does in New York City. Determining your market value will require you to do some research.

A good place to start is with professional organizations and publications. Many professional organizations conduct annual surveys of a range of job titles in various geographic regions. This information may be published in a research report or whitepaper or on their website. They also typically discuss any salary trends they are observing. Note that you may need to be a member of the association to access these data.

There are also a large number of commercial online resources for salary research. Although some charge users for detailed searches, most allow basic searches by job title and geographic area for free. The data may be a bit dated, because it is often based on research that is as much as a year old. However, most online resources allow users to dig down for both job titles and cities or geographic regions. Many supply a median salary and ranges of salaries. Some of the most popular online resources are Salary.com, Glassdoor.com, and Payscale.com.

The United States Department of Labor Employment and Training Administration also provides a very good online resource, O*NET OnLine (www.onetonline.org). In addition to listing the job requirements, interests, and skills for a huge range of job titles, O*NET provides data about the projected demand in coming years. Salary information is available both nationally and broken down to the state level. This is a rich resource of information for determining your market value.

Friends and colleagues working in your field can also be a good resource for salary information. In fact, they can probably provide the most up-to-date figures based on their knowledge of your field. Rather than asking colleagues exactly how much money they are earning, instead ask them for their insight into what a realistic range is. If possible, find a colleague working in the industry in which you are considering an offer, because she will probably provide the most accurate information for your purposes.

Negotiating: The Personal Aspects

After your salary research is complete, there are still variables that make every negotiation unique. These are subjective aspects, based on your personality and comfort level, and are entirely within your control.

Negotiation does require a certain level of assertiveness. Even initiating the process requires that you be fairly assertive. A big difference exists, however, between assertiveness and aggressiveness. Being overly aggressive could offend a potential employer and even result in an offer being rescinded. So what level of assertiveness is called for?

Most important, keep your negotiations with your potential employer positive. This is not the car dealership scenario described at the beginning of the chapter. You and your employer need to conclude the conversation feeling as if both sides got a fair shake. But what does this mean?

First, make a case for your value. What skill sets do you bring to the table that will benefit the employer? How will you help them solve their problems? Better yet, how will you help them move their performance to the next level? This conversation is not about what you need from them, but about the value you can add to their organization.

Second, understand the employer's constraints. Some employers (particularly nonprofit or government employers) may not have a lot of flexibility in the negotiation process. Don't be unrealistic in your expectations.

Finally, don't issue an ultimatum. Nothing will take negotiations to a negative place more quickly than issuing an ultimatum about what you want or need. Even if you have a bottom line in mind, making demands will not get you what you want. Instead, negotiate from a positive place. If you do end up having to walk away from the offer, keeping the process positive will result in both parties feeling good even though the negotiation was not successful. And who knows, another opportunity may come up in the future for which you will be viewed favorably.

After some of my negative early career and personal experiences around negotiating, I detested even seeing the word *negotiate*. I promised myself that I would never again put myself in a scenario in which I needed to negotiate anything. That promise was, of course, not realistic. As I began to realize that the process did not necessarily have to be negative, I realized that I could develop the expertise to negotiate both positively and effectively.

Realize that your future employer truly wants you both to be happy. If you accept a job with a salary that you view as being unacceptable or a benefits package that is inadequate, you likely will not perform at your maximum.

In short, you need to adjust your attitude about the negotiation process by adopting a mindset that the process should result in a win-win situation. While that adjustment may be easier said than done, it's important to see that your job offer discussion is much different from the negative process you may experience when you purchase a car. A win-win benefits both you and your potential employer. Keeping that concept in mind will help you diminish your negative feelings about the negotiation process.

How Will My Potential Employer Respond?

The good news is that most private sector employers expect some kind of negotiation process. Negotiation of the various aspects of an offer has become a widespread practice. In a 2015 Salary.com survey, 73 percent of the employers surveyed said they were not offended when people negotiate. Even more interesting, 84 percent of the respondents said they always expect job applicants to negotiate salary during the interview process. And for those concerned about losing an offer if they try to negotiate, 87 percent said they've never rescinded a job offer after the negotiation process.

The bad news is that there is some risk. If the employer you are trying to negotiate with is not one of the 87 percent, you do run the risk of offending them and your offer being rescinded. Refer to the earlier part of this chapter about when and when not to negotiate for assistance in making your decision about whether to move ahead.

Getting to Win-Win

Regardless of whether you are negotiating salary, benefits, or work schedule, these tips will help you be successful and achieve the win-win scenario that both you and your potential employer are striving for.

Remember to stay positive. The theme of remaining positive is woven through this entire chapter, but it is the single most important thing that you must do throughout the process. If you become negative by making unreasonable demands, for example, the entire process will break down. Regardless of your previous experiences with any kind of negotiating, stay positive.

To best make your case during the negotiation process, you have to be prepared with any back-up information that you will need. With salary negotiation that means knowing your market value. For other issues (benefits, work schedule, and so forth), you need to help the employer understand how everyone will benefit. For example, if you are trying to negotiate a telecommuting arrangement two days a week, you should first assure your employer that you have the technology in your home to make the arrangement work flawlessly. You should also try to have some evidence (perhaps from past experience) that you may actually be more productive when working from home.

Finally, be realistic about the eventual outcomes from the negotiation process—you may not get everything that you want. You may not get the full salary you desire, or you may end up telecommuting one day a week rather than two. However, in a true win-win scenario, both you and your new employer will feel satisfied with the outcome of the process.

Wrapping Up the Deal

You have moved through the negotiation process successfully and have received an offer that is acceptable. Congratulations! What steps do you need to take to finalize the deal?

First off, do not accept the offer on the spot, even if you've already gone through negotiations. You may have a spouse or significant other with whom you need to discuss the details of the offer. Absent that, you simply deserve the opportunity to review the offer one last time in detail to be absolutely sure that you understand every aspect. Any reputable employer should be willing to give you at least 24 hours before you respond.

Secondly, be clear about all the details and make sure you understand what you are accepting. One of my clients received an offer that included a very complex system of awarding her company stock options. Although the situation sounded good on the surface, she did not understand the process. Her initial reaction was to just go ahead and accept, but I convinced her that she really needed to go back and clarify. When she did, the employer modified the process.

Third, get the offer in writing. A verbal offer is not enough and needs to be followed up with a formal offer letter. Learn from this example of a colleague of mine who did not heed this advice. She negotiated an extra week of vacation with her recruiting contact at the organization she was joining, but the agreement about the extra vacation was verbal. By the time she started work, her recruiting contact had left the company and no one knew anything about that extra week of vacation. Fortunately, the company did eventually go ahead and honor the verbal commitment, but my colleague could easily have ended up without that extra time off.

Finally, respond to the final offer in writing. Once again, a verbal acceptance is not enough and should be followed up with a formal letter. With a written offer and a written acceptance of the offer, you have a paper trail that ensures both you and your new employer are on the same page about the circumstances around your employment.

Summary

The negotiation process can be complex and frustrating, yet rewarding. First, research your circumstances to determine whether negotiation is recommended. Discover your market value and then consider what can be negotiated. It is important to keep a positive attitude and strive for an arrangement that will work well for both you and your future employer. A successful negotiation process will truly result in a win-win for both you and your new employer.

Part III

Managing Challenges and Special Situations

In Part II, you covered the steps you need to take to find a new position that suits you. In this section, we discuss some steps you can take to grow in your current situation, make a career change, go out on your own, or seek international employment.

Should I Stay or Go: Managing a Successful Career Transition

Marilyn A. Feldstein

If you are feeling uncertain about how to make a smooth career transition, you are not alone. A generation ago, we were expected to select one career or job after college that we would remain in for the rest of our working lives, until we received the gold watch by which we would observe the remaining time in our lives tick down. This is no longer the case. You should view your career as a journey, not as a destination. And often, as with most journeys, you will need to make changes. So, how do you know when it's time for a change? Here are some clues that you may be ready to make a move:

- You wake up each weekday dreading going to work.
- You are bored because your skills are underused.
- Your values conflict with your manager's or the company's.
- You have not had a raise in a while, and your salary has not kept up with inflation.
- You didn't receive the promotion you thought you would.
- Your company recently hired someone whom you now report to, and you have to train her. You believe that you should have been selected for this position.
- Your company is going through a merger, acquisition, or downsizing, and is offering a severance package to help you make a smooth transition.
- You feel trapped. You can't imagine being in this position or career one year, two years, or five years from now.

Before you jump ship, make sure you know why you're leaving. This will help guide your conversations with your managers and leaders to see if there is another position in which your skills are better served. Sometimes new energy and interest can be gained by simply transferring your skills into a new position at your current company. However, if you do decide to leave, at least you will know why, which should make your next career move a more rewarding one.

What Is Your Level of Job Satisfaction?

To help you decide if it's time for a change, take the quiz in Figure 12-1. Answer yes if the statement is true for you most of the time.

Figure 12-1. Job Satisfaction Quiz

1. Do you enjoy most of the tasks and activities that you perform on a daily basis?	Yes	No
2. Do you feel reasonably challenged by the tasks required by your job?	Yes	No
3. Do you like working with the people at your organization?	Yes	No
4. Do you feel that you fit in with the culture at your company?	Yes	No
5. Do you get clear direction and support from your boss most of the time?	Yes	No
6. Do you respect and trust your boss?	Yes	No
7. Are you proud of the products and services your company provides?	Yes	No
8. Is your company on solid financial ground and moving in the right direction?	Yes	No
9. Is your work environment safe and conducive to getting your work done?	Yes	No
10. Do you feel that your work life and personal life are reasonably in balance?	Yes	No
11. Do you receive reasonable compensation for your work, including benefits?	Yes	No
12. Do you think there are growth opportunities for you at your company?	Yes	No

Count up the number of yes answers to get your score and review your results below.

Score:

10-12: You are in a good situation if you answered yes to most of the questions. Review your no answers and work on making changes at your current organization that will address the issues you uncovered.

7-9: You answered yes to a majority of the questions, so you still may be able to salvage the situation. Continue reading to determine if you can resolve the problems.

0-6: You answered no to at least half the questions, so a change is probably in order. Read on to determine how to address some of your concerns.

If you answered no to question number:

- 1 or 2, you may have a skills gap
- 3 or 4, you may have a culture clash
- 5 or 6, you probably have a manager mismatch
- 7 or 8, you may be in a values bind
- 9 or 10, your work environment may be the problem
- 11 or 12, you are experiencing a failure to thrive.

Skills Gap

One of the most common reasons people leave their jobs is that they dislike or don't feel challenged by the daily tasks they have to perform at work. If you answered no to questions 1 or 2 of the quiz, you may be experiencing a skills gap. If you dislike your daily tasks, ask yourself why:

- Do you feel incompetent at work? If you feel incompetent at work, it may be that your natural skill set is simply not a good fit for the job. Consider whether additional training could solve the problem or if the tasks just feel beyond you. There are many ways in which you might gain additional experience or training that could help you resolve the problem. Review chapters 13 and 14 for more guidance on this issue.

- Do you think you are the wrong person for the job? Examples include introverted people in jobs that require a great deal of people interaction or extroverted people in jobs that require them to be chained to a computer all day. If this sounds like you, you may be experiencing a personality mismatch. Explore the exercises in chapter 1 on personality and interests to help you identify the root cause of the problem.

- Do you find the tasks boring? If your work doesn't interest you, you are not doing yourself or your company any favors by staying in the position. As a next step, determine what skills you most enjoy using the exercises in chapter 2. Then explore whether there are any opportunities that you could pursue at your own company.

- Do you feel underutilized or underemployed? If your daily tasks don't challenge you or require little of your experience or training, you may have outgrown your job. If you like your company, talk with your manager about stretch assignments or look into opportunities to move up or make a lateral move to gain skills. Chapters 13 and 14 provide guidance on moving up and managing your own professional development.

Culture Clash

Another common reason people leave their jobs is that they think they don't fit in with the people or corporate culture at work. If you answered no to questions 3 or 4, you may be experiencing a culture clash. Ask yourself the following questions:

- Do you dislike most of the people at your company or just a few? If you dislike most of the people at your company, then moving to another department or area won't help. If you don't get along with those in your department, but there are other departments with people you do like, consider exploring a transfer.

- Are many of the people you work with abrasive or abusive? If the management team allows this sort of behavior to flourish at your company, it's probably time for a change. If this type of behavior is more of an exception, you should speak with the HR department or take advantage of Employee Assistance Program services if your company offers them.

- Do you believe that you don't fit in at the company because of your age, race, or ethnicity? Are there few employees "like you" at your company? In this case, finding a more diverse company might be the solution (see the annual Top 50 Companies for Diversity at www.diversityinc.com for ideas). Another solution is to work on building relationships with people at your company so that you get to know them on a more personal level. Or you may be able to start or join an employee affinity group within your company to begin gathering a group of peers with whom to network.

- Do you think that your personality doesn't fit with many of the people at your company? In this case, you may have a different style from those around you; for example, a highly creative person with a flamboyant personality working for a conservative firm where most people wear suits. While this situation can be comfortable if your company embraces different personalities and work styles, you may find that you can't be yourself at work. Chapter 1 provides guidance on personality type and chapter 3 explores finding the right workplace for you.

Manager Mismatch

Having a bad boss is one of the most common reasons people leave their jobs. If you answered no to questions 5 or 6 of the quiz, the problem may be a manager mismatch. Ask yourself the following questions:

- Is your manager open to feedback about your working relationship? If you generally like and trust your boss and your skills are valued, she may not realize that you prefer a different style of supervision. Schedule a time to talk that is not during a performance review or other charged situation. Explain what you like and don't like about how you work together. Most people will accept feedback if it is provided in a professional and collaborative manner.

- Have you examined your part in the working relationship? It's important to be honest with yourself about your relationship with your boss. Are you contributing to a dysfunctional relationship or giving your boss a reason to feel you can't be trusted? If he is micromanaging you, it may mean that he thinks your work has been sloppy or not on target. Before meeting with your boss, take some time to consider what you might do to improve your relationship.

- Are there other departments or areas in the company with better leaders? If you believe there are other leaders within the company who would be a better fit for you and they have a need for your skill set, you may be able to approach them about a transfer. Your HR department, if you have one, may be helpful in this regard. You can also seek a mentor who may provide some insight on other departments. Chapter 13 includes guidance on finding a mentor.

- Do you believe the relationship cannot be repaired? If you think the relationship is beyond repair and few other options exist within your company, it is probably time for a change. When looking for a new position, make sure that you thoroughly explore the type of manager that is right for you. Networking with colleagues in your industry can help you identify companies that have good management teams.

Values Bind

People often leave their jobs because they are concerned about the company's future or feel that the company is on the wrong track. If you answered no to questions 7 or 8, you may be in a values bind. Ask yourself the following questions:

- Are you comfortable with the mission of the company? If you don't believe in the company's mission, or are opposed to it, you may be experiencing a values bind. For example, if you are asked to take over a department that sells tobacco products, but you are opposed to smoking, you may become conflicted. Most of the time, the situation is more nuanced, but lack of alignment with your company's purpose makes it difficult to stay committed to your job. If this sounds like you, a change to another company or industry is in order. Review chapters 3 and 4 to help you identify companies that may be a better fit.
- Do you believe in the products and services that the company provides? If you don't believe in the company's products and services, it is difficult to do a good job unless you can influence change. If you have tried and failed to make improvements, target companies in your industry with a reputation for excellence.
- Are you concerned about the financial health or direction of the company? If you are worried about the financial health of your company or strongly feel that it is headed in the wrong direction, you owe it to yourself to look for a new position. Many people stick their heads in the sand when signs of financial distress appear. Instead, be proactive and look for a company that is in a stronger position. Chapter 10 provides guidance on evaluating companies before you accept a position.
- Have you been asked to do something that goes against your personal ethics? Another situation that can arise is when an employee is asked to do something that feels unethical or sleazy. If you find that this happens more than once, it could be a pattern. Be wary of staying at a company that is willing to put its (and your) reputation at risk.

Work Environment Issues

People often leave their jobs if they find the environment to be a poor fit with the way they work. This can include everything from the physical work environment, their commute, or the sheer amount of work they are expected to complete on a daily basis. If you answered no to questions 9 or 10, you may have a work environment issue. Ask yourself the following questions before exiting:

- Does the job and workplace support my desired lifestyle? If you find that your job is significantly interfering with the life you want to lead, think about what is causing you the most distress. Is it the number of hours you are expected to work? Your commute? Lack of flexibility in your schedule? You may be able to negotiate some of these issues with your employer. Before leaving a job or company you otherwise like, try discussing your concerns with your boss or an HR representative.

- Does the physical environment help me to do my best work? If there are aspects of the physical environment that are interfering with your work, discuss them with your boss before looking for a new position. For example, if you are introverted by nature, you might have a difficult time working in an office with an open floor plan. By explaining the problem, you may be able to negotiate some work-at-home days or quiet time in a conference room when working on intensive projects. Chapters 3 and 4 provide guidance on identifying your workplace preferences.

- Is the physical environment unsafe or unhealthy? If your work environment is putting your health at risk and you are not in a position to improve the situation, it's time to make a change. Look for companies with a better safety record (www.osha.gov) or a reputation for a healthy work environment (search "Best Places to Work").

Failure to Thrive

Employees commonly leave their jobs when they believe they are not being compensated enough or there are few opportunities for them to grow. If you answered no to questions 11 or 12, you may be experiencing a failure to thrive. Ask yourself the following questions:

- Do you know your fair market value or what comparable companies are paying people in your field? If you are a high performer, but believe you are being paid below your fair market value, it helps to share those data with your boss when discussing the possibility of a raise. Chapter 11 provides guidance on negotiating your salary and includes some sources for finding salary data.

- Does your company have a career or leadership development program? More companies are creating career development programs to help retain and engage employees. Ask to be included in the program and take advantage of the growth opportunities that are provided.

- Are there other opportunities at your company that might be a fit? If you like your company but are worried that your job is a dead end, talk with your boss about stretch assignments or determine if there are other opportunities at your current company that will help you gain skills. Chapters 13 and 14 provide guidance on moving up and managing your own professional development.

- Have you been passed over for promotion or given only small increases, despite high performance? In this situation, you may need to move to another company to get the compensation you desire. You may have started at a lower salary, and your company's pay structure may be inflexible. In other cases, you may have been pigeonholed and simply need a fresh start elsewhere. To be sure you are moving to a company with a better compensation structure, network with colleagues and review Glassdoor.com and Payscale.com to find companies that pay well.

What's Holding You Back?

If, based on these scenarios, you believe you need to make a change, what is stopping you? There are many fears, myths, and false career beliefs that can hold us back from making a change. Here are some of the most common ones:

- **It's safer to stay where I am.** If you are unhappy at work, it is probably affecting your performance. As much as you try, it is hard to stay committed when you mentally have one foot out the door. Remember that you are not doing yourself or your employer any favors by staying where you are if you are highly dissatisfied.

- **No one wants to hire someone older than 35, 40, 50, and so forth.** You're never too old, unless you think you are. You're much more valuable when you're older and can command a higher salary because of your experience. Look at annual reports, and you'll see that leadership teams are usually composed of men and women who are 50 and older. Why? Because they have the skills, experience, and talent. Is there age discrimination in the workforce? Yes. We all have biases, and as long as people hire people, these biases will exist. However, it's important to remember that as you age, your experiences and knowledge increase, and so does your potential value to employers.

- **No one is hiring, there aren't any jobs, and the economy is still bad.** Here's the challenge with this myth: Finding your next position has nothing to do with whether the economy is bad or good, or what unemployment rates are. There always will be open positions despite how well or poorly the economy is doing.

People are moving around every day, and here's why:

- Employees accept promotions or lateral moves internally and externally.
- Companies merge or acquire other companies and may hire and downsize simultaneously.
- Women take maternity leave and may not return to their positions.
- People move to other cities, states, and countries.
- Companies expand and add new positions.
- Entrepreneurs create new companies for which they will be hiring.
- People retire.
- And, unfortunately, people die.

These movements occur in every organization, leaving openings for you. Whenever you hear that there aren't any jobs, read this list again. You need only one position. The best time to look is when you are ready. So what's stopping you?

- **What if it's worse at the new job?** This is why doing a thorough self-inventory is critical. Researching companies before you take the leap will also help you avoid making an ill-advised move. Chapters 1-4 and 10 provide more guidance on these topics.

- **I'm afraid I will look like a job hopper.** Having short tenure at many jobs can raise concerns for potential employers. However, job mobility has increased substantially in the past 10 years, so "job hopping" has less of a stigma. If anything, someone who stays too long at a company in the same position is now often viewed as having a lack of ambition or flexibility. So, while you should definitely "look before you leap" and try to resolve issues before moving to a new company, just keep in mind that staying too long in a bad situation can hurt you too.

- **My education is outdated.** The wonderful thing about education is that once you've earned it, it's yours, and it does not age. Even though you may retain only a fraction of what you learned, you still have many opportunities to continue learning: on the job, by attending conferences and seminars, through reading, working with others, taking on stretch assignments, and leading projects. Chapters 13 and 14 provide guidance to help you decide if you need more training or certification before making a change.

- **I'll have to start over.** Starting over connotes for most taking an entry-level position. However, many people make career changes without having to totally start over. Use your transferable skills to market yourself differently on your resume and in your branding statements. Employers are looking at you based on how you can add value and make a difference with your skill set.

Now that we've refuted many of the common excuses for not making a change, how do you get unstuck? How do you turn the truth about change into the swift kick you need?

If you've decided you need a change but staying at your company is a viable option, look at open positions within your organization, talk with HR, and network within your organization to ferret out departments and positions that might be a good fit (see chapter 13 for additional suggestions). On the other hand, if you've decided to leave your current company, start by looking at open positions at other organizations to see what skills employers want. Resist the urge to apply! Treat this as research to determine the types of companies and positions that might be a good fit for you.

The website Indeed.com, which acts as a spider and searches for posted positions across the web, is a great resource. When you search on the website, the first thing you see is two boxes asking you *What?* and *Where?* Be creative. Don't limit your possibilities to titles like instructional designer. Use transferable skills, such as curriculum design, program planning, project management, or developing training programs. If you have a current certification or training that is in demand, enter that in the what box to see which employers value your credential. Enter specific cities where you want to work or leave the where field blank, so you can see all the open positions. This will give you a much broader picture of the types of positions available, along with the skills and experience typically required by employers.

Next, fill out a transferable skills worksheet for the types of positions to which you could apply (Table 12-1 shows a few sample jobs). Compare your skills and qualifications to typical employer requirements to determine if this type of position might be a good fit for you.

Table 12-1. Transferable Skills Worksheet

Job Title	Technical Skills	Interpersonal Skills	My Skills and Qualifications
Corporate Trainer	• Developing sales and leadership classes • Creating agendas • Developing course materials • Creating student plans • Delivering presentations	• Excellent grammar • Verbal and telephone skills • High energy • Multitasking • Flexible • Work well with all levels of employees and vendors	
E-Learning	• Analysis • Design • Development • Implementation • Evaluation • Strategic planning • Graphic design • Blended learning	• Partner with others • Flexible • Adaptable • Organized • Detail-oriented	

Once you have homed in on the types of positions that would suit you best, revisit chapter 4 to clarify your career goals and preferences, and start identifying your target companies.

Should I Move Into a Different Career or Industry?

If, based on your analysis of your situation, you believe you want to move into a new field or industry, you will need to do some additional work. Moving into a new field or industry is more challenging than finding a new job in your current field. But it can be done!

The first thing you'll want to do is make a thorough assessment of skills you most enjoy using and compare those skills to careers that interest you (chapter 2). It is important to understand how your transferable skills are used in the new career or industry you are targeting. Once you have identified a few possibilities, you'll need to do some field research. Two of your best tools for learning more about a career or industry are informational interviews and job shadowing.

Similar to the networking meetings that were discussed in chapter 7, informational interviews are generally 15-30 minutes long and their purpose is to gather information. Most people love to help others. If you explain that you are seeking advice and information about their chosen career, most people will be more than happy to give it. Why? By asking for advice, you're implying they are an expert and you value what they have to say. Chapter 7 goes into more detail about arranging for and following up on this type of meeting. Bring a list of questions to your meeting to ask, such as:

- I'd like to hear more about your career journey. How did you get into your position or profession?
- What parts of your job are the most challenging or interesting to you? Why?
- What would make someone successful in this field?
- What skills, qualifications, or training are required?
- Would my current skills and training be valued in this industry or field? What else do I need to do to be marketable in this field?
- What resources do you recommend I read or obtain to learn more about the field or industry?
- What are the educational or licensing requirements?
- What is a typical career progression?
- Can you recommend two to three other people I can talk to? May I say that you referred me?

After you have done several informational interviews, you should have a sense as to whether the field holds promise for you. The next step is to arrange a job shadowing experience. Observing the day-to-day activities of someone in a potential new career provides invaluable information with which to make a sound decision before committing to a new path. More information about how to arrange for and benefit from a job shadowing experience can be found in the article "Research Companies and Careers Through Job Shadowing" by Katherine P. Hansen.

Once you have chosen a new direction, you'll need to revise your resume to highlight your transferable skills using the terminology that is used in your new field or industry. Chapter 5 has tips for formatting a resume if you're trying to transition careers. Don't start looking for a job until you can explain how your transferable skills apply in your new industry. This is a common problem for ex-military job seekers because they have difficulty translating their military experience into civilian terms (so much so that the federal government has created a skills crosswalk for those leaving the military, www.onetonline.org/crosswalk/MOC). To be sure your skills and terminology match your new industry, compare job postings and job descriptions from your targeted field with what you've entered on your transferable skills worksheet (Table 12-1).

How Can I Make a Successful Career Change and a Smart Financial Decision?

We often spend more time planning our vacation than we do planning our career and managing our finances. It's imperative that you have a plan so you can be prepared for any bumps in the road. Going through a downsizing or losing your job may be the swift kick you need to make your next career move. Following the tips below will help you protect your finances while you make the transition:

- **Have a financial cushion:** Living paycheck to paycheck adds a lot of stress and affects how you make career decisions. A financial cushion allows you to manage your career from a rational point of view rather than an emotional, irrational one. Financial advisers will tell you to save three to six months' salary, but in my experience it is wise to have at least a year's worth. This allows you to pay your bills while you make a successful career change. Appendix I provides a monthly expense worksheet to help you develop a budget.
- **Negotiate salary:** Make sure to negotiate your salary when you get a promotion or take a new position. See chapter 11 for advice on how to do this successfully.
- **Invest:** As soon as you're eligible, invest in your 401(k), 403(b), or other retirement and pension account. Prepare for your future so that when you're ready, you can leave the workforce early or retire.

You may not think you'll get a new boss with whom you disagree, lose your position, or be in a company that closes or merges, but these things happen daily. Prepare for them by having a sound financial plan so that you are not desperate to secure a job if you find yourself "in transition."

Real-Life Career Change Success Stories

Making a job or career change can be daunting—whether it's within your current company or in an entirely new field. To help you envision your own change, here are four true stories of successful transitions to fuel your imagination. The names have been changed.

Same Industry and Function in a Different Company

John had been in sales with the same company for 15 years. He joined right out of college. He had always done well, but over the years the company had decided to change the compensation and commission plans. As a result, even though John was working harder, increasing revenue, and breaking sales records, his commissions and total compensation were going down each year. He was also frustrated that when he gave a sales lead to a colleague in a different territory, his company didn't reward his efforts. In addition, because the company was having trouble retaining sales managers, he had had numerous new bosses in the past several years and was not impressed with their leadership abilities.

One day as he was expressing his frustrations to a new boss, she replied, "You should be happy that you have a job." At that moment John decided to stop vacillating and pursue external positions. A colleague had gone to a competitor the year before and had been trying to get him to consider joining him, but John hadn't been ready until now. He called his friend, and interviews were set up. John did all his homework and was made a very lucrative offer, which he accepted.

Final Result: John has been in this new position for several years now and is very happy he found a company that shares his values and he is financially rewarded. He is also pleased with the company's leaders, who understand the business and take care of its top performers.

Industry Change With Same Functions

Harry had worked at the same helicopter company in the Northeast for 25 years. For a long time, he and his wife talked about moving to Florida to be closer to his in-laws; then they finally made the move. His wife was a nurse and quickly landed a position in a hospital. However, Harry felt trapped. There were only two companies that manufactured aircraft, and he wasn't having any luck talking with either, despite having "supervisor with 25 years' experience in helicopter manufacturing" on his resume. After he completed some assessments with his career coach, it became clear what Harry's transferable skills were, and he repackaged his resume and branding statements.

At the time, the housing business was booming in Florida. Harry was also building his own home then, and he started talking with the superintendent who was overseeing the construction. Harry conducted an informational interview with the superintendent and felt confident that his project management, supervisory, inventory control, and operations skills would transfer well to the construction industry. After reaching out to several other home-building companies, Harry was offered a position.

Harry, however, was more interested in another company because it had a six-week training program, which he thought would be beneficial to gain more confidence in this new industry. After successfully selling himself in the interview with this second company, he received an excellent offer that has served him well for many years.

Final Result: Only after Harry understood that his skill set was transferable was he able to consider working in a different industry.

Career Change

Denise earned a master's degree in library and information studies and had been a librarian for 14 years. She began her career setting up a new library for a law school and then worked for 12 years in the public school system as a librarian. However, Denise was ready to pursue other careers after she injured her back and realized that she could no longer lift hundreds of books each year and that she was feeling stymied in her job.

But she had no idea what to do next. To get a better idea, she took some assessments with her career coach and learned that she was very good with technology and enjoyed conducting research and teaching others. Denise enrolled in an instructional design certificate course at the local university. She also approached the co-owners of a new e-learning business and asked if she could apprentice with them to learn more about their business and to help with some projects. They were delighted to assist her because they had also re-branded themselves and wanted to help others.

Denise was very excited about acquiring new skills that were a good fit, and she made the critical decision to change careers. She also reached out to her friends to let them know of her new interests. One of her friends managed a staffing company and was able to hire her immediately to fill some part-time training positions at several major companies while she continued to look for a full-time position.

After a few months, Denise was offered an open position for a learning technology specialist at a local hospital, where she would be responsible for the learning management systems and training staff members.

Final Result: This position turned out to be the perfect skills and industry match and instantly doubled her salary. Denise has thoroughly enjoyed continuing to learn and acquire new skills and is actively involved in her local professional association.

Transition From a Corporate to Nonprofit Environment

Ginger had worked for two major corporations for 27 years in manager- and director-level positions. When she was downsized the second time, she decided that what she really wanted to do was transition to a nonprofit position. She had volunteered for many years and really enjoyed being on boards and making a difference in the community.

After learning of a perfect position as a program manager for a social services agency, she updated her resume to brand herself for a nonprofit position. Ginger thought that the biggest hurdle would be convincing the executive director that she could transition from a very large corporation to a small nonprofit with limited resources. However, that wasn't an issue because Ginger had worked in small departments with limited resources before and understood the challenges. She was among numerous candidates who interviewed for the position, most of them coming from other nonprofit organizations, but because she was able to convince the executive director and HR manager of her transferable skills, she landed the position.

Final Result: Ginger successfully transitioned from a corporate to a nonprofit position. Her main goal was to work in an environment where she knew that she was contributing to society, and she also enjoys having some flexibility to work from home, which she didn't have before. She has been happily employed for four years.

Summary

Uncertainty and change are inevitable. In fact, the only certainty is change itself. By thoroughly understanding your skills and preferences, as well as why you are making the change, you can take control of your own career journey. Be alert to the warning signs that it is time to leave and be proactive, rather than wait until the change is made for you.

Whatever the reason for your change, think of the situations described in this chapter as your swift kick to get moving toward a job you'll love.

Gaining Experience and Moving Up

Vivian Hairston Blade

Are you eager to move ahead in your career? Whether you're just starting out or have been at it a little while, you may expect your career to progress pretty quickly if you feel you've put in the time. So, you may occasionally find yourself somewhat impatient at how long it's taking to move ahead. Many say you have to pay your dues to earn the right to move up. This means spending time in jobs along your career path contributing to the company's goals and gaining valuable experience. This chapter focuses primarily on how you can gain the valuable experience you need to move up.

Leaders would argue that the quality of your career path is more important than how long you've been on your journey. But what constitutes quality from their perspective? Quality is the value of your experiences over the course of your educational and professional careers—the longer you've been in the workforce, the more important your professional career experiences.

The value of your experiences is characterized by three factors, which are key in landing a job and moving up:

- What have you delivered?
- What do you have to offer?
- How do you manage your career?

What Have You Delivered?

Whether hiring from the outside or promoting from within, hiring managers need a level of confidence in your ability to do the job. Among the most telling about your abilities are your resume, interview discussions about the positions you've held, and experiences you've had across your education and career.

When considering talent for positions, organizations are looking for people who have a proven track record of outcomes in their education and work. They want to know:

- What have you actually accomplished?
- What is your track record of educational achievement?
- How have you made things better along the way?
- Have you been able to solve problems?

The deeper meaning of your story is in the difference you've made while in school, as an individual contributor, or as a manager, not just the titles you've held or the tasks that you've performed. The organization has ongoing goals for meeting customer and stockholder expectations, so it needs a team that can hit the ball out of the park on these goals.

What Do You Have to Offer?

Employers realize that your experience is only part of your story. More and more, human resource and hiring managers are evaluating how your track record translates into your potential. They are looking for the knowledge and skills you've developed during your educational and professional experience, but they also want to see your work ethic and how your personality traits fit the role and organizational culture. A variety of assessments are often used to project how well suited you are for specific roles and types of work (see chapter 10). A work inventory can help you recall, organize, and list your marketable knowledge, traits, and skills (Table 13-1). This work inventory is similar to the Personal Inventory Tool in Appendix B, but it is focused on what you have to offer employers instead of what you want from an employer.

Table 13-1. Your Work Inventory

In column 1, list the skills and experience you've accumulated. In column 2, list the special knowledge and credentials you have gained. In column 3, list the key characteristics of your personality that best describe you. In the proof section, list the documentation that can support your inventory items.

Skills and Experience	Knowledge and Credentials	Personality Traits
Example: teaching, writing	Example: history and grants	Example: extroverted and detail oriented
Proof:		

Another big part of what you have to offer is evaluated by your "runway." This is the future that potential leaders and hiring managers see in you. Do they believe you have the potential to grow into roles of increasing responsibility, and continue to deliver results in a big way? Your runway is evaluated on six key characteristics:

- **Ability to deliver results:** Have you been consistent in delivering results?
- **Integrity and values:** Can you be trusted to do the right thing when decisions of integrity confront you? Do you represent the company's values?
- **Coachability:** Are you open to feedback to help you develop and grow?
- **Developing skills and competencies:** Are you developing the technical skills and leadership competencies to be able to handle bigger roles?
- **Emotional intelligence:** How you work with, engage, motivate, and influence subordinates, peers, and leaders indicates what your interaction and leadership style will be going forward.
- **Representing the desired company image:** Do you represent what the company wants to stand for? If you were with a client or in public, would the company be proud to have you represent what it wants to be known for?

Evaluating these six characteristics helps the company get a feel for whether they will get a return on their investment from betting on you. The combination of your capabilities, experiences, and runway demonstrate what you have to offer.

How Do You Manage Your Career?

Many professionals float along in their careers waiting for good things to happen to them. They've been in the same job for many years, head down, working hard. They expect to be tapped for the next role. You may have this same misperception—that keeping your head down and working hard will get you noticed. When reviewing talent and interviewing candidates, leaders look for patterns of achievement. Has your journey been more intentional than accidental? Do you have a career plan that you've been working on, expanding your experiences and skills along the way?

You need to be intentional about seeking opportunities that will give you the experiences and help you build the skills you need to be successful and get ahead. In short, you need to take ownership of your career. It may seem like people around you have someone just offer them jobs, or they always get tapped for the promotion. These people are not just lucky; there are other factors at play that influence the availability of those opportunities. You may have heard the saying, "Luck is what happens when preparation meets opportunity." Make sure you're prepared. This chapter will provide strategies and resources to help you leverage the experiences you have, gain the experience you need, and propel your career forward so that you, too, can be lucky.

What Experience Do You Need?

If you're going to be hired or promoted, hiring managers need to feel confident you can do the job and are a good long-term investment for the company. Your selection comes from having relevant experiences that can demonstrate your readiness for the position. Note the word *relevant*. To ensure you gain relevant experience throughout your career, take the time to identify the types of experience you'll need to realize your career plan. You need experiences that help you develop fundamental professional skills, as well as a specialized skill set for your technical area of expertise.

Develop Fundamental Professional Skills

There is a fundamental set of skills that companies look for when they hire and promote employees. Companies need employees who are prepared and ready to contribute to achieving their goals. These five fundamental skills are considered to be the standards for high performance:

- **Problem solver:** Proactively identifies potential problems and takes responsibility for finding and implementing sustainable solutions.
- **Accountable**: Delivers on commitments. Doesn't become victim to challenges or let excuses handicap willingness to take action. Works effectively with the team to deliver results.
- **Consistently exceeds expectations**: Gives an all-out effort to consistently deliver above and beyond what's expected.
- **Gets things done**: Works smart on the right things, identifying and accessing the resources needed to complete every job.
- **Customer focused:** Advocates for customers, ensuring there's an outside-in, reality-based perspective driving priorities and decisions.

These fundamental skills can be gained from a variety of experiences, whether from your education or your professional career. Take advantage of opportunities to develop these skills and build a track record demonstrating them. You will enhance your skills in these areas as you gain more experience in your education and work over time. As you move up in your career, you'll add leadership competencies to this toolkit as well.

Use the gap analysis to assess your qualifications for a desired position in comparison to the company's requirements for the role (Table 13-2). This will help you identify areas of focus for your future development and career plans.

Table 13-2. Gap Analysis

Gap Analysis	
Their Requirements	**My Qualifications**
Experience:	
Knowledge:	
Skills:	
Personality Traits:	
Education and Certifications:	

Adapted from Kaiden (2015).

Develop Specialized Skills

In addition to this fundamental set of skills, make sure you have the specialized experiences and skills needed for your technical area of expertise. As you look ahead one, two, and even three roles into the future, what experiences and skills are required for those positions?

Do you need to do more research? Here are some sources to help you investigate the type of work involved, the expertise, skills, and experiences required for your area of interest.

Industry Associations

Industry associations are a great resource for professionals to explore careers. Many have job boards, where companies post open positions in the hopes of reaching talent with experience in the industry. Here, you can get information on the types of positions, and link to job postings where you can see the qualification requirements. You'll also find information on certificates and certifications you can obtain. You can search for associations in your industry or areas of interest at www.directoryofassociations.com.

Information Resources

There are a variety of online information resources that provide insight into different industries and associated careers. O*NET onLine (www.onetonline.org), Career Builder (www.careerbuilder.com), Experience (www.experience.com), and Indeed (www.indeed.com) provide information on required skills for different careers, the latest career news, links to job postings, blogs, and other resources.

Colleges and Universities

Whether you're in school or have graduated, colleges and universities provide a variety of resources.

- **Work with your career placement office**: Their reference materials on careers and the qualifications can give you a good bit of information. Try to set up an appointment with an adviser familiar with the industries and employers you're interested in.
- **Attend career fairs**: Organizations send HR and other successful professionals to represent them at career fairs. They are very knowledgeable about a number of positions and the associated qualifications and experience required. You also can gain practical insight from their personal career experiences. Even if you're not in the market for a job, attend the fairs, visit the booths, pick up their brochures, talk to the representatives, and ask questions.
- **Attend interview preparation workshops**: These prep sessions help students get ready for the interview process, and the facilitators are often familiar with employers who attend their career fairs and what they're looking for.

- **Tap into the alumni network**: Many colleges and universities have alumni chapters in cities across the country. Your school's alumni office can also connect you to other alumni in your geographic area or potentially in a particular profession. Offer to buy fellow alumni coffee or lunch to get insights on their career path and advice on experience and skills required for your area of interest. Most people are willing to help.

In Your Community

Most communities have a number of groups that meet for the purpose of networking. These groups can be great places to learn more about various industries. Search "local networking groups" or visit Meetup (www.meetup.com) to find local groups you can join.

Within Your Company

If you're already working or even a seasoned professional, you have a variety of internal and external sources for information.

- **Informational interviews**: Identify colleagues who are in positions of interest in your career path. Meet with them to get insights on the day-to-day and what they believe is required to be successful in the role. Refer to chapter 12 for more guidance on informational interviews.
- **Colleagues**: Who are the people you work with across the organization day to day in roles of interest to you? Offer to buy them lunch. Ask questions about their department, goals, daily responsibilities, skills, and work experience they find important to be successful.
- **Human resources:** Use discussions with human resource managers like you would an informational interview. They have a wealth of information about the organization and what hiring managers look for. Your discussion also can help them learn about areas you're interested in, and give you a chance to update them on your current work and contributions to the business.
- **Your manager:** You should be having periodic career discussions with your manager. Use these meetings to get her insight on important experiences for roles that may interest you in the future. If you are uncomfortable bringing up career plans with your boss, instead talk about how you can increase your skills and provide more value to the organization.
- **Professional associations**: Are you a member of a professional association? Join your local chapter to build your professional network. Get to know members who hold the type of job to which you aspire. Ask them how they got there and what, if anything, they would do differently.

With this research, you'll have a wealth of information on the experiences you need to gain. As you look ahead at your career plan and consider the required experiences, determine whether you need to adjust any steps in your plan to get to where you ultimately want to be.

Gaining Experience

Now that you have a good feel for the experience you need, let's explore how to get it. You may already have some relevant experience that will help demonstrate your track record of accomplishments, and show you have developed many of the fundamental high performance and specialized skills employers seek. Keep a record of your experiences, skills, and accomplishments as you complete projects or key milestones in your education and work. This will help you maintain a more complete story of your experiences and impact over time. (Refer to chapters 5 and 9 for best practices on how to quantify and share your accomplishments). Consider the following sources for gaining experience and where you can point to examples.

Begin While You're in School

Even as a student, you can gain practical work experience for your ideal career. You may not think of some of these opportunities as ways to gain experience while you're in school, but a wide variety of opportunities exist around you.

Student Organizations

Student organizations are a great way to gain experience because they are constantly recruiting students to join and be involved. You can run for an officer position and even hold multiple positions during your tenure. Volunteer to lead a committee or chair an event. These types of opportunities help you build leadership and organizational skills.

Community Service

You could volunteer for a nonprofit organization for short- or long-term stints. These organizations often need volunteers to help deliver programs and services to their clients, or to lead or serve on committees for special events. Sometimes they need people with specific skills, such as social media or graphic design. Contact the organization to find out where they need help and how you can serve. Not sure where to volunteer? Your local United Way and websites such as Volunteerconnection.com have information on and connections with many local organizations.

Class Projects

Think of the number of times your professors assigned group projects in your classes. Most of the time, students view these as an annoying inconvenience. Instead, see group projects as opportunities to gain experience. Take the lead and offer to coordinate the assignments and meetings. Pull together everyone's pieces into a cohesive project package and then give the presentation during class. Even if you're not the group leader, you can influence the team's effectiveness and gain from the experience. See if you can get your team members to work effectively as a group.

Part-Time Jobs

While you're in school, secure a part-time job working a few hours a week. Even if your job is not in your field, you can still gain some fundamental professional skills. Many employers will be flexible with your school schedule, and some, like UPS, even help you pay for school.

Internships and Co-Ops

These are another great option for gaining work experience as a student. Businesses and nonprofits often partner with colleges and universities to hire students for short-term assignments. You can find lists of opportunities on websites such as internships.com or experience.com. Employers look for students who are studying in fields that align with job opportunities within the organization. It's a win-win for both the organization, which gets to access fresh talent at a lower cost, and students, who can gain valuable, practical work experience, college credit, and may even earn a paycheck. Assignments often last a semester, but can extend for multiple semesters if the relationship is a good fit. Some internships even result in full-time employment after graduation. Some websites post paid and unpaid internships, including www.internships.com and www.idealist.org.

Externships With Nonprofits

Externships are similar to internships, but they're nonpaid and noncredit. Don't discount the value of gaining valuable work experience when these opportunities arise. You're essentially volunteering, but you gain practical experience you can add to your resume. If the organization you want to work for doesn't specifically offer an externship, you may need to ask for the opportunity and negotiate the details of the arrangement. Specify what you would like to learn and gain from the experience, as well as what you have to offer. That will help the organization create an experience that is beneficial and worthwhile for both parties.

Work Study

This option is located on campus, so it is convenient to your classes and where you live. Seek opportunities that have some practical responsibilities so that your time invested has a return benefit. Get an understanding of the work you'll be doing before you commit.

Temporary Agencies and Freelance Contract Work

Find jobs using temporary agencies or find freelance contract work through online services, such as Upwork, Freelancer, Guru, Fiverr, and others. This type of work is a good option because of the short-term commitment. You can build your experience by working with the same organization or individuals repeatedly, or working with a variety of clients. (Check out chapter 15 for more information on these types of opportunities.)

Gaining Experience in Your Professional Career

You may have already started your professional career and need to gain additional experience to continue on your career track or to change career paths. How do you go about gaining that experience? Look for opportunities both within and outside your day-to-day role.

Professionals often don't take full advantage of opportunities to expand their skills within their current role. Instead, they get into the routine of their daily tasks, just trying to keep up with day-to-day responsibilities. You have to be intentional about seeking opportunities to broaden your experiences. Go back to your gap analysis in Table 13-2 to review the skills and experiences you need to develop. Just be careful not to overextend yourself, ensuring you focus on doing a great job in carrying out all your responsibilities. Try doing the following:

- **Deepen skill development:** Consider what skills you can develop within your current role. Are there areas you can stretch yourself a little more? What opportunities arise, shuch as making presentations or working on project teams, can you take advantage of?
- **Add responsibility:** Ask for additional or expanded responsibility to gain specific experience or skills you need.

Other opportunities often are available within the company to gain experience outside your current job responsibilities. To avoid adding more to your plate than you think you can handle, determine which opportunities provide the best experience while balancing your bandwidth. However, be willing to stretch. You can often find ways to work smarter so that you can fit in some of these opportunities.

- **Special projects:** These help implement important company initiatives. Tell your manager you're interested in being on the project team and why. These projects often are sponsored by and have exposure to senior business leaders.
- **Company service projects:** Many companies support their communities by sponsoring volunteer projects with local nonprofits. These are great opportunities to develop your skills by joining the planning committee or signing up to work at the event.
- **Employee resource groups:** Companies sponsor these as resources for personal career development and employee engagement. You can gain experience and develop your skills by serving as an officer, chairperson, or member of a standing committee or event committee.
- **Nonprofit organizations and professional associations:** Nonprofits and professional associations often need people with more seasoned skills to serve on their boards. Becoming a board member may require a more formal vetting

process that works to connect volunteers with the skills and community relationships the organization needs at the time.

- **Contract or part-time work:** Evaluate your skills. What do you have to offer that others may need? Research job postings to get an idea of where companies seem to have skills gaps. Where do you need to expand your experience? If you're trying to change fields, contract work or a part-time job can help build new experience. A part-time job also can help you get a feel for whether this new area fits well with your interests and career goals.

Moving Up in Your Career

As you gain experience and develop relevant skills, you'll position yourself to move up. Remember, you don't just automatically get promoted when it's "your turn." You have to keep your head up while working hard and proactively manage your career so opportunities will open up for you.

Take Ownership

Moving up in your career means taking ownership. Like many professionals, you may have the misperception that your manager is responsible for your career. Even in companies that have outlined career paths, advancement is not guaranteed for everyone. Make sure you communicate your career plan to your manager, your human resource manager, your mentor, or even other leaders. People won't know how to help you or when to keep you in mind unless they know your skill set and your goals.

Consider Lateral Moves

Another career misperception is that if you're not moving up to higher-level positions, you're not advancing. Moving up sometimes means taking a lateral position to get the experience you need. Think of it more as a corporate "lattice" or "climbing wall" than a ladder. Senior-level executives often held lateral roles that gave them either a depth of experience in a functional area, or breadth of experience across the organization. See taking lateral roles as making a strategic move, like in a chess game. Identify and target roles that will help you add the skills and experiences you need to continue moving up.

Always Do Your Best Work

You may find yourself in a position that is not ideal for you, doesn't seem important, or has its unfair share of challenges. It's hard to see the value of your work and stay motivated in situations like these. Whether you're in your dream job or a less desirable position, do great work every day. Execution is the foundation for getting promoted. Companies have to stay competitive to thrive in their markets, and they need a team of high performers to meet those demands. So, they look to professionals who have a solid track record of getting the job done for bigger roles and greater responsibilities.

Always Be Prepared: Continue to Learn and Grow

Market dynamics for your company are always changing—the economy, technology, and the needs and demands of your customers. If you are stagnant in your knowledge and skills, you won't be prepared to contribute what the company needs from you. You also need to advance and expand your skills to be prepared and well positioned for higher-level roles. Work with your manager to determine the options available to you for training and development and what the company is willing to pay for. Consider your ongoing development a personal investment as well. Be willing to pay for some training programs yourself.

Manage Your Reputation

Whether you realize it or not, you have a reputation, or what we commonly refer to as a brand. Do you know what your brand is? Does it represent what you want and need it to? When considering a promotion, leaders assess whether you have the kind of brand they want to invest in. See chapter 6 for details on managing your brand.

Reach Out

In addition to your reputation, decision makers must experience and build confidence in your skills and abilities. Be intentional about creating opportunities—both inside and outside your day-to-day responsibilities—to make these strategic connections and experiences happen. Find resources outside your typical network to assist you with your work. Engage in special projects to connect with other professionals and leaders you wouldn't have the opportunity to work with otherwise.

You also have to be intentional about how you decide to show up and engage at work. I recently interviewed the director of engineering for a fast-growing technology company. She observed that in meetings, some of the junior-level female professionals would take seats around the wall, rather than at the meeting table, immediately diminishing their value and ability to contribute to the discussion. Others sit at the table, but don't say anything. What impression does that give others? Be intentional about creating interactions with others that demonstrate your capabilities.

Build Relationships

Relationships are a critical part of moving up. You've heard the saying, "It's not who you know, but who knows you." I add to that saying ". . . and what they know about you." You need a network of people who know you and what you're about. There are three types of relationships that are especially important: acquaintances, allies, and advocates.

- **Acquaintances:** People you know both within and outside your organization whom you can call for information or referrals. Be strategic about identifying the individuals with whom you need to build relationships.
- **Allies:** People with whom you have a strong working relationship. Allies can be at any level within your organization and can be counted upon if you need help with a problem.
- **Advocates:** People who are willing to recommend you to others because they are aware of your good work.

Building Your Strategic Network

Start building your strategic network by listing your current relationships and thinking about the type of relationship you need to develop with each individual (Table 13-3). Then, use Table 13-4 to help you further strategize.

Table 13-3. Identifying Your Strategic Relationships

Person's Name and Title or Role	Current Relationship Type *(Acquaintance, Ally, Advocate)*	Desired Relationship Type and Why *(Acquaintance, Ally, Advocate)*

Table 13-4. Relationship Strategy Planning

List your allies. What can you do to further support these relationships? How can you add value?

Allies	How can I further support these relationships?
1.	
2.	
3.	

List your advocates. What can you do to ensure they can continue to advocate for you?

Advocates	How Do I Earn Continued Advocacy?
1.	
2.	
3.	

Are there important relationships you need to build as acquaintances or allies that would make an impact on business performance? What advantage can you bring to the relationship?

Potential Acquaintance or Ally Relationships	Strategic Benefit	What I Bring to the Relationship
1.		
2.		

What adversarial relationships do you need to give strategic attention to? What do you believe might be the cause of the strained relationships? Are there actions you can take to improve these working relationships?

Adversarial Relationships	Likely Causes	Actions I Can Take
1.		
2.		

The timing to execute my plan will be:

I will measure my progress by:

Navigating the Corporate Environment

The corporate environment is complex, with formal and informal processes and networks, and plenty of office politics. You need someone to help you navigate this environment. Both mentors and sponsors are important relationships in your career.

Mentors—people senior to you, peers, or even subordinates—can help you understand the corporate environment and avoid career mistakes. A mentor's primary purpose is to assist with specific development areas. Identify a development area where you could use some assistance, and determine a specific goal or outcome you wish to accomplish. Then, identify potential mentors who have the expertise in that area. You may ask a senior-level mentor to share experiences and provide feedback as you develop strategies to enhance your business knowledge or leadership skills. A peer or subordinate may help you learn new systems or technologies. Schedule a time to meet with potential mentors to see who might be willing and able to work with you. Call the person to request a meeting, even if you have to leave a voicemail; don't send an email, text, or instant message. In your conversation, say you are looking to work with a mentor on specific career-related goals.

Sponsors, also known as champions, are usually senior-level leaders who have gotten to know you and believe in your potential. They hold a level of influence in the organization and become your promoters, speaking up about your track record and the capabilities they see in you. The degree of certainty and passion they have when they speak about you will heavily influence the perception of others. Always look for opportunities to demonstrate your capabilities among influential leaders; a potential sponsor may be among them.

Before you can successfully navigate your corporate environment, you must understand the organizational hierarchy. Does your organization have bands or levels into which every job is categorized? Where do the positions you aspire to obtain fall within that organizational hierarchy? Knowing this will help you see whether the career path you've designed realistically gets you to your goals.

You also need to find out how talent decisions are made and how your company invests in talent. Companies often have leadership development programs for identified high-potential talent. Participating in these programs usually opens doors to move up in the future. If leaders are seriously considering you for promotions, your profile will be part of the talent review process. If you understand how this process works, you can figure out how to influence that review process. This is why having strategic connections is so important—you want leaders to be aware of you, your contributions, and your potential.

Employee resource groups are a valuable source for helping you navigate the corporate environment. They offer social events and programs, which are often presented by senior leaders, on a variety of professional development and career management topics. Participating in these group activities helps broaden your network; you'll be able to connect with professionals in other internal networks who are knowledgeable about the corporate landscape and rules. You'll also have a better chance of meeting and talking with senior leaders during the events.

To Stay on Track, Reflect and Reassess

At some point, you'll need to step back, take a look at how things are going, and evaluate if you can achieve your career goals with your current plan. How are you progressing compared with your plan? Does the career path you've mapped out still make sense? Do you need to adjust some of the roles or timing? Is achieving your goals possible at your current employer? Do you need to go work elsewhere to gain additional experience or credibility? Do your personal values and career goals still match the values and needs of the organization?

Summary

Determine your goals and what you need to do to achieve them. Your career path will not be linear—rather than progressing straight up, it will take side steps, twists, and turns as you gain the experience you need to be successful.

Gaining experience prepares you to progress in your career, but the value of your experience is also important because it demonstrates your capabilities and potential. Evaluate the skills you've developed from the experiences you've already had so that you can communicate to a boss, mentor, or advocate what you've gained. Be strategic in taking advantage of available opportunities to gain additional experience.

To move up, you've got to do more than keep your head down and work hard. Always be prepared and do your best work, while continuously managing your career. Understand the environment you're in, so you can better build and leverage your connections and relationships as you navigate the corporate world.

Managing Your Professional Development

David Hosmer

We all are empowered to manage our careers. No matter where you are in your career journey, be sure to have a destination in mind. This chapter assumes you have already either established an overall career target (chapter 4) or decided to make a career change (chapter 12) and determined that you may need to pursue a new credential.

Your goal is to weigh your professional development options, and determine whether additional education or credentials are necessary. In the Foreword, Dick Bolles wrote of "disconnections—things that seemed always connected until now." Education, as it is imagined, takes place in a classroom with a lecturer and a group of students. But in practice, education has become more disconnected from this image. This chapter reviews alternative ways to achieve your professional development goals beyond the traditional approach to learning.

Regardless of what career path you chose, earning a professional degree or certification can catapult your development and strengthen your qualifications. In some cases, they constitute bona fide requirements for specific job opportunities for you to be an eligible candidate. Fortunately there is a plethora of professional development resources available for nearly every profession, from traditional brick and mortar institutions to flexible virtual options to blended methodologies. The information in this chapter will help you understand the differences between several traditional curriculum-driven credentials, as well as noncredential custom choices. This chapter compares the pros and cons of each to give you a better understanding of what options are most suitable for your situation.

Is a Credential Required?

The first question to answer is whether a credential is required to progress further in or enter your chosen field. There are several circumstances that might warrant a credential:

- Your career goal requires a specific course of study to gain licensure or certification: accounting (CPA), attorney (JD), health professions (RN, MD, PT), or trades (plumbing and master electrician).
- You must fulfill specific requirements before you are eligible for a targeted position on your career path.
- Your goal is to earn an advanced degree, which requires a prerequisite degree; that is, a bachelor's degree is required before you can enroll in a master's degree program.
- You need to learn new material outside your current realm of competencies to facilitate a career transition or to gain increased breadth or depth of knowledge in a particular discipline.

Is there an entry-level education requirement for your field? A more advanced credential? If you're not sure, here are two places to get answers:

- *Occupational Outlook Handbook* is a site maintained by the Federal Bureau of Labor Statistics (BLS) that has extensive information about various occupations, including any required entry-level education.
- O*NET OnLine, maintained by the U.S. Department of Labor, has information about existing and emerging occupations, including typical education requirements and what percentage of those in the field have various levels of education. These data are updated frequently and are some of the most extensive available on occupations.

However, with the rapid changes in many fields, the most current education and experience qualifications will be found in individual employer job postings. Job search sites, such as Indeed.com and Simplyhired.com, are also rich sources of information on the current job market and multiple employers' job-specific requirements.

In relatively high growth or emerging fields, job requirements tend to be more flexible if no legal license is required to enter the occupation. When growth tapers off, or if your field becomes saturated with applicants, requirements generally become more stringent.

Does It Improve Your Job Prospects or Salary?

Some professions require a master's degree to enter the field, while others merely prefer one. For example, managerial positions in the marketing, sales, and financial fields, depending on the level, do not require a master's degree. According to the Bureau of Labor Statistics, 51 percent of marketing and sales managers and 41 percent of financial managers had bachelor's degrees in 2013; 17 and 19 percent, respectively, had master's degrees. On the other hand, nurse anesthetists and nurse practitioners require a minimum of a master's degree, a subsequent state license, and passing the national certification exam.

Often, positions don't require a credential, but it can improve your job prospects. Again, the Bureau of Labor Statistics and O*NET OnLine are excellent resources. The summary reports for occupations on O*NET provide the percentage of people in the field with different levels of education. If more than 50 percent of people in your field have a master's degree, you will be in the minority without one, but this won't necessarily preclude you from getting hired.

One way to determine if a credential is valued in your chosen field is to talk with people currently employed in the occupation. You can do this by conducting informational interviews (described in chapter 12), posting queries to LinkedIn or other online groups, or participating in local chapter meetings of relevant professional associations. Some professional associations survey their memberships to determine how educational attainment affects salaries and career growth.

Does having a degree affect salary? For some, this is an important question. The short answer is, yes, more education can have a correlation to salary. For example, the U.S. Bureau of Labor Statistics has found that there is a 14 to 44 percent wage premium for workers with master's degrees over those with a bachelor's degree in selected education occupations. Similarly, for healthcare and social service jobs, workers with master's degrees earn a 19 to 44 percent higher premium over those with bachelor's degrees. However, it is important to note that not all healthcare and social service occupations at the master's level earn higher wages than those with a bachelor's. It is wise to conduct your own research of salary ranges and relationship to degrees before investing valuable time and money in a formal educational credential.

What Are Your Options?

Once you determine that you need further professional development based on the requirements for your targeted jobs, the next step is to decide which educational option to pursue. The good news is, there are so many learning opportunities that you can create a learning strategy tailored to your specific needs. Which option you pick comes down to your criteria and whether you need a formal credential from an accredited education provider to achieve your career goal.

Degree and Certificate Classifications

Many careers require a relevant degree or certification, but it varies, depending on the industry, occupation, and company in which you want to work. For example, if your career choice is to become a school principal, your state board of education will require a master's or doctorate in education. If you want to teach as a full-time, tenured faculty member at the college level, you will need to have a doctorate. However, if you want to teach online courses or at the community college level, a master's degree and relevant field experience should be sufficient. Adjunct faculty typically require a master's degree, not a doctorate. High school teachers typically require a bachelor's degree and a licensure certificate, although a master's degree is helpful for getting hired at a private school.

Explore what you will be eligible to do with your degree and how far you want to take your education before investing time and money in a degree or certification that might be unnecessary for your desired career path.

Associate's Degree

An associate's degree typically requires at least two years of full-time college work. It is a higher level of education than a high school diploma or GED, but lower than a bachelor's degree. They can be general, such as an associate in science (AS) or arts (AA), or career focused, such as an associate's degree in nursing (ADN). The Bureau of Labor Statistics lists 40 occupations that require an associate's degree, including occupational therapy assistants and physical therapy assistants, which are two of the fastest-growing occupations.

Bachelor's Degree

A bachelor's degree typically takes four years to complete and can prepare you for a specific vocation, such as computer science, or a more general, liberal arts education. Bachelor's degrees are sometimes referred to as the new high school diploma, because they are the minimal requirement for many professional and entry-level positions. Obtaining a four-year degree no longer guarantees a job and the rising cost of college has led some to believe that it is not worth the cost.

Certificate

These credentials—which can be earned in a year or less—can provide specialized training for people who have already earned diplomas or degrees. They are also helpful for those who want to quickly learn the knowledge and skills required for a specific job, such as home health aide. Many university extension and continuing education departments offer such certificates.

O*NET OnLine and the *Occupational Outlook Handbook* can provide helpful guidance on available certifications and training programs. You can also explore trade and profes-sional organizations in your field to see if they offer relevant certifications.

Note that *certificate* does not equate to a licensed *certification*. The American Speech-Language-Hearing Association offers a good example:

> *Professional certification* is the voluntary process by which a non-governmental entity grants a time-limited recognition and use of a credential to an individual after verifying that he or she has met predetermined and standardized criteria.

ASHA's Certificate of Clinical Competence is a professional certification. A *certificate program* is a training program on a specialized topic for which participants receive a certificate after completing the course and passing an assessment instrument.

As you explore certificates and certification, beware of the hard sell from representatives at for-profit online colleges and schools. Some have been found guilty in class-action lawsuits for their aggressive tactics to pressure potential applicants to enroll. Nevertheless, certificates are a sensible option for people who want to take the next step in gaining a new or deeper area of knowledge without the rigor of a full academic degree program.

Master's and Doctoral Degrees

A master's degree is earned after a bachelor's degree and normally requires one to two years of in-depth study in a chosen field. Some examples include master in business administration (MBA), master of library science (MLS), master of public health (MPH), master of education (MEd, EdM), or master of engineering (MEng).

The highest degree for graduate study that you can earn is the doctoral degree. Examples of this classification include doctor of education (EdD), juris doctor (JD), and doctor of philosophy (PhD).

Professional Certification and Licenses

Professional certifications and licenses are credentials earned after the completion of a program of study in order to practice in a profession. These typically involve meeting the requirements for professional licensure granted by federal and state authorities (a licensing board) in which the holder practices, and require a minimum of two years of prior college work and at least six additional academic years to complete studies. Example disciplines include veterinary medicine, dentistry, law, medicine, pharmacy, and optometry.

Other certifications require completing specific criteria, including proven knowledge, experience, and applied skills. These certifications are organized and granted by credible professional field and industry organizations, in addition to colleges and universities. They are not licenses. Examples in the talent management field include the Certified Professional in Learning and Performance (CPLP) and the Senior Professional in Human Resources (SPHR). The U.S. Department of Labor sponsors a comprehensive database on careeronestop.org.

Some professional certifications and licensures do expire, and require ongoing learning and earning of continuing education units (CEUs) to renew.

Which Option Should You Choose?

If you decide to pursue an additional credential, you will find many formal learning options from which to choose. Using a credential decision matrix makes the selection easier (see

Table 14-1 for an example). List your criteria across the top and the credential options down the left column. Then, assess each credential against each criterion and place a check in the appropriate box. As you complete the table, your best options become clearer. If you prefer to use different criteria than what you see here (for example, geographical location, online access, accreditation status), the matrix is intended to be flexible. Simply modify it by replacing those criteria that are less important to you.

Table 14-1. Credential Decision Matrix

Career Goal: Secure instructional design position
My current credentials: Bachelor's degree in an unrelated field with some work experience in the field

Criteria	Option 1 Master's Degree		Option 2 Certificate Program From University		Option 3 Online Courses From Association or MOOC	
Required?	No		No		No	
Preferred qualification?	Yes, for some; 65 percent have a master's degree		Yes, for some		Not mentioned very often	
Growth or outlook?	Good		Good		Good	
Impact on salary?	May command a premium; average salary is $61,000		Could help demand premium		Unclear	
Cost to acquire?	$30,000		$15,000		$3,000	
Time to acquire?	1 Year		6 months to 1 year		3 months	
Can it be applied toward other credentials?	Yes, but probably not necessary		Can be counted toward a master's degree		Maybe, depends upon the program	
Other considerations	Will likely need to complete full time		Evening classes		No face-to-face contact	
Total						

Emergent Learning Options

Unprecedented trends in the labor market, technology, and work-life balance over the past several years have afforded remarkable new ways of learning. The "partnership between man and machine," as Dick Bolles coined it, makes managing your professional development easier than ever, with flexible options that enable you to reach your individualized learning goals. However, along with so many choices comes complexity and a mind-boggling array of options. The following is a summary of learning alternatives outside traditional academic curriculums that anyone can pursue without cost.

Instructional Design Example

Suppose you have decided you would like to pursue a career in instructional design. You have some related experience, but no formal credentials in the field. What steps can you take to decide how to proceed?

A first step is to visit O*NET OnLine and search for instructional design, which will yield a summary report for instructional designers and technologists. The report reveals that the field has a "Bright Outlook," which means there is a demand for professionals in the field. Job growth is projected at 5 to 8 percent, with 25,000 job openings projected in the next 10 years. This is healthy growth. The average salary is listed as $61,000 per year; 65 percent of people in the field have master's degrees, and the rest have bachelor's degrees or less. The summary report also links to a number of degree programs and training options across the country.

You then search for jobs posted to Indeed.com, and find 17,000 openings that list instructional design as a needed skill. A spot-check shows that master's degrees are not typically required, but they may be able to replace years of experience. Based on the job postings, the requirements appear to be flexible.

Next, you search for education and training options and you find:

- master's degree in instructional design or learning technologies
- certificate programs from colleges
- certificate programs from associations such as ATD.

Your research shows that a master's degree could take two years to complete and will be costly ($30,000+ per year). Certificate programs from a university are less expensive and can be completed in a year or less. In addition, you may be able to apply some coursework from your certificate program as earned credit toward a master's degree, should you decide to pursue one in the future. There are also options from recognized associations that could help you get your foot in the door, but may not apply toward a degree.

You decide to further explore three certificate programs that provide the training you desire, and ask each organization to provide a list of alumni with whom you could speak to learn more about their experiences.

MOOCs

The term *MOOC* (massive online open course) was first introduced in 2008 and has emerged as a popular mode of free, unlimited participation, open-access online learning. Stanford University designed and led the first MOOC in 2011 with 160,000 participants. Subsequently, many universities branded their own version of MOOCs, such as MIT's Open Courseware. The number of MOOC provider sites has grown as rapidly as the massive volume of courses offered by them. Yale University offers courses on a variety of online platforms, including Coursera, iTunes U, YouTube, and Open Yale Courses. edX is a collaboration of academic institutes offering more than 950 programs in subjects such as humanities, math, and computer science. A few other easy-to-use sites include Udemy, Class Central, and Udacity.

Universities worldwide now offer MOOCs in their native languages that can be translated into English at the click of a button. For example:

- Alibaba and Peking University sponsor a platform called Chinese MOOC.
- Edraak is an Arab MOOC platform that is an initiative of the Queen Rania Foundation.
- France Universite Numerique (FUN) is France's national MOOC platform.

MOOCs are basically a no-cost resource for exploring unlimited topics and fields of interest. They are convenient, self-paced, and accessible at home and on mobile devices. Users can interact with one another from all over the world. Additionally, some courses are facilitated by professors from leading Ivy League universities. Be aware that some sites advertise "free" online courses, but then request your credit card information for payment at the point of registration. Paying for online courses should not be necessary with so many open-access options.

Not all employers take MOOCs as seriously as traditional academic programs. Like anything new, this could change over time. For now, MOOCs should not be pursued in lieu of recognized credentials; instead, treat them as supplemental to your overall professional development. MOOCs are also not degree-granting programs, although some do offer certificates (not to be confused with certifications as described earlier). In summary, MOOCs offer rich content and engaging experiences for avid learners.

Online Education

In addition to MOOCs, other online programs have arrived to provide a convenient mode for learning and earning a degree. In addition to traditional face-to-face offerings, many colleges and universities now provide online programs. These programs allow participants to obtain college degrees, with minimal in-person attendance required—some without having to ever step foot on campus. Instead, participants engage in dialogue through virtual classroom formats. You can find a list of accredited online degree programs at Geteducated. com. As with MOOCs, not every employer takes online degrees seriously, but more and more are realizing that online learning is a suitable mode of education in the modern world.

Microlearning

Continuous learning does not always warrant a curriculum or a course. Microlearning is another emergent strategy that has become a popular means for quick, on-the-spot learning. The potential topics are almost limitless—from how to grow a lawn to communication models to how to create a strategic plan for your organization. YouTube is a great delivery source for this form of learning.

Instructional designers also use microlearning as a component of their design strategies. Microlearning has numerous benefits, some of which include learner-centric, just-in-time, accessibility, time- and cost-effective, and rich media for retention. Microlearning can act as a supplement to any ongoing professional development plan, especially in this dynamic world of fast-changing content.

Academic Credit for Nonacademic Accomplishments

Do you want to spend more time learning what you already know? Learning experiences outside the walls of the traditional classroom may be eligible for academic credit. The following are four ways adult learners can earn educational credit for prior study and work experience.

Recognition of Prior Learning (RPL)

RPL is the umbrella term for Accrediting Prior Experiential Learning (APEL), Prior Learning Assessment (PLA), and Prior Learning Assessment and Recognition (PLAR). RPL is a process used by adult learning centers, academic institutes, military organizations, and other organizations globally to evaluate learning acquired outside the traditional classroom. It constitutes a consistent set of standards or competencies by which to evaluate a person's skills and knowledge for a given topic. In essence, an RPL assesses a claim provided by individuals to support their request for credit for prior experience that they wish to apply toward college degree requirements. The prior experience might be gained by volunteer work, paid or unpaid employment, standardized exams, and employer-provided training. Make sure you keep a portfolio of learning experiences and programs you have completed as a record for submitting your request.

The Council for Adult and Experiential Learning (CAEL) provides resources for translating your work experience into college credits.

Transfer College Credit Earned at Other Institutions

Many universities and colleges will honor credit from other accredited institutes toward a matriculated course of study. Criteria regarding course content, minimum grade, accreditation, and timeframes can usually be found on your target college's website.

Standardized Exams

Most colleges will allow you to test out of a course if you have a proficiency in specific topic content, such as a language. The most common standard examinations for this purpose include:

- College Level Examination Program (CLEP)
- Excelsior College Examinations (ECE)
- Thomas Edison Credit-by-Exam Program (TECEP)

- Defense Activity for Non-Traditional Education Support (DANTES)
- Advanced Placement (AP).

Each exam tests for specific topic proficiencies. The exams that are accepted by your target college will be listed on its website.

Noncollege Sponsored Learning

Another way to seek college credit is by leveraging nonacademic learning from professional development programs, employer training, military, and professional associations. The American Council on Education (ACE) qualifies many of these programs. ACE also has a page for personnel who seek formal courses and occupations offered by the U.S. military.

Summary

With so many learning options, there is no one-size-fits-all professional development plan. Rather, your strategy should reflect a unique blend of experiences and education that meet your assessed needs. A college degree is not a panacea or a replacement for experience. Nor does professional development always necessitate a formal education. For example, you can create an individual development plan (IDP) with your manager to gain valuable experience that aligns with your employer's goals. This will strengthen your portfolio, and your value to the team and your company. Working through your self-assessment to determine your career and development goals is necessary and worth your time.

If you decide that a new credential is necessary, matching various credential options to your criteria using a decision matrix will help narrow your focus. With the many traditional and emerging options available, the online databases and robust information contained in the suggested web resources will help narrow your choices even further.

Learning is ongoing and may be as formal or informal as you wish. Prudent, successful, career-minded professionals will continually assess their portfolios to make sure they are ready for the next milestone in their career.

Self-Employment and Contract Work

Barbara Seifert

By now, you've learned how to identify your skills and talents, how to create and follow-through on a job search plan, how to craft the perfect resume that gets noticed, and how to get through the interview that will get you the job. Perhaps you've been in your career for quite a while. What's next? You may be questioning if you should continue on your current career path. Perhaps retirement is on the horizon, or you may be undecided about your next step. This chapter offers some alternatives to consider as you continue to plan your career and career development. Self-employment and alternate work arrangements enable you to use and monetize your identified skills and talents.

The Current World of Work

The world of work has changed drastically in the last decade, and there are lingering elements that will continue to affect the way people seek and perform work. Today, self-employment is also called on-demand work, gig, contract, or freelance work. What is leading to these alternate ways of doing work and earning an income? There are four major influences:.

First, during the recent Great Recession, millions of people lost jobs and many remained unemployed as the economy inched toward recovery. Workers who survived a layoff now had to learn to do more with less: less time, fewer resources, and fewer people. While these workers may have been thankful to have a job, they soon started to feel the effects of this overload. The labor market shifted from employee driven to employer driven. With so many job candidates, employers now could be selective in who they kept and who they hired. Those who were ready to retire saw their retirement accounts shrink, leaving many Baby Boomers in the workforce or looking for work. With increased pressure and few benefits, workplace disengagement levels reached 70 percent, and have only recently dropped, merely to 67.3 percent (Gallup 2016).

Work roles are also being defined by the second influence: the continued presence of Baby Boomers in the workforce, amid the arrival of Millennials and Generation Z to the job market, which is the third influence. Some research suggests that younger workers are attracted less to a corporate ladder and more to a "lattice," which is less hierarchical and can offer more alignment between life and work (Benko 2010).

The fourth influence on the definition of work is the revolutionary effects of technology on systems and processes, both public and private. Mobile devices allow people to connect and work how they choose as never before. Globalization has become the way of the workforce and technology is the bridge between them. On the one hand, it is now easier than ever to have people from all over the world working for the same company; at the same time, technological advances have led to economic dislocations in some industries. This has all led to a new world of opportunities, possibilities, and challenges for those seeking work.

Alternate Work Arrangements

Alternate work arrangements are often thought of as workplace based; these include flextime, job sharing, and telecommuting (Robbins and Judge 2016). But alternate work arrangements can also be worker-focused, such as self-employment (or entrepreneurship), contract or part-time work, and leveraging skills and experiences with multiple streams of income.

These are all viable options and have pros and cons for consideration. Be open to each option before you make any type of decision. Take notes in your job journal, which will allow you to capture any related ideas.

Self-Employment

You are working for yourself. Starting your own business can involve employing others or employing only yourself (sometimes known as a "solopreneur"). There are two main tracks your business can take:

- product based
- service based.

A product-based business involves having an actual product to sell with a physical location, such as a restaurant or store for goods and wares, where people pay for the products you sell. Money is involved in starting one of these types of ventures, as well as heavy marketing and hiring employees. We don't focus on this area in this book, but know it is a viable option.

The easiest and fastest way to leave your regular job is by creating a service-based business, which provides a service to consumers (such as a dog walker) or businesses (for example, consulting or marketing services). A service-based business can be based in your home, have a separate office location, or share space with other small businesses.

Service-based businesses involve trading a service for a fee; a talent, knowledge, or past experience that can be translated into a service people need or want and are willing to pay money to have. Some of the most common services provided are consulting, coaching, training, speaking, and writing for a living.

Consulting

One of the main ways people become self-employed is by leaving a corporate job and becoming a consultant; someone with subject matter expertise who comes into a business to act as the third eye to detect problems or issues. The consultant helps the company overcome issues to increase performance and profitability. There have probably been many times when you've looked at a work situation and thought, "I'd change or improve things if I were in charge." This is one reason why individuals leave the workforce and go out on their own.

Consultants work independently, helping organizations of all sizes with whatever problems are identified. To succeed as an independent consultant, you need to have expertise that is in demand and enough experience to give you the credibility to advise potential clients.

Here are some examples:

- John was a project manager but now consults with industrial firms to ensure their projects are completed on time.
- Lisa was a human resources director who now helps other HR departments with their policies, procedures, and systems to ensure compliance and provide oversight for any issues that arise.
- Luke worked in quality improvement (QI) and now helps small companies develop their QI programs.
- Jack, whose focus is on change management and organization development activities, advises nonprofits to manage change more effectively.
- Jennifer, who started her own consulting firm, now focuses on helping new consultants and business owners to build their firms.

When working in this capacity, you have the option to make recommendations and then leave the work up to the organization to complete, or you can be directly involved as the work is being done. This will depend on the needs and requests of the organization and how involved you want to be.

If you decide to go this route, there are a number of professional associations that cater to consultants who may have useful resources for you:

- Institute of Management Consultants USA (www.imcusa.org)
- Society of Professional Consultants (www.spconsultants.org)
- Professional Consultants Association (www.professionalconsultants association.org).

Coaching

Another route to self-employment is to set up a coaching practice to work one-on-one with individuals. There are many niche areas to consider when forming this type of business, such as:

- business coaching; helping individuals start and build a business, or advising small businesses
- executive coaching; working with individual performers, teams, and leadership development
- life coaching
- health and wellness coaching; enhancing the physical and emotional wellness of employees through stress reduction, healthy eating, and personal development.

To gain credibility in the marketplace and ensure you have the requisite skills to become a successful coach, you may want to consider earning a coaching credential before striking out on your own. There are many types of coaching credentials, but an excellent place to start is the International Coach Federation (ICF). The ICF sets standards in the coaching field and approves the coaching programs provided by a wide range of organizations.

Training

Training is another self-employment option, which can include going into an organization and providing seminars and workshops on a variety of topics, including communication, conflict management and time management. You can also hold your own seminars and workshops in which you invite others to come to a location and then provide the training. Typically, those who provide training as a service have a niche in which they specialize, which gives them credibility when training others on the topic.

Training can also be done online, such as through Skype, or teleseminars and webinars. This allows more attendees to participate and gives you a broader, more global reach. Developing training programs and packages are two ways to enhance your reach and income.

Speaking

Speaking may include giving keynotes or presentations at corporations, universities, conferences, and conventions. This can be a very lucrative career path because you can command high fees for your services if you have a good reputation and respect in your field. If you are a well-versed speaker, you could coach others to become more effective speakers as a way to grow your business. Some resources to learn more include *Speak for a Living* by Anne Bruce (ASTD Press, 2008), Heroic Public Speaking (www.heroicpublicspeaking .com), Red Elephant (www.redelephantinc.com), and the National Speakers Association.

Writing

Freelance writers contribute to online and print publications, professional associations, and online directories, as well as books, e-books, whitepapers, and their own blogs. Another way to use your writing skills is writing for others, such as ghost writing or creating training programs that you are paid for. Editing the work of others, such as books or journal articles, also falls under this category. For more information, visit The Writer's Circle (www.writerscircle.com), Freelance Writing (www.freelancewriting.com), or UVOcorp (www.uvocorp.com).

Contract Work

Another way to move from a full-time job to a more flexible option is to do contract work. This could entail working directly for a company or several companies, or by working as an independent contractor.

When you do contract work for a company you are not considered a full-time employee, although you may work full-time hours, and you don't get the same benefits. This type of arrangement should be spelled out prior to accepting a position. Normally, the hourly pay is much higher than a regular employee's, because you will be paying for your own benefits. When considering contract work, be sure that the proposed wage is high enough to cover your expenses, including health insurance and self-employment taxes. The rule of thumb is that to break even you should be paid twice what you are paid as a full-time W-2 employee. Review the monthly expenses worksheet in Appendix I to help determine a rate that will cover all your expenses.

There are also companies you can work through; ones that pay you to essentially become a subcontractor. The company obtains and negotiates the contract, and then hires workers to complete the contracted work. Employment length is dependent upon the length of the contract, which can vary from a month to a year (or more). But, if you do good work and get good reviews, you can make this a full-time job. If you decide to work through an agency, one good source of local companies is the American Staffing Association's member directory.

Companies that do federal contracting often offer great opportunities to become a subcontractor. The Small Business Administration, the Federal Business Opportunities, and Supplier Connection (www.supplier-connection.net) are three good resources. Another way to pursue contract work is to do so on your own. You can market yourself as an independent contractor, meaning that you are responsible for your own taxes and reporting. The difference between marketing yourself as an independent contractor rather than a consultant is that independent contractors typically perform a function that is needed on an ongoing basis, as opposed to consultant work of solving a specific problem or advising clients on how to improve their business. Finding contract opportunities involves less marketing than consulting, which is typically a shorter-term proposition. Building a portfolio of your work, along with solid testimonials, will go a long way to staying "employed." Some websites that advertise contract opportunities include FlexJobs (www.flexjobs.com), Freelance.com, Guru (www.guru.com), Upwork (www.upwork.com), Sologig.com, Mindbench (www.mindbench.com), and JobCrank.com.

A final way to pursue contract work is by becoming an affiliate or partner with a company that sells products or programs, such as software programs, assessments, or training packages. With this model, you market and sell these programs to organizations and receive compensation, typically in commissions. Depending on the company, you may also provide the initial training for implementation, and then return to check up and be the go-to person when problems arise. Most companies offer affiliate programs; look at current programs or applications you are using (such as Microsoft Office, Kapersky, AWeber, Amazon, or eBay) or look at people you follow or have taken classes from (for example, Tony Robbins or Everything DiSC). These companies want to spread the word about their services and are happy to pay others to do so.

Several Part-Time Jobs

If you don't want to go out on your own to full self-employment, you can also choose to work at several part-time jobs, which can replace or exceed your full-time salary. The difference between this type of arrangement and independent contracting is that you receive a W-2. Depending on the company, you may also receive benefits on a prorated basis. Working for two or more companies, which can be complementary or in different industries or topics, can give your career a nice skill variety while you continue to gain experience and contribute to the success of several organizations. Some resources to peruse part-time positions include FlexJobs (www.flexjobs.com), Indeed (www.indeed.com), Snagajob (www.snagajob.com), and Craigslist.

The Portfolio Career

You can also use your skills and talents in alternate ways to create multiple streams of income. This is sometimes called a portfolio career. Some examples of this option include:

- working in an HR role while consulting on the side
- working a full- or part-time job while teaching in the evening
- working a full- or part-time job while contracting or freelancing on the side
- using your writing skills to create programs for a speaker, coach, or consultant
- using your curriculum design experience to edit and provide feedback for a scholastic or book publisher.

Franchising

A fifth path to independent employment is to buy and operate a franchise business. As a franchisee, you purchase the rights to open and run a local location of a larger organization. Some examples of well-known franchise businesses include McDonald's, Starbucks, Allstate Insurance, and CrossFit. Lesser-known business franchises include Action Coach, the Growth Coach, Transworld Business Advisors, or Renaissance Executive Forums.

Buying into a franchise has some advantages in that you are getting:

- an established business with systems and processes in place
- a known brand with name recognition
- extensive training and support from the parent company.

However, there are also some disadvantages to the franchise option, including:

- high investment to start: in addition to the rights, there may also be royalty and other fees (some cost as low as several thousand dollars to buy in, while others can cost up to $500,000)
- ongoing costs to maintain the business
- strict compliance to the parent organization's policies and procedures, which can lead to a termination of your contract if not followed
- possible lack of communication and support.

You could also start your own franchise. For instance, if you have a training program and established system around it, you could then recruit others to buy into and sell your system to others.

If you are thinking about whether franchising is the right option for you, these resources are great for more information: *The Franchise Handbook* (Atlantic Publishing, 2006), *The Franchise MBA* (Neonakis and Rambhia, 2013), *Franchise Your Business* (Mark Siebert, 2016), and entrepreneur.com/franchise. There are also companies that advise people on how to select a franchise, such as www.frannet.com and www.fransource.com.

Motivation, Temperament, and Timing

Before you can decide if you are ready to become self-employed, it is important to assess your motivation. Two questions to ask:

- Am I running away from a bad situation that I don't know how to change?
- Am I running toward a compelling idea?

Many factors can lead you to consider self-employment—stress, boredom, family obligations, and personal needs can all factor in to feelings of dissatisfaction and the need to do something different. However, the decision to walk away from a job and start your own business should not be based on job unhappiness or because you are running away from a bad situation.

If you answered "yes" to question 1, ask yourself a follow-up question: "Have I done everything I can to make the situation better?" Review chapter 12 for guidance on improving your current situation. Starting your own venture is stressful and will occasionally take priority over your personal needs, so ensuring that job dissatisfaction is not the main reason you are pursuing self-employment will help you make a good, informed decision.

If you answered "yes" to question 2, ask yourself a follow-up question: "Have I done the research to determine if this idea can succeed?" Creating a credible plan, even a simple one, will help you to think through the various steps you will need to take to make your business a success.

Temperament

Being on your own is not for the faint of heart. There will be work and sacrifice involved, so you need to be sure you have what it takes and are willing to do what you need to do. Successful entrepreneurs possess five essential traits: passion, resilience, a strong sense of self, flexibility, and vision (Rampton 2014). Other helpful attributes include risk-taking, creativity, personal sacrifice, the ability to market and sell, and independence (Greenhaus, Callanan, and Godshalk 2010). If you think you possess these attributes, you may have the temperament to go out on your own.

Moving to self-employment may be harder for some generations than others. Millennials—who are just leaving college or not finding fulfillment in the workplace—seem to be starting their own businesses at faster rates (Miller 2016). In fact, a study by Bentley University found that 67 percent plan to start their own businesses, leading the generation to be nicknamed "Millennipreneurs" (Petrilla 2016). As fewer older workers view retirement as a time for rest, many Baby Boomers and Gen Xers who have left the workforce are starting their "second or encore careers" (AARP 2016). But they may have difficulty due to the impact of the recent economic downturn, which can affect all groups. This does not preclude anyone from starting an alternate work arrangement; it's just important to assess and do the proper research to determine whether an entrepreneurial venture is for you.

Timing

How do you know when it's time to leave your job and start your own venture? Making a quick jump is not advisable, so it's important to do your research and plan before making such a move. However, you may find yourself in a situation that will "force" such a decision; for example, if your company is downsizing. Sometimes a life event acts as a catalyst, such as the death of a loved one, a divorce, or retirement. Whatever your reason for starting your own business, taking the time to be prepared for the day you walk away and begin anew will pay dividends down the road.

Planning for Making the Leap

If, after doing a self-assessment and pre-planning, you decide to move forward and begin your own venture, the following sections show how you can safely make the leap.

Create a Business Plan

The best way to determine if your business has a chance to succeed is to develop a business plan or road map. If your business is going to be self-funded, your plan doesn't need to be fancy, but creating one will still force you to answer key questions about how to proceed. If you're thinking of starting a business, you most likely already have an idea or niche area on which your business will focus. Your plan will help you spell it out by including a vision, mission, target market, what you are offering, your marketing plan, your financial plan, and other considerations. Let's look more closely at each item.

Vision and Mission

The vision and mission answer the big "why"—what is leading you to go out on your own, and why do you want to help people? The vision is the idea you have and how you will help people. The mission defines the direction you want your business to go.

Your Niche and Target Market

In this section, you identify the focus of your business, as well as further clarify whom you want to help. You may have a lot of great ideas and the experience to back it up, but you can't be all things to all people. Focusing on a specific area and identifying the people who need and want your services will help you get started and grow in a bigger and faster way. Your niche area is the specific topic (leadership development, team building, or change management) or industry (healthcare, information technology, or human resources) in which you will offer your product or service.

Your target market is the group of people who need and will buy your products or services. Who would be an ideal client? It could be someone you worked with in the past that led to great results or whom you resonated with. Identifying one area and the ideal client will help you find and attract them faster and grow your business and income quickly.

Your Offering

Identify exactly what you are offering, or selling, to the market you've identified. As discussed, there are many ways to put your knowledge and experience into an offering:

Consultants act as the subject matter experts and come into an organization to be the outside eyes. Consultants either solve a problem or enhance the skills and performance of a company's employees. As a consultant it's important to identify a niche in which you can become a recognized expert.

Coaches help all levels of workers with performance and productivity (or whatever quality your niche is focused on). You can work individually or in groups at all levels, such as lower-level workers, executives, or teams. You can deliver hourly sessions or offer a package for a set amount, such as 12 sessions for a set dollar amount.

You can offer **training programs**—either delivering a program you designed (or are an affiliate of) or creating one that an individual or a company buys. It is easier than ever with technology to put one together, and programs can be conveyed through video, audio, manuals, or a combination. You can also develop a train-the-trainer program to expand your reach and income.

There are many **products** that you could develop to help others and get your message across. Some examples include:

- developing a game around a particular topic
- filming videos and packaging them
- writing a book or e-book
- recording a training program to create a CD or an iTunes download.

Writing is one of the best ways to get started and get your message out to the masses. The Ezine Directory, Hub Pages, Info Barrel, Freelance Writers, and The Write Life are some great resources. You could incorporate writing using:

- blogging (for yourself or others)
- articles or newsletters (for publications, professional associations, or magazines)
- whitepapers
- editing or proofreading
- developing programs that you sell to others.

Masterminds, groups, and retreats allow a group of people to develop greater inclusion and ideas to grow their business. Based on Napoleon Hill's *Think and Grow Rich* (1937), masterminds bring a group of people together to share best business practices, problem solve, and get feedback on ideas. Groups bring together like-minded people to share their experiences around a specific topic and get some type of education. Retreats offer people the opportunity to get together at an off-site location to focus on a topic or training idea; this is ideal for busy executives to unwind and decompress.

One of the best ways to grow a business and gain a broader, more global reach is by holding a **webinar, teleseminar,** or **workshop** around your topic. A webinar is conducted on the Internet, and you usually provide the training while the audience looks at a Power-Point slide. In a teleseminar you provide the same training, but you are on the phone with a group of people, so the interaction is live and people can ask questions. You can record the webinar or teleseminar and offer it again, post it on your website or as a podcast, or package the presentation with a product. Resources include www.livemeeting.com, www.gotomeeting.com, www.zoom.com, and www.freeconferencecall.com. Workshops are live, in-person meetings during which you offer a specific program to a group of people; you can be the featured speaker or bring in other speakers to offer more variety.

Marketing

In the marketing section, you identify all the ways you plan to promote the programs and services you will offer. Where do your potential clients "hang out," both physically and online? Are they members of a local association or community group? Think about all the ways in which you could reach potential clients, and don't forget that the power of technology gives you the ability to reach global markets. For example, on-ground marketing could include business cards, networking events at professional associations, cold calls, flyers and brochures, follow-up calls, meetings, workshops, speaking engagements, and interviews in print, television, or radio. Online marketing could include a website, logo, blog posts, newsletters, search engine optimization (SEO), email marketing, e-books, videos, webinars, a membership site, educational series, or online learning programs.

The National Federation of Independent Business has some excellent resources for small business marketing.

Budget and Finances

Include all aspects of the money you will need to spend on the business, as well as how you will make money, such as through fees for your products and services.

One of the first things you need to determine is the type of business you're setting up:

- **Individual or solo-practice:** This type of structure blends your personal and professional assets, so you are taxed on all income at the personal income tax rates after your business expenses are deducted. This is the simplest structure to use. However, if you are sued or need to declare bankruptcy, your personal assets will be at risk.

- **Limited Liability Company (LLC):** This type of structure protects your personal assets from the business. In most states, you can file a fairly simple form to create an LLC. Your income is still reported through your personal tax return and taxed at personal income tax rates, but you also file a separate informational return.

- **Corporation:** This type of structure is more involved and requires paperwork and a quarterly tax report. There are two main types of corporations:
  - S-corporations are "pass-through" entities, in that the profits and losses of the business are passed through to the owner's personal tax return as with an LLC. S-corporations provide limited liability but can sell stock.
  - C-corporations are the most complex to create, but the income earned is taxed at corporate rates. There is also the possibility of double taxation if corporate income is distributed to business owners as dividends or salary.

It is important to review your model with either a business attorney or an accountant to ensure compliance with tax laws and reporting; good record keeping is essential. Most states have a department that provides information on how to start a business. You can always get free help with your local Small Business Administration or SCORE, and Edward Alexander's book *10 Common and Costly Business Killing Legal Mistakes and How to Avoid Them* is another great resource.

You should identify how you are funding your business, which can include personal funding, bank loans, grants, credit cards, or a loan from family. You may also be able to get funding from investors, such as an angel investor (see Angel Capital Association for a list), or from a crowdfunding site, such as Kickstarter or Indiegogo.

Identify any future needs or projections as the business grows. You will want to determine how you will set aside money to live on while you are growing your business, or for any unforeseen circumstances, such as taxes or if equipment breaks down. This is an individual determination for what is "acceptable"; but you do need to have resources and a back-up plan in case any adverse situations arise.

Other Financial Considerations

Last, you need to consider how you will set up your business and what start-up needs you'll have to pay for. Some examples include:

- office space: space in your home or a physical location elsewhere
- office equipment: phone, Internet, computer, printer, fax machine, desk, filing cabinet, whiteboard, decorations
- office supplies: pens, copy paper, stationery, printer ink, file folders, expense log, mileage book, brochures, business cards
- forms: office policies, checklists, and assessments
- personal services: bookkeeper, CPA, Internet help (website design or SEO), virtual assistant, business coach
- personal and professional development: health insurance, attending conferences, workshops, and business meetings.

You need to identify how you will price your products or services to ensure your business is profitable. If you are offering consulting services, remember that you will need to build in time to sell and administer your business. A rule of thumb for consultants is that you should charge at least three times the hourly rate you would earn as an employee. Identify if you will offer one-on-one or individual services, group rates, different price points, a package of your services, or a contracted rate. Some helpful resources include *The Irresistible Offer* (Joyner 2005), *What Should I Charge* (Price 2015), *Pricing Consulting Services* (Shays 2008), and *The $100,000 Entrepreneur* (Enelow 2007).

Depending on your state, you will need to get a business license (through your county government) and register the name of your company (check with your state's department of labor or your local small business development center for rules and regulations, as well as assistance). Both are minimal in cost. You also may want to have business cards or a flyer advertising your services, but they are not necessary to start.

Then, set a date and take the leap!

Moving Past Fear and Indecision to Freedom

Now that you're set up with your business model, have written your business plan, and identified your ideal client and market, you're ready to become a business owner on the target date. However, at this point you may be feeling hesitant or questioning your decision. This is perfectly natural, but you should address it before moving forward.

What you're experiencing is fear—the worry about a perceived outcome. Fear can present itself in many ways: fear of failure, fear of success, or fear of rejection or not being good enough. You may compare yourself with others already out there and worry you won't be as good or that no one will buy your services, or you might worry that you won't have the money to sustain your business. Again, these are all natural feelings, but they can get out of control if they're not dealt with and resolved.

In moving past any fear it is important to recognize the source. The basic fear is the fear of not being good enough, which offshoots to failure, rejection, and the like. Fear creates anxiety, which is worry about a future outcome that can't be known or controlled. When you are in business for yourself, fear can creep up and delay you from fulfilling your dream and why you went into business in the first place.

To overcome any fear, you must first acknowledge and then challenge these thoughts. "Do I know this to be absolutely true?" is a great question that will help you dispel any fears. Having confidence in yourself and what you can offer others is the key to putting yourself out there (Katie 2002).

Keep your focus on "why" and not "how." It might be helpful at this point to seek out the services of a consultant or coach. But remember, feeling fear is not bad because it can spur you on to greatness. "Feel the fear but do it anyway," psychologist Susan Jeffers (2006) once wrote. "What matters is that you begin now to develop your trust in yourself, until you reach the point where you will be able to say: Whatever happens to me, given any situation, I can handle it!"

Summary

Self-employment and contract work opportunities are widely available in today's digitally driven economy. It is important for those interested in independent work to understand the steps to setting up a business, of whatever size, and their rights and legal protections in the marketplace. Self-employment isn't for everyone; review the common personality traits of the self-employed and what is required to be personally successful. Understand your motivations so that you can identify any roadblocks and how to work to resolve them. Take time to be as fully informed as you can, and make sure you do the proper planning and have a determined mindset—these will all help you make the leap and be successful in your own business or in leveraging your knowledge and skills in alternate ways.

International Employment

Nicole Miller

In this world of rapid-fire market change, open borders and global expansion offer tantalizing possibilities. Employees now interact across the globe, either in person or using some type of remote tool, and their companies have a real need for new recruits experienced in world affairs. According to a study by the World Economic Forum, a not-for-profit foundation based in Switzerland, 64 percent of employers worldwide consider international experience to be important during their recruitment (Santiago 2015). So, if possessing the "golden key" of international experience is something that has always intrigued you, there is no better time than the present.

According to the Federal Voting Assistance Program, as many as 6.5 million U.S. citizens were living and working abroad at the end of 2015. While some of these expatriates were transferred to a specific locale by their employers, for others the decision is theirs alone, and it is not an easy one to make. Ideals and choices about where to live have no doubt been influenced by the media glamorizing travel and living overseas. For example, who could forget film classics like *Roman Holiday*, featuring Audrey Hepburn and Gregory Peck on their Vespa in Rome; *The Great Race*, starring Natalie Wood and Tony Curtis; or Julia Roberts's around-the-world escape in *Eat, Pray, Love*? Certainly these conjure up images that romanticize living in a foreign land, but what is it really like to live and work there? How could you begin to make this dream a reality?

Choosing the Right PLAN

When setting out on any traveling adventure, the first thing you need to do is plan. This gives you direction and itemizes exactly what you have to do to reach your destination. The same rings true with an international job search; you need to start by creating a job search PLAN:

preparation, location, action, and netting the rewards. This chapter will help you find the right path and deliver the fundamentals of how to land an international position.

Preparation

There are no shortcuts to any dream worth having; therefore, the hours and days you spend preparing for your international job search will save time in the long run. Self-reflection is a strong tool that can help crystallize the answers to some very important questions.

Determining the Who

A vital consideration in your preparation deals with your personal situation. If your family is moving with you, there will be a whole different set of challenges than if you are going overseas alone. You have to take into account not only the wants of your family unit, but also the costs and finances, which in the end could actually dictate who accompanies you.

Either way, as with all job searches, your success hinges on support. If you do not have buy-in from your family, especially if you are expecting them to accompany you, then this could seriously hinder the process. Take the time to explore the options with them, as well as presenting how you will gain a unique life experience as a family. Be sure to include every member in the initial decision process to get a clear picture of the pros and cons from their perspective. The Let's Move Overseas guide in Appendix K has many tips and will assist you in facilitating buy-in from everyone.

Determining the Why

Before choosing where your new adventure will take you, you must reflect on the goals and career expectations you have for your overseas experience. American expatriates have very different reasons for living abroad—there are retirees in Paris pursuing their interest in art by being tour guides; English teachers who use their teaching skills to travel the world and live in different countries; and businesspeople eager to settle in a new country and climb the corporate ladder. But their target is the same: a desire to experience different cultures and enrich their lives.

An effective job target identifies a career path that combines your personal interests with your skills. So, what are some of your choices?

- **Do you want to study abroad?** Contact an exchange program either sponsored by your college or offered through a reputable student exchange organization to find out which countries are offered for study abroad. Often a student visa provides a great opportunity to work in your field of study while obtaining extra spending money. (The website www.goabroad.com has a variety of information to help you decide which program would be best for you.)

- **Would you like to gain a volunteer experience?** If money is not a consideration, some of the most rewarding overseas positions are nonremunerated. Examples of such programs include the Peace Corps, Projects Abroad, UN Volunteers, and Doctors Without Borders.
- **Are you retired and want to earn money to sustain a lifestyle in another country?** Although living abroad in retirement may be your dream, it may not be a fiscal reality. However, a working retirement has become the means for some people to achieve their goal of moving to a new country.
- **Does moving up the career ladder in another country appeal to you?** The first step you should take is to check with the company you are currently working for. You may find that they have an international office you can transfer to, or that they are planning an expansion to another country.

Once you have a clear target, then you can effectively pursue that goal. Without one, your international job search might become aimless and its results unsatisfying.

Determining the What to Start With

Regardless of your job target, you'll need to prepare. The U.S. Department of State's website has a traveler's checklist, which is a good start. Two additional things you can begin to do to assist in your preparation are learning a new language and learning about cultural differences.

Learning a New Language

If you are moving your job search away from countries that are primarily English speaking, learning a new language is definitely a marketable skill that will help you get an edge on your competition. Did you take Spanish, German, or French in high school or college? This might be very useful if you hope to relocate to Europe or Latin America. Brush up on your language skills by taking a conversational course at a local community center or volunteering with a cultural group to reinvigorate your language skills. If you are more of a self-study and want to learn a brand-new language, there are many apps and websites you can use; for example, Duolingo offers web-based lessons for free.

Another avenue, if you have the financial resources, is to take a month or so and embark on an immersion experience. La Maison Française is one such program that is offered by Canada's University of Victoria; it is a five-week total immersion program in French. If learning Spanish will serve you best, there are many programs in Mexico, Central and South America, and Spain, depending on your needs and interests. Take a look at the language forums on the websites Go Overseas and the Lonely Planet for more information. Remember that living with a family or studying at a language school in the country you are interested in serves a twofold purpose: learning the language and experiencing life in the country before making a longer-term commitment.

Learning About Cultural Differences

Cultural differences can affect every single part of your search—the job application process, marketing materials, how you interview, and even whether you negotiate your salary. Without understanding the rules of the game in your target country, your chances of successfully securing a new job are not as good as they could be.

To successfully seek a job abroad, research the cultural differences and respect them in every step of the process. The website Expat.com is an excellent place to begin because it gives you access to more than 5,000 blogs written by expats from all over the world; another great resource website is Expat Exchange.

As you prepare to make your dream of working abroad a reality, commit fully to the idea. Don't worry about opportunities you might be missing back in the United States. Even if you can't find your ideal position in the beginning, the experiences and insight you gain will definitely act as a stepping-stone to better opportunities.

Location

Narrowing down where, in the vastness of the world, you would like to secure your next career opportunity is paramount. Once you have your job-type target, the locale where you want to move will help frame your efforts and assist in securing the most coveted of international experiences.

Determining the Where

The Bureau of Consular Affairs at the U.S. Department of State has an excellent website detailing the conditions of each destination, including visa requirements, safety assessments, healthcare, and a brief overview of local laws. You should also consider your target country's average salaries, cost of living, safety, and whether your industry is in demand.

Average Salaries

So, how much can you expect to be paid when you move abroad? The following two sources have compiled an extensive list of salaries:

- Payscale uses crowdsourcing and big data technology to compile 54 million individual salary profiles.
- The 2016 "Robert Walters Global Salary Survey" analyzes job data across 24 countries, including the United Kingdom and Ireland, Europe, the Middle East, Africa, Asia, Australia, New Zealand, and North and South America.

Cost of Living

Being aware of the expenses you could incur while living in your chosen country is also important information to consider when making your choice. Numbeo is a free online database of worldwide indicators that allows you to research cost of living by city or country.

When budgeting, do not forget to factor in the proximity of your new locale to the United States. Will you want to return home on a regular basis for business or family reasons? Having to travel longer distances is not only more expensive, but also more time-consuming.

The final consideration in cost of living surrounds tax implications related to being an American working out of the country. You are a U.S. citizen and the IRS does not care where you are earning your salary; therefore, you will still need to file a return every year. Understanding the tax guide (found on the IRS website) is not that simple, so it's advisable to consult a tax accountant that specializes in U.S. expatriates.

Is It Safe?

No country is absolutely safe. You need to decide whether your preferred destination has a crime rate that is acceptable to you. The amount of risk you are willing to take will directly affect the choices you make. In addition, every country has its own set of rules, some very different from the United States. What we might take for granted may not be acceptable, or even against the law, in your country of choice.

A great resource is *The World Factbook*, compiled by the Central Intelligence Agency, which presents detailed country profiles in standard categories, such as geography, people and society, government, economy, energy, communications, military and security, and transnational issues.

What Country Has a Need for My Skill Set?

Is your specific skill set in demand in the country you are considering? The online career development website Live Careers has a thorough geographic listing, including job sites organized by country.

Action

In every job search effort, action is what enables a job seeker to land the opportunity, but where do you start? Making the decision to embark on this journey and knowing where you want to go is half the battle. As you have probably noticed, there are some real challenges when looking for a job overseas; however, the PLAN has tools that will help alleviate some of the hurdles. The following are some actions you should take to be successful in your search.

Is Google Your Friend?

When snooping out international opportunities online, using Google is helpful; however, in the massive world of online resources, you could get lost. Try using job search engines instead, which can help refine your search and can actually save you time. Transitionsabroad.com has listed a series of portals organized by global regions that will be very useful as you start your job search. Here is a sample of the portals from their website:

- Africa: CareerJunction.co.za is a searchable job site portal with the majority of jobs in South Africa.
- Asia: JobsDB.com provides job listings for positions across Asia.
- Australia: Jobsearch.gov.au is a government site that lists jobs by occupational category and location.
- Canada: Simplyhired.ca was touted by *Canadian Living* as the best for one-stop searching.
- Europe: Jobsite.co.uk has extensive listings and sister sites in several other European countries, including France, Ireland, Spain, and Italy.
- Latin America: LatPro.com lists positions in Latin America and the United States for professionals who are bilingual in Spanish or Portuguese. All positions require previous experience.
- Middle East: Bayt.com is an extensive job posting site with positions available across the Middle East.

Growing Your Social Network

Social networks are not just for keeping in touch with friends. The most important tool in your job search, no matter where you are, will always be your professional network. It is not what you know, it is whom you know. This very common saying rings true when looking for an international position, and although you may think you don't have a network in your target country, there are a few ways you can grow it without too much effort.

Online networking is definitely a way to easily connect globally with decision makers. However, it is very important to choose the right network. LinkedIn is the largest international online professional network, and connecting with individuals and groups through that site is very user friendly (see chapter 6 for more information about LinkedIn). But, there are additional, lesser-known networks you might be able to tap into based on your target country or region.

- VK is the number one social media site in Eastern Europe, beating out even Facebook with more than 100 million active users. The one caveat is that most interaction on the site is in Russian.
- XING is a Western European business network with more than 7 million members.
- QZone is China's most popular social media site, and with more than 645 million registered users, it is the largest social network in the world.
- Taringa! is a popular networking site with Spanish-speaking users.
- Mixi is a must-use resource if you want to build your network in Japan.

Job Fairs

Another great option is to attend an overseas job fair because in the course of a few hours, you'll get to meet dozens of employers who may be hiring in your target locale. Attending a job fair in your own city is a good start; you can find a list of international job fairs on the U.S. Job Fair directory. Attend these fairs ready to interview, dressed to impress, and carrying resumes to hand out. Make sure you network and ask questions about any positions available. Even if you do not get an on-the-spot interview, you will start gathering contacts who may be able to assist you in landing an opportunity in the future.

Resume or CV?

Always write your documents with the target reader (and that reader's cultural expectations) in mind. For example, to apply for jobs in countries with a North American influence, job seekers should create a resume—a short (no more than two pages) summary written with bullet points to describe skills and work experience. (Refer to chapter 5 for more information on resume crafting.) However, a curriculum vitae (CV) is widely used in European countries. This document is longer than the traditional resume, usually more than three pages, and tends to be written using descriptive paragraphs. Very recently, the EU created the Europass CV to help you present your skills and qualifications effectively and clearly. There's even an online portal to help applicants generate a CV through an online template.

A quick call to the human resources department of your target company or your recruiter can help sort out which format is appropriate to use. Note that what to include in your resume or CV is based on where you are applying; for example, including a photo or indicating marital status is not acceptable in the United States, but is very common in many other countries. Researching these intricacies can ensure that your application is competitive.

Keeping Track of Your Search

Organization is paramount once you start applying to international positions. If you plan to manage your job search on your own, setting up a tracking document in Excel is the easiest way to keep the information at your fingertips. Brighthub has a free Excel template you can use.

You could also decide to use an employment agency. There are thousands of such services worldwide, but most have a fee. They can certainly be worth the money; just make sure you understand exactly what they will be offering and for how much. If possible, talk with a few past clients to find out about how their experiences. *Verge* magazine has a great listing of job placement agencies across a broad spectrum of job types.

Consider hiring a professional career coach, who can assist with everything from picking your target country to creating winning marketing documents to interview prep and salary negotiations. Although this process can be costly, Career Directors International states that it is money well spent. Before hiring a coach, ensure she has industry recognition, expertise in your target country, and great references.

Interviewing Internationally

Chapter 9 included many great tips for acing your next interview. However, you'll need to take a few more things into consideration when interviewing for an international job. The Goinglobal website lists interviewing advice in its country profiles, so that is an excellent place to start. Here are a few more things you should consider when preparing for international interviews.

Language

If you only speak English, confirm that your interview will be conducted in English. If not, make sure you have enough verbal ease to portray yourself as professional. Even if your interview is conducted in English, one tip is to greet the employer in their native language. It shows that you're culturally aware and helps to sell your flexibility.

Time Zones

When scheduling an interview, remember that 6 p.m. in New York is actually 7 a.m. the next day in Tokyo.

Phone vs. Video Call

Wherever possible, use Skype or some other videoconference tool. There is something to be said for being able to see whom you are speaking to. Chapter 9 includes additional guidance on video interviews.

Cultural Differences

Ignoring culture differences can get you into trouble during an interview:

- Keep the interview professional and serious—this is no time to crack jokes.
- Keep your accomplishment statements toned down—you don't want to come across as boastful.
- Always be conscious of social hierarchies—never become familiar with the interviewer.

Dress Conservatively

Keep in mind that the industry you are applying to will probably have certain dress codes. For example, in London's business world a suit and tie are prevalent, but as you go into northern England, the dress relaxes.

Always Be on Time

Whether your interview is in person or by phone, don't be late for your interview. But keep in mind cultural preferences. In some Asian cultures it is extremely rude to not arrive early (15 minutes) for your interview. Compare that with the United States, where arriving more than 15 minutes early to an interview is inadvisable. You definitely do not want to send the wrong message, so make sure you are adhering to the preferences of the country you are interviewing in.

Netting the Rewards

Congratulations! You've secured a job! But what do you do now? Once the excitement over landing the job wears off and the reality of the offer sinks in, there are some things you need to consider before signing on the dotted line.

Can I Negotiate?

The short answer is yes, all contracts are negotiable. Before you contemplate a counteroffer, make sure you have something in writing. Treat this as a starting point. In some cultures negotiating is rude, so make sure that is not the case for your position; however, the majority of the business world will entertain a well-thought-out and researched counteroffer.

What Will I Be Paid?

It may sound fantastic to be offered a six-figure salary, but how does that salary relate to the average salaries in your industry? Remember that there are differences in buying power around the world; you do not want to get stuck with a lower standard of living than what you had in the United States. Most industries use location pay when reassigning employees across the world. For example, an executive moving from New York to London can expect a pay hike of approximately 10 percent, due to the increased cost of living in London. If you are working in a country with instability, ensure that at least part of your salary is still paid in U.S. currency.

Compensation Package

The typical expatriate compensation package will include visa requirements, accommodation allowance, relocation costs, healthcare coverage, paid vacation, and an education allowance for children. Try to speak with employees who have been hired previously by the company to get a feel for what they were offered.

Visa Requirements

Visa requirements should be discussed with your new employer. Things such as who makes the application, what is involved, who pays, who in the family needs to be covered, and how long it will take need to be cemented before you accept your offer. Many deals have gone sour over not being able to get a visa to work within a country, so make sure you cooperate fully in this process.

Accommodation Allowances

Before you sign your contract, your new employer should be able to offer you a realistic view on housing costs, where to live, and how much of the costs (if any) they will cover. Depending on where you relocate, things such as utilities, domestic help, security services, electric generators, inverters, and water storage and purifiers may be in the realm of what your employer is willing to pay for. Monster.com indicates that some companies incorporate these costs into a foreign-service premium, which is usually between 10 and 15 percent, depending on where you will live (DeZube nd).

Relocation Costs

Relocation costs can include movers, real estate fees (for selling your U.S. property), hotel accommodations, meals, and airline tickets. You may also want to include the cost of employment services to help your spouse find work.

Healthcare Coverage

If you are going to a country where you will not have access to universal healthcare, make sure to bring this benefit to the negotiation table. Healthcare can be one of the most costly items when making the move to a new country and most employers will include it in the package.

Paid Vacation

According to most headhunters, it is very common for your benefits package to offer at least one trip home for you and your dependents. Depending on the seniority of your position, you may be able to request business class travel or multiple trips back to the United States. The number of paid vacation days you receive depends on the country and industry you are working in. Some countries also have mandated paid family leave (maternity and paternity), so make sure you are aware of your rights. Research this before making a counteroffer. The International Labour Organization is a great resource.

Education Allowance for Children

This is an important item if you are moving with children because their education costs have the potential to be very high. An English-speaking private school in China, for example, can cost more than $100,000 a year. The average school fees allowance sits at about $20,000 per year (Botten 2014); in the Middle East employers typically cover upwards of 75 percent of tuition costs (Clarke 2010).

What Will My Work Environment Be Like?

Make sure your work hours and duties are clearly spelled out in your written contract. Not all countries have the same labor laws as the United States, so make sure you have clearly looked into these laws and that they mesh with what you are willing to do. For example, the typical Japanese employee works more than 60 hours a week, but never on weekends. This means they routinely work 12-hour days Monday through Friday.

It is very important to look into the occupational safety and health legislation of your destination to make sure you are not being taken advantage of. The International Labour Organization maintains a database that will help with your research.

Culture Shock

Once the excitement of your new surroundings dissipates, you will soon realize your new locale is different. You'll notice the little things first; shopping in a grocery store and not being able to speak the language, perhaps driving on the opposite side of the road, or even a slower pace of life. This can lead to culture shock; everyone will experience it to some degree or another. So, what can you do to counteract it?

Learn about your new country. Research the people and their lifestyle. Reach out to various expat social networks and ask questions.

Remember that patience is a virtue and it will serve you well. The more you interact with the people in your new country, the more comfortable you will become. Join a sports team or two, accept any invitations to social events; in short, do anything you can to start integrating into the fabric of your host culture. This will help ease the awkwardness that you are feeling about your new home.

And remember, this does not need to be a permanent move. All jobs are temporary; you moved for this one, and you can move again to find another.

Despite the initial culture shock, many people ultimately find relocation to be a rewarding endeavor. Take the time to reflect on your decision, then move forward with your eyes wide open, ready to experience the change of a lifetime.

Summary

An international job search requires a strong PLAN. The concept of preparation, location, action, and netting the rewards presented within this chapter is a simplified way to structure your efforts to be successful.

Appendices

The following pages contain the appendices referenced throughout *Find Your Fit*, including the Interest Profiler (Appendix A), Personal Inventory Tool (Appendix B), and Career Plan (Appendix E). You'll also find sample resumes, cover letters, and a value proposition letter.

Interest Profiler

Fill in the circle next to the statements that sound like you most of the time. Then count the number of circles darkened in each column and enter the number in the appropriate column of the last row. The two or three columns with the highest totals are your theme codes. Note your theme codes and then review chapter 1 for a description of each.

	Statement	R	I	A	S	E	C
1	I can usually carry, build, or fix things myself.	o					
2	I need to understand things completely. I like to have all the details.		o				
3	Music, color, or beauty of any kind can really affect my moods.			o			
4	People make my life better and give it meaning.				o		
5	I have confidence in myself that I can make things happen.					o	
6	I appreciate clear directions so I know exactly what to do.						o
7	I don't mind getting my hands dirty.	o					
8	It's satisfying to explore new ideas.		o				
9	I always seem to be looking for new ways to express my creativity.			o			
10	I value being able to share personal concerns with people.				o		
11	I enjoy competing.					o	
12	I need to get my work space in order before I start a project.						o
13	I like to buy sensible things that I can put to good use and do by myself.	o					
14	I see education as a lifelong process of developing and sharpening my mind.		o				
15	I have a great imagination.			o			
16	If I have a problem with someone, I prefer to talk it out and resolve it.				o		
17	To be successful, it's important to aim high.					o	

	Statement	R	I	A	S	E	C
18	I take pride in being very careful about all the details of my work.						o
19	I don't enjoy spending a lot of time discussing things. What's right is right.	o					
20	Sometimes I can sit for long periods and read or just think about life.		o				
21	I love to try creative new ideas.			o			
22	When I feel down, I find a friend to talk to.				o		
23	After I suggest a plan, I prefer to let others take care of the details.					o	
24	A good routine helps me get the job done.						o
25	It's energizing to do things outdoors.	o					
26	I need to analyze a problem from all angles before I act on it.		o				
27	I like to rearrange my space to make it unique and different.			o			
28	Close relationships are important to me.				o		
29	It's exciting to take part in important decisions.					o	
30	I prefer being in a position where I don't have to make the decisions.						o
31	I like my space to be plain and practical.	o					
32	I keep asking why.		o				
33	I look forward to seeing art shows, plays, and concerts.			o			
34	I want you to tell me how I can help you.				o		
35	Promotion and advancement are important to me.					o	
36	I'm usually content where I am.						o
37	A strong system of law and order is important to prevent chaos.	o					
38	I'd like to learn all there is to know about subjects that interest me.		o				
39	I don't want to be like everyone else; I like to do things differently.			o			
40	I feel concerned that so many people in our society need help.				o		
41	It's exciting to influence people.					o	
42	When I say I'll do something, I'll follow through on every detail.						o
43	Good, hard physical work never hurt anyone.	o					
44	I like people who challenge my thinking and help me learn more.		o				

	Statement	R	I	A	S	E	C
45	The beauty of nature touches something deep inside me.			o			
46	I often go out of my way to pay attention to people who seem friendless.				o		
47	I'm willing to take some risks to get ahead.					o	
48	I hate it when things change just when I get them down.						o
49	I usually know how to take care of things in an emergency.	o					
50	Just reading about new discoveries is exciting.		o				
51	When I'm creating, I tend to let everything else go.			o			
52	People often seem to tell me their problems.				o		
53	I love to bargain.					o	
54	I don't like to do things unless I'm sure they're approved.						o
55	Sports are important in building strong bodies.	o					
56	Don't get excited. We can think it out and plan the right move logically.		o				
57	I like to create exciting events.			o			
58	I believe that people are basically good.				o		
59	If I don't make it the first time, I usually bounce back with energy.					o	
60	I appreciate knowing exactly what people expect of me.						o
	Total						
		R	I	A	S	E	C

Adapted from: Michelozzi, B.N. 1998. *Coming Alive From Nine to Five: The Career Search Handbook*, 3rd ed. Mountain View, CA: Mayfield Publishing Company.

Personal Inventory Tool

Personal Mission Statement (chapters 3 and 4)		
Personality Traits (chapter 1)	**Interests (chapter 1)**	**Skills and Strengths (chapter 2)**
	Enter your the me codes from the Interest Profiler here.	
Principles and Values (chapter 3)	**Logistics (chapters 1 and 4)**	**Work Environment (chapter 3)**
	Company Size: Type of Company: Location: Commute: Salary: Level:	Corporate Culture: Type of Boss:

Appendix C

Assessment Tools

Interest Assessment Tools

Name of Assessment	Founder	Where to Find	Framework
Strong Interest Inventory	E.K. Strong	www.discoveryourpersonality.com/stronginterestinventorycareertest.html	• Compatible with Holland's R-I-A-S-E-C framework • General occupation themes • Basic interest scales • Occupational scales • Personal styles scale
Occupational Interest Card Sorts	Richard Knowdell	www.careercentre.dtwd.wa.gov.au/toolsandresources/toolsandresourcestohelpyouplanyourcareer/findingouttoolsandresources/Pages/SkillsCardSort.aspx	• Degree of readiness, skills, and knowledge needed to perform a job • Competency-building steps • 110 occupational cards
CareerLeader	Timothy Butler and James Waldroop	www.careerleader.com/individuals.html	• Business career interest inventory • Leadership motivations profile • Leadership skills profile
Interest Profiler	U.S. Department of Labor, Employment and Training Administration	www.onetcenter.org/IP.html?p=3	• Compatible with Hollands's R-I-A-S-E-C framework
Self-Directed Search	John Holland	www.self-directed-search.com	• Realistic • Investigative • Artistic • Social • Enterprising • Conventional

Personality Assessment Tools

Name of Assessment	Founders	Where to Find	Framework
Myers-Briggs Type Indicator (MBTI)	Katharine Cook Briggs Isabel Briggs Myers	www.myersbriggs.org/my-mbti-personality-type/take-the-mbti-instrument www.mbtionline.com	• Extraversion/Introversion • Sensing/Intuition • Thinking/Feeling • Judging/Perceiving
DISC	William Mouton Marston	www.discprofile.com/what-is-disc/history-of-disc	• Dominance • Influence • Steadiness • Conscientiousness
Kiersey Temperament Sorter	David Keirsey	www.keirsey.com/default.aspx	• Guardian • Artisan • Idealist • Rational
The Big Five	Paul Costa and Robert McCrae Warren Norman & Lewis Goldberg	www.outofservice.com/bigfive	• Openness • Conscientiousness • Extraversion • Agreeableness • Neuroticism
Motivational Appraisal of Personal Potential (MAPP)	Henry Neils	www.assessment.com	• How you relate to: • Tasks • People • Things • Data • Reasoning • Math • Language

Skills Checklist

Skills Working With Things	✓ when used in story	Skills Working With Ideas	✓ when used in story
Assembling things		Acting or dancing	
Being good with your hands		Adapting	
Building or constructing things		Brainstorming	
Driving and operating vehicles		Communicating abstract ideas	
Finding out how things work		Composing music	
Fixing or repairing things		Creating programs or events	
Gardening and farming		Designing processes and programs	
Good hand-eye coordination		Developing strategies	
Inspecting things		Drawing, painting, or sculpture	
Installing equipment		Expressing ideas through art	
Making things (crafts, furniture, etc.)		Graphic design or photography	
Monitoring equipment, machinery		Innovating or imagining concepts	
Raising, training, tending animals		Inventing products and processes	
Restoring objects		Seeing different perspectives	
Tending plants		Singing or playing an instrument	
Using computer software		Using color, shape, and form	
Using tools, equipment, or machines		Visualizing physical space	
Working well in three dimensions		Writing and editing	

Skills Working With People	✓ when used in story	**Skills Working With Data**	✓ when used in story
Advising or mentoring		Analyzing information and data	
Advocating for people		Applying statistical analysis	
Building relationships and rapport		Attending to detail	
Coaching		Auditing records	
Conducting meetings		Budgeting	
Conflict management		Calculating and manipulating numbers	
Delegating tasks		Checking for accuracy	
Demonstrating diplomacy		Classifying and sorting data	
Developing people's abilities		Comparing and evaluating information	
Directing or leading others		Compiling numbers or information	
Explaining or instructing		Creating efficient systems	
Facilitating groups		Developing plans	
Influencing, persuading, or selling		Finding and gathering information	
Interviewing		Forecasting or estimating	
Listening		Interpreting plans and diagrams	
Motivating others		Keeping financial records	
Negotiating		Organizing and improving systems	
Presenting and public speaking		Preparing or following instructions	
Providing customer service		Presenting data visually	
Providing physical or medical care		Researching	
Teaching or training		Scheduling	
Working well with a team		Tracking progress of projects	

Career Plan and Target Companies Worksheet

My Career Plan
Career Target (title or titles commonly used for the type of position you are targeting):
Skills needed for this type of position (review 2-3 current job postings that would be a good fit):
Industry Preferences (industries that interest you or where your skills are in demand):
Location (geographic area you are targeting. Be specific):
Work Environment Issues (corporate culture, mission, physical environment):
Target Salary/Level (what is the going rate/your market value?):
Timeline (what is your target date for achieving this career goal?):
Next Logical Position (beyond this one to which I aspire):

Action Plan	
Next Steps:	Date:

Target Company List		
Company Name	Location	Contacts

Resumes

This appendix includes four sample resumes that illustrate some of the key points made in chapter 5.

- The first sample is a functional resume for a financial executive who is planning a career change into real estate development.
- The second sample is a hybrid resume for a senior executive who spent a fair bit of time at one company. In this case, the accomplishments were subdivided into categories to break up the text and avoid a long line of bullets under one employer.
- The third sample is for a recent college graduate with multiple internships.
- The fourth sample illustrates a deconstructed resume, which can be used for online applications, as explained in chapter 8.

We recommend having a nicely formatted resume for use in face-to-face meetings, networking, and when applying for positions that request you to email your resume in for review. For online applications, we recommend using a resume with simple formatting, like the last sample in this appendix.

JOHN M. FINANCE, CFA

44 Monroe Lane, Port Jefferson Station, NY 07856

Phone: 888.222.1111   **jfinance1001@gmail.com**

REAL ESTATE DEVELOPMENT—SALES

MBA Architect with financial acumen and design expertise. Known for ability to analyze markets and recommend sound investments. Seeking to work with real estate developers and investors to research real estate markets, opportunities and properties in order to maximize value for all stake holders.

- Real Estate Development & Planning
- Property Renovation & Sales
- Investment Research & Management
- Financial Analysis
- Persuasive Written & Oral Communication

- Asset Value Maximization
- Chartered Financial Analyst (CFA)
- Licensed Real Estate Sales Agent VA & MD
- MBA
- Master's in Architecture

PROFESSIONAL ACCOMPLISHMENTS

Real Estate Development & Planning
- Seven years of experience vetting development and subdivision applications, providing action recommendations as member and chair of township planning commission
- Seeking, analyzing, financing and planning valued-added renovations of existing properties for resale.
- Design development and construction documentation leader for the central building of a large office facility for a major technology firm.
- Managed designed and construction of residential properties.

Property Renovation & Sales
- Bought and upgraded residential property to generate rental income in excess of operating expenses. Designed landscaping and negotiated related contracts. Market value has risen 15%+ since 2011.
- Conceptualized, designed and managed complete functional, visual and operating systems renovation of 3,600 SF home. Repurposed surrounding property with hardscaping, landscaping and pool.
- Licensed VA and MD Sales Agent, ABC Real Estate company.

Financial Research & Analysis
- Researched markets and industries to determine the trends and components for success in order to predict which companies and stocks will perform best.
- Analyzed companies in a variety of industries and provided recommendations to institutional investors that met their goals and risk tolerance.
- Developed convincing and clear rationale for reasons to buy and sell stocks, and executed persuasive presentations of investment ideas.
- Institutional Investor All America Research Team, Barron's Best of the Boutiques and Wall Street Journal Best on the Street citation.
- StarMine Top 3 Stock Picker, TheStreet.com Best Stock Picker.

Continued . . .

WORK EXPERIENCE

Entrepreneurship In Investing   **2008–Present**
Investments Unlimited, LLC, New York, NY, *Partner, 2012-2013*
Partner in real estate-focused specialty research and investment firm
ABC Securities, LLC, *Principal, 2007-2008 and 2010–2011*
Well Known Investment Group, New York, NY, *Managing Director, 2008-2010*
Spearheaded development of research products for distribution to institutional investors

Equity Research & Financial Analysis   **1988–2007**
Forecasts, LLC, New York, NY, *Consultant, 2005-2007*
First Bank, New York, NY, *Senior Analyst, 2000-2005*
Investment Firm, New York, NY, *Senior Analyst, 1992-2000*
Bank Of New York, New York, NY, *Buy-Side Equity Analyst, 1988-1992*

Architecture Experience
XYZ Architecture Firm, *Associate, 1981-1985*

EARLIER CAREER

Abc University—Anywhere, Usa
Master of Business Administration (MBA), School of Business (1987)
Master of Architecture (M.Arch), School of Design (1978)
Bachelor of Arts (BA), Design of the Environment (1976)

Series 7-, 63-, 86- and 87-qualified

CFA Charter holder since 1991

Industry Awards:
- Institutional Investor All America Research Team
- Wall Street Journal Best on the Street citation
- StarMine Top 3 Stock Picker
- Barron's Best of Boutiques designee
- TheStreet.com Best Stock Picker

Community Involvement:

Township Planning Commission Chairman 2004-10

JACK BLOOMBERG

210 Pole St., Port Jefferson, NY 10077
631.555.8888 | jbloom@sample.com

GENERAL MANAGER | CHIEF OPERATING OFFICER

Private Club, Hospitality, and Culinary Expert with an unwavering appetite for success

Member, Club Managers Association of America

Uniquely diverse hospitality expert with an ever forward moving career path that began as a pre-teen boy and has reached an all-encompassing, executive level. With a lifetime of industry experience and achievements, driven and focused about each daily challenge and opportunity; begin each and every day with positive enthusiasm.

Fun Fact: As a culinary extern, prepared dinner for President Clinton at Four Seasons. Special clearance by Secret Service.

EXECUTIVE ASSETS

High-Yield Business Growth Strategies	Facility Enhancement & Capital Projects	Event & Tournament Planning
Strategic Planning & Execution	Multi-facility Management	Human Resource Management
Capital & Operating Budgeting	Culinary Expertise	Golf, Tennis & Pool Operations
Financial Analysis & Management	Board Collaboration	Clubhouse Management
	Membership Engagement	Rapport & Relationship Building

EXECUTIVE ASSETS IN ACTION

Ardsley Country Club, Belle, NY | 1999 to 2002, 2004 to Present
www.ardsley.com
Private, family-oriented Country Club that offers full service golf, tennis, swimming, paddle, dining, curling, summer kids camp, member events, and world-class dining.

General Manager and Chief Operating Officer (2004 to Present)
Assistant Manager (1999 to 2002)
Executive leadership role; accountable for success of entire operation. Established reputation at the Stanwich Club and demonstrated ability during earlier tenure at Ardsley Country Club that earned a confident invitation to return as general manager and COO. Direct a large, cross-functional team of department heads and professional staff (155 in season and 75 off season). Initially challenged to complete $8.8M golf course and clubhouse renovation that was 50 percent finished, and to turnaround the existing financial crisis.

Relationship Management and Member Satisfaction: An approachable, visible, and collaborative leader who engages staff, members, vendors, and community in the overall goal of creating a heartfelt, high-quality establishment.

- Created standard of excellence to ensure all areas of club, staff, and facility exceeded member expectations.
- Rebuilt pool (capital project $2.1M) to reestablish a family friendly atmosphere and boost membership morale.
- Repaired relationships with local municipalities; enabled club to have productive negotiations, community support, and successful completion of capital projects.

JACK BLOOMBERG | 631.555.8888 | jbloom@sample.com | Page 2 of 2

Management Style and Success: Expert in assessing existing talent pool, restructuring workforce to meet set objectives, restaffing to ensure the right team is in place, and developing a cohesive team of individuals who take ownership responsibilities and deliver exceptional, high-quality service. Educate staff in multiple facets of the operation to create understanding of how each role is an integral part of the whole.

- Created culture of respect and confidence in management that resulted in an environment where employees desired to work and strived to perform well.
- Developed and facilitated success-driven training programs that provided management with practical tools for real results; invested in staff, identified high potentials, and mentored individuals for career advancement.
- Renegotiated professional golf and tennis contracts to better align long-term goals of pros with the long-term goals of club.

Cost Savings and Revenue Generation: Saved money without sacrificing quality and scope of offerings and services. Ensured realistic budgeting and forecasting of revenues, managed expenses to those revenues in all areas. Developed fresh programs and services that bolstered membership participation and generated additional revenue streams.

- Curbed skyrocketing labor costs on grounds and greens team; renegotiated property taxes and water rates to benefit the club.
- Reinvigorated junior camp and kids programs; generated modest profit of $40K.
- Worked closely with insurance carriers; ensured proper reimbursement of losses due to Hurricanes Irene and Sandy.

Financial Management: Bottom-line oriented and fiscally responsible. Proven ability to generate revenue and rescue an underperforming organization, even during times of economic downturn. All financial goals achieved with membership satisfaction at the helm of initiatives.

- Achieved 10 consecutive years of forward financial progress.
- With operational losses in the $450K range during first year, achieved a break even on operational budget within two years and have sustained through present day.
- Successfully restructured repayment terms on debt incurred on large capital project from 2004; currently tracking better than budget.

The Stanwich Club, Freehold, NJ   **2002 to 2004**
Top 100 course rated by Golf Digest *Internationally recognized golf course and club.*

Assistant General Manager
Managed all aspects of clubhouse. Trained staff ensuring exceptional service while fulfilling events and member holiday gatherings.

Process Improvement: Designed and implemented back office and point-of-sale computer network for accounting, restaurant, and proshop.

Event Planning: Spearheaded start to finish planning efforts for 2004 Amateur Golf Tournament televised on CNBC.

EARLIER CAREER

Manager—Hola Restaurant, New York, NY | **Culinary Extern, Four Seasons Hotel,** New York, NY | **Food and Beverage Manager,** Excalibur Events, Miami, FL

EDUCATION, CERTIFICATIONS, AND LICENSES

Degree in Food & Beverage Management, Johnson & Wales University, Providence, RI

Food Service and Management Certification | Food Sanitation Certification | Wines Certification

ROY M. PENN

508.266.1535 | roympenn@gmail.com
www.linkedin.com/pub/roy-penn

ENTRY-LEVEL ENGINEERING

Systems Engineer | Test Engineer | Business Intelligence Analyst

VALUE ADDED

- Project Management
- Team Leadership/Motivation
- Technical Writing
- Budgeting
- Cost Accounting
- Cost/Benefit Analysis
- Requirements Verification/ Validation
- Requirements Testing/Allocation
- Systems Integration
- Critical Path Analysis

RELEVANT COURSEWORK

Economics
Fundamentals of System Engineering
Logistics and Supply Chain Management
Modeling and Simulation
Probability and Statistics
Project Management of Complex Systems
Systems Integration
System Architecture and Design
Thermodynamics

TECHNICAL SKILLS

AutoCAD | SolidWorks | MS Excel w/ Solver | MS Word | MS PowerPoint | MS Sharepoint | MiniTab | Salesforce | Mac OSX | Windows 10 | Internet (Explorer, Firefox, Chrome)

Motivated student completing undergraduate degree in **engineering management**. Well-rounded individual with a unique blend of academic development, athletic training, and hands-on business insight, attained through numerous long-term, field-related internships (civil, mechanical, and systems engineering). Cultivated strong work ethic and lifelong passion for learning in a homeschool environment, culminating in college-level and advanced study of engineering. Began college courses at age 15, demonstrating ability to make independent decisions regarding subjects to study and learning schedule.

EDUCATION

Bachelor of Engineering in Engineering Management
Minor: Economics
SSE Graduate Certificate, Systems Engineering & Architecting
Brooks Institute of Technology, Grand Island, NY
Anticipated graduation date: June 2016 | GPA: 3.7

HONORS AND PERSONAL ACHIEVEMENTS

Howard T. Brooks Scholarship | Scholars of Excellence Scholarship | Brooks Honor Society | Five-Time All-American NCAA DII Swimming | Brooks Scholar | Dean's List

Demonstrated ability to successfully juggle numerous diverse activities.
- Three-time individual event All-American in NCAA swimming.
- Triathlon and ski team participant.
- Trained more than 20 hours a week while maintaining an exemplary grade point average and full time internships.

ROY M. PENN   508.266.1535 | roympenn@gmail.com | Page 2 of 2

INTERNSHIPS

Proven commitment to professional growth and gaining valuable, hands-on experience.

The Carriage Firm, Albany, NY (6 months)

A full-service broadcast engineering firm providing systems consulting planning, design, and integration of advanced digital and high definition facilities. www.thecarriagefirm.com

Systems Engineering Intern

Gained valuable experience as part of the company's engineering department. Collaborated and provided input on specific projects; surveyed and implemented basic changes to project documents in AutoCAD, Excel, and MS Access. Worked with the planning department to update and format vendor price lists in Excel.

- Organized and formatted backlog of vendor pricelists to TSG standard.
- Created functional drawings in AutoCAD to represent vendor products.
- Managed Sharepoint database of project drawings and documents.

Dansville Corporation, Utica, NY (7 months)

Dansville Corp. is a developer and owner and operator of solar power projects. www.dansvillecorp.com

Sales and Marketing Intern

Reported directly to senior vice president of sales and marketing. Championed various responsibilities including client identification and sourcing by utilizing Hoovers, PropertyShark, and Google Earth; ensuring positive direct client interaction; and database management (in Excel and Salesforce).

- Refined company database to improve data retrieval and increase efficiency.
- Introduced Google Earth as a client identification tool. Linked database with Google Earth document enabling the company to map current and potential clients across New York and parts of Vermont without overlapping information from extensive existing database.

Rickland Toys, New York, NY (6 months)

Rickland Toys manufactures various toys for children. Its products include learning toys, toys based on preschool characters, baby gear, and children's products. www.ricklandtoys.com

Mechanical Engineering Intern

As mechanical engineer on the Clinging Critters toy line, served as an integral member of cross-functional team comprising designers, electrical engineers, and packaging engineers. Collaborated with team members to ensure product standards were met. Reported to the director of engineering and the senior project engineer.

- Received toys in various stages of development; worked with team to identify needed changes and report findings to manufacturing engineers in Hong Kong.
- Served as direct line of communication with Hong Kong for assigned product lines.
- Challenged to discover innovative solutions to various mechanical issues.
- Successfully assumed and performed responsibilities of senior project engineer during a two-week leave.

Mary Smith
Philadelphia, PA
215.123.4567
marysmithmarketing@gmail.com
www.linkedin.com/in/marysmithmarketing

Digital Strategist | Opportunity Prospector & Business Development | Creator of Strategic Partnerships & Alliances

Outstanding record of success in penetrating new markets, building relationships, and partnering with vendors and clients to develop win-win solutions in the media, entertainment, and other fields. Problem solver, skilled negotiator, and talented supervisor who builds cohesive teams to produce results. Strategically incisive thought leader who generates new ideas to create effective and innovative digital solutions across client engagements. Creative catalyst able to balance complex situations for multiplatform product launches.

Core Competencies
- Analytics
- Brand Management
- Business Development
- Corporate Sponsorships
- Cross-Functional Team
- Digital Marketing
- E-Commerce
- Innovation Planning
- Integrated Marketing
- Leadership and Training
- Negotiation
- New Product Launch
- P&L Management
- Revenue and Profit Generation
- Social Media Marketing
- Strategic Partnerships
- Strategic Sales and Tactical Alignment
- Team Building

Work Experience
QVC, West Chester, PA   2014–Present
SVP Customer Experience and Business Services
- Researched and developed a unique digital solution plan with media and entertainment companies, as well as industry aggregators, coordinating a cross-functional team to help formulate and facilitate the plan for a company with revenues of $28M.
- Include other accomplishments under this employer.

QVC, West Chester, PA   2010–2014
VP Digital Branding
- Generated $28M revenue channels while increasing brand exposure utilizing strategic partnerships and restructuring policy, pricing, and procedures.
- Include other accomplishments under this employer.

Sony Pictures Entertainment, Culver City, CA   2007–2010
Senior Business Development Executive
- Negotiated content and pricing with media companies including book publishers, music labels, and film and video studios.
- Include other accomplishments under this employer.

Image Entertainment, Chatsworth, CA   2004–2007
Director Business Development for Special Markets
- Reduced administrative expenses by 32 percent driving small business clients to e-commerce intranet site after minimum order amounts were removed.
- Led a task force to develop an online ordering system to streamline company-wide catalog and create visibility of products transforming revenue generators from money losers of more than $1M.
- Include other accomplishments under this employer.

NBC Universal, Los Angeles, CA   2001–2004
Online Sales and New Product Launch Manager
- Planned and managed more than 20 Google AdWords campaigns and paid search for 2 million SKUs followed by actionable web analytics to increase online sales conversions and optimize online marketing.
- Include other accomplishments under this employer.

Stream Companies, Malvern, PA   1997–1999
Account Coordinator
- Developed key initiatives in revamping business plan to double business within two years.
- Include other accomplishments under this employer.

Various School Districts, Southeastern, PA   1980–1997
Teacher
- Taught high school English, business, and technology courses.

Education
University of Pennsylvania, The Wharton School, Philadelphia, PA   2001
- Master of Business Administration, Dual Major in Strategic Management and Marketing

West Chester University, West Chester, PA   1980
- Bachelor of Arts, Psychology

Awards and Honors
- Leadership Ovation Award, NBC Universal
- Innovation Award, Sony Pictures Entertainment
- EPIC Award, QVC

Volunteer
- Philadelphia Area Great Careers Group, Membership Chair

Interests
- Technology, running, fitness, skiing, cooking, traveling, social media, news, movies, Disney, and scrapbooking.

Personal Marketing Plan

ALANA SMITH

MA in Curriculum & Instruction, ATD Credentialed Master Trainer Candidate

TRAINING / INSTRUCTIONAL DESIGN & DEVELOPMENT MANAGER

10+ years' expertise developing and delivering training solutions for corporate performance optimization

- Learning and development professional with success in start-up environments. Consultative approach to building training with proven ability to deliver best practices for adult learners in multicultural environments in both academic and business settings.
- Experience with the full scope of the instructional design process, including blended learning, face-to-face training, e-learning (asynchronous, virtual classroom, mobile), and real-time facilitation. Familiar with all aspects of the learning and development design cycle, including needs assessment, gap analysis, and evaluation.
- Taught, presented, and worked in the United States, Saudi Arabia, Dubai, and Antarctica.

Job Title and Level	Geographic Location	Industry or Company Size
Training/Instructional Design & Development Manager	Washington, D.C.	Midsized Company

Target Companies and Organizations		

Value Proposition Letter

Google Inc.
Attention: People Operations Team
1600 Amphitheatre Parkway
Mountain View, CA 94043

Dear People Operations Team,

Do you need a presence in the Greater Philadelphia area to tap into the talent of a smart, well-educated, and determined wannabe Googler?

As a seasoned educator, event planner, and local mentor with an entrepreneurial mindset, I have instituted some innovative ideas in the local career transition community that have empowered others to become more tech savvy as they are seeking their next opportunities.

Here are some initiatives that I can spearhead for Google when you are ready to set up a branch in this area:

- Provide curriculum and instruction for workshops on the Google platform and apps that would be available to local small- and medium-sized businesses, children, and adults, including the career transition community.
- Initiate networking groups to build community, relationships, and good will in a territory where Microsoft and Apple have existed for some time.
- Partner with the local business development team to integrate the product training in the sales skill curriculum.

I look forward to hearing from you so we can explore this strategic partnership and plan together for the future.

Sincerely,

Lynne M. Williams
Director, Philadelphia Area Great Careers Group

Monthly Expenses Worksheet

Fixed Expenses	Monthly Amount	Discretionary Expenses	Monthly Amount
Housing		**Recreation**	
Mortgage/Rent		Entertainment	
Property Taxes		Media	
Heating		Hobbies	
Electricity		Sports/Health Clubs	
Telephone		Other	
TV: Cable/Satellite			
Internet Provider			
Other		**Clothing**	
Insurance		Purchase	
House		Upkeep and Repair	
Automobile			
Health			
Life		**Contributions**	
Other		Church	
Credit Payments		Donations	
Automobile		Gifts	
Credit Cards		Other	
Other			
Food			
Groceries		**Personal**	
Meals Out		Barber and Hair Stylist	
Transportation		Pets	
Auto Maintenance		Personal Items	
Gas		Other	
Parking and Tolls			
Public Transport			
Other			

Family			
Child Care			
Child Support			
Medical Expenses			
Prescriptions			
Other			
Other Expenses Not Listed Above			

Cover Letters

This appendix contains two samples that illustrate the type of information that should be included in a cover letter, as referenced in chapter 8.

- The first sample is a standard cover letter that highlights key selling points for the position, as well as why the applicant is interested in the job.
- The second sample letter is in a "T" format, which identifies key job requirements in one column and applicant qualifications in the other. This format works well for applicants who need to clearly show how their background fits the stated job requirements.

While there is some debate about the value of cover letters, in our experience, having a cover letter can definitely help you, while not having one can hurt you. So, we recommend taking the time to create a solid master cover letter that includes all your potential selling points, which can be easily tailored to specific positions.

MARY SMITH

Philadelphia, PA | 215.123.4567 | marysmithmarketing@gmail.com
www.linkedin.com/in/marysmithmarketing

October 20, 2016

Director of Human Resources
Google
9701 Wilshire Blvd., Suite 1000
Beverly Hills, CA 90212

Re: Position of Manager, Content Partnerships, YouTube and Google Play Transactional Partners

To whom it may concern:

In this present economy, customer service and new business development are key components that are vital to successful campaigns. With a track record of engaging internal teams and external constituents to embrace the corporate mission and drive growth initiatives, I am a results-oriented leader who can clearly define your company and differentiate its value proposition. I have consistently returned millions of dollars in incremental revenue by leveraging unique opportunities and developing long-term strategic partnerships and penetrating new business verticals, with company product and service offerings. In addition, I transformed a significant loss into an income machine. I define challenges and seek solutions that meet and exceed goals, delivering stellar results for win-win opportunities. Aside from providing excellent customer service on day-to-day partnership activities, I also focus on growth activities by developing and recommending business strategies.

For the past twenty plus years, I have worked in the entertainment and media industries with high profile partnerships, as well as other fields and have cultivated strong deeply rooted strategic relationships with key partners in order to drive objectives and execute initiatives across cross-functional teams. My passion lies in facing the daily challenges of a fast-paced, continuously changing environment, where I am put to the test to resolve conflicts while being accountable. Not only do I challenge thoughts and ideas, but I contribute to cutting-edge ways of thinking about, creating, and executing ideas while juggling multiple priorities. My prior experiences include digital entertainment, movie studios, television broadcast/cable networks, advertising agencies, and digital platform. In addition, I have negotiated contracts and other legal documents with attorneys to meet tight deadlines and have made presentations about products and programs with analytics and models.

Examples of some selected career accomplishments include:

- Negotiated alliance with ABC Company to promote company's offerings when it was a new entity, securing revenue of $32 million within two years.
- Saved $600,000 on shipping costs through development of promotional website that streamlined access to catalogue companywide, transforming money loss into revenue generator.
- Drove small business clients to e-commerce intranet site by removing minimum order amounts, potentially reducing administrative costs by 55%.

I am focused on being a change agent and influencing others to support the mission. If you are seeking a Business Development Executive and Manager of Content Partnerships with the experience, insight, and vision to secure a new, viable future for your company, I would welcome the opportunity to further discuss my qualifications. Thank you for your consideration, and I look forward to hearing from you soon, as I am extremely interested in this position and know I would be an asset to Google.

Sincerely,

Mary Smith

MARY SMITH

**Philadelphia, PA | 215.123.4567 | marysmithmarketing@gmail.com
www.linkedin.com/in/marysmithmarketing**

Date: 10/20/2016
Attention: Director of Human Resources, IMDb
Subject: Position of Principle Business Development

While reviewing job postings on LinkedIn, your listing for a principle business development position was of considerable interest to me.

Key Requirements for Principle Business Development	Qualifications of Mary Smith
1. 10-15 years relevant experience.	✓ More than 20 years of experience in the entertainment and media industries, as well as other fields.
2. Ability to form relationships, develop business plans, and close partnerships.	✓ Equipped with more than 20 years of existing industry relationships, plus an outstanding record of success in new business development. ✓ Experienced in developing business plans and writing RFPs. ✓ Skilled at forming strategic and close client partnerships.
3. Ability to prioritize resources, create a product road map, develop product specifications, and work with engineers.	✓ Able to prioritize resources and innovate when faced with limited resources. ✓ Implemented innovative product features on new packaging to drive sales. ✓ Liaison that communicates and works well with diverse individuals at all work levels.
4. Able to create a story and value proposition, develop presentations, and present in front of clients	✓ Strategically incisive, connected, and productive thought leader with an outstanding record of success in penetrating new markets and driving increased revenue through client presentations. ✓ Skilled negotiator and problem solver, partnering with clients and vendors to develop solid solutions and a win-win value proposition.
5. Willingness to work at all depths of issues with general manager/owner mentality and entrepreneurial drive	✓ Created and implemented cross-sell strategies. ✓ Expanded product marketing program. ✓ Self-driven, talented manger able to build a cohesive team to deliver results.

In this present economy, customer service and relationship development are key components that are vital to successful campaigns. With a track record of engaging internal teams and external constituents to embrace the corporate mission and drive growth initiatives, I am a leader who can clearly define your company and differentiate its value proposition. I have consistently returned millions of dollars in incremental revenue by leveraging unique opportunities and developing long-term, strategic partnerships, even transforming a loss into an income machine. I define challenges and seek solutions that meet and exceed goals, delivering stellar results.

Examples of my career accomplishments include:

- Negotiated alliance with ABC Company while at Sony Pictures Entertainment to promote the company's offerings when it was a new entity, securing revenue of $32 million within two years.
- Saved $600,000 on shipping costs through development of promotional website that streamlined access to the catalog company-wide, transforming money loss into revenue generator.
- Drove small business clients to e-commerce intranet site by removing minimum order amounts, potentially reducing administrative costs by 55 percent.

I am focused on being a change agent and influencing others to support the mission. If you are seeking a business development executive with the experience, insight, and vision to secure a new, viable future for your company, I would welcome the opportunity to further discuss my qualifications. Thank you for your consideration, and I look forward to speaking with you.

Best,

Mary Smith

Let's Move Overseas

Use this guide to prepare you and those around you for a move overseas.

Moving Abroad Alone?

If you are a job seeker looking for greater opportunities in a foreign country without the responsibilities of a spouse or family, your physical move will probably be straightforward. However, there are still some things you need to put into place to set yourself up for success:

- **Friends and Family**
  - Do they have any objections to you leaving? Are they justified? What can you do to alleviate their fears?
  - Create a Facebook page or blog to keep everyone abreast of your adventures.
  - Make a list of phone or Skype numbers for your core group for moments when you need to connect with home.
- **Banking and Money**
  - Keep at least one bank account open in the United States. This will be helpful when you return for visits or move back at the end of your sojourn.
  - Calculate your finances and make sure you have enough money to begin life in a new locale.
  - Find out what documents you will need to open a bank account in your new country. Gather them into a file, either paper or electronic.
  - Organize power of attorney for someone within your immediate circle in the United States, just in case anything needs to be taken care of financially or otherwise.
- **Housing**
  - Do you own your own home? Deciding whether you will rent or sell is of utmost importance because leaving your home empty while you're abroad has insurance implications.
  - Do you want to store most of your belongings or will you take the opportunity to declutter and have a yard sale?
  - Try to secure housing in your new locale before leaving the United States. This will make your transition easier.

- **Language Skills**
    - You might want to take a conversational language course. Learning basic phrases will assist in your integration, even if you will be working primarily in English.
- **Medical and Health**
    - Look at what healthcare plans are being offered either by the country or your employer. Pay attention to any costs associated with supplementing your plan.
    - Verify if any vaccinations are required to enter your new country, as well as any health risks associated (for example, travelers to Ghana are required to have yellow fever vaccinations).
    - Ask your healthcare professional in the United States if you have any pre-existing conditions that will make it difficult to live in your chosen new country, and what plans you will need to put in place.
- **Driver's License**
    - Renew your stateside license for at least one year. Some countries will allow you to drive with your U.S. license.
    - Find out if you'll need an international driver's license, and if you qualify for it.
- **Pets**
    - Can you legally import your pet? What are the procedures to do so? Will you be able to bring it back when you're ready to move back to the United States?
    - Is your pet healthy enough to transport? Some countries require you to have a certificate from a USDA veterinarian; check this website for one in your state: www.aphis.usda.gov/animal_health/area_offices.
    - Will it be too costly for you to import your pet? What will you do if you cannot?

Moving Abroad With a Partner?

When moving with a partner, everything involved with moving alone is still applicable to you; you're simply fortunate enough to be able to share the journey with another person. A *trailing spouse* is the term that identifies someone who moves with a partner. What do you do when your partner is reluctant? How can you persuade your partner to make your dreams his or her dreams? Here are a few things that could help:

- **Creating the "WE" in Your Decision**
    - This is a huge decision that deserves input from the one with whom you share your life. Open the communication lines early in the process and keep them open.

- Spend some time researching together and separately. Don't just look up information; check out forums in which you can gather real-time information on your new potential country of residence.
- Remember that there are two of you in this decision. This is paramount.
- **Finances and Budgets**
  - The number one reason couples fight is money. Make sure you are on the same page when it comes to spending.
  - Do both of you have access to bank accounts, both stateside and overseas?
  - Have at least three months of expenses set aside as a reserve. This will give you a sense of financial security, which can help calm fears.
- **Should We Have a Test Drive?**
  - Before selling all your earthly possessions and flying to your new locale, consider having an end date in mind. Forever is a scary concept for some people, and your spouse might fall into this group. Give your new locale a no-strings-attached trial for a specific period of time.
- **To Work or Not to Work?**
  - This might be your spouse's opportunity of a lifetime. Maybe she has always wanted to write a book, learn to paint, or volunteer for an NGO. All of these could be packaged as her dream come true.
  - Within relocation packages, the norm is to include a transition allowance for trailing spouses. These services include resume writing, career counselling, recruiting assistance, or providing actual employment. Make sure you verify with the employer once an offer is made that this is included.
  - For the entrepreneurial spouses, the ability to start a retail business, an English tutoring service, or even a freelance Internet company may help ensures their dreams are realized as well.

Moving Abroad With Children?

Depending on the age of your children, involving them early in the process of moving internationally is definitely the key to getting buy-in. Each age group offers its own set of challenges; here's a list of tips and tricks on how to involve them.

Toddlers and Pre-Schoolers

- **Explaining the New**
  - Talk openly about the new country, new house, and new friends with your children. Although they are too young to grasp everything that will occur, they will be much more willing to accept what is explained at their level.

- **Routine**
  - The primary item you need to address in this age group is routine. Keeping consistency in their lives will ensure that there is not a marked difference in their behavior.

School-Aged

- **Researching the Country**
  - Get a globe or map, put it in the child's room, and map out where you will be going. School-age children are visual and concrete.
  - Create a fun and exciting game out of learning new items about your destination.
  - Contact the school your child is attending and involve the class in learning about the country you are going to move to.
- **Schooling**
  - When choosing a school, remember to take the child's interest into account. As in the United States, some schools abroad stress sports, while others focus on the arts.
  - Connect the child with the school you have chosen as soon as possible (maybe through chat or Facebook).
- **Language**
  - Children learn languages quickly, but getting a head start could help with the initial barriers of not knowing the language.
  - Hire a language tutor or register them in classes.
- **Friends Back Home**
  - Until they create a new peer group, they need to maintain their present friend group. Create a way for them to exchange conversations, such as Facebook, chats, or emails.
- **Allow Them to Communicate Their Feelings**
  - Keep the lines of communication open at all times. Always give honest answers, even if you have none to give.
  - Ask them to create a list of what they will miss the most, and check to see if these things will be available in the new country.
  - Involve them in deciding what to put in storage and what to bring with you.
  - Recognize that the process is different for each child. Just be there for them.

Teenagers

- **Discussion Table**
  - Although the decision to go does not lie with your teens, including them in the discussions from day one will create a sense of participation. This is the first step of buy-in.
- **Social Networks**
  - Friends are an important part of their life. The more you include and try to garner the assistance of their peer group in helping with the transition, the easier it will be.
  - Encourage your teenagers to have friends help them pack or organize a going away party.
  - Make sure your teenagers connect virtually with friends. They will want to stay in regular contact with everyone they know, at least at the beginning.
- **Schooling**
  - Research the schools together. Knowing what your children are looking for in a school and weighing the options is paramount.
  - Try to find schools with the same curriculum as their current school.
  - Visit the schools before making a final decision, if this is in your budget. This is a great way to ensure the school will be a good fit.
- **Extracurricular Activities**
  - Sports teams, music lessons, church youth groups, and so forth are all activities that could be a great segue into creating excitement in your teens for the move. Imagine a soccer player getting the opportunity to attend a summer camp at a European club, or a budding ballet dancer joining a renowned dance school. These are opportunities that might not be available to teenagers in the United States and may entice your teenagers into an easier transition.
- **Leaving Your Teenager Behind**
  - Sometimes due to schooling issues, a child must be left behind. Include your child in this decision. There may be alternatives, such as distance learning, that your child could make use of, rather than staying behind at a boarding school or living with family or friends.

A Resource Guide for
Find Your Fit

General Career Books

- Lou Adler, *The Essential Guide for Hiring & Getting Hired* (Workbench Media, 2013).
- Richard N. Bolles, *What Color Is Your Parachute? 2016* (New York: Ten Speed Press, 2016).
- Debra A. MacDougall and Elisabeth H. Sanders-Park, *6 Reasons You'll Get the Job* (New York: Prentice Hall Press, 2010).
- Barbara Sher and Annie Gottlieb, *Wishcraft: How to Get What You Really Want* (New York: Ballantine Books, 2004).

General Career Websites

There are many useful resources online for job seekers and career changers. Here are some of our all-time favorites:

- O*NET OnLine is an occupational website managed by the U.S. Department of Labor. In addition to listing the job requirements, interests, and skills for a huge range of job titles, O*NET provides data about the projected demand in coming years. Salary information is also available both nationally and broken down to the state level. (www.onetonline.org)
- The *Occupational Outlook Handbook* is a resource from the U.S. Department of Labor that includes a large quantity of information on a variety of different industries and career fields, including work environment, education, pay, and job outlook information (www.bls.gov/ooh).
- Live Career is the new home for the Quintessential Career website archives. It holds a vast array of how-to information on topics such as informational interviewing, job shadowing, and job search abroad (www.livecareer.com).

- Dick Bolles's *What Color Is Your Parachute* website, Job Hunter's Bible, has a wealth of information for job seekers and career changers (www.jobhuntersbible.com).
- JT O'Donnell's website, CareeRealism, has a wide range of information and articles on career topics (www.careerealism.com).

Industry and Professional Association Directories

Industry and professional associations are key resources for networking and industry research. Here are two directories to help you find appropriate associations:

- Industry Week (www.industryweek.com/associations)
- Directory of Associations (www.directoryofassociations.com)

International Resources

If you are interested in working abroad, here is a list of some of the most helpful resources:

- GoAbroad.com has information about studing, volunteering, teaching, and interning abroad (www.goabroad.com)
- Goinglobal has information about international careers (www.goinglobal.com)
- Quintessential careers has job and career resources for global job seekers (www.livecareer.com/quintessential/global-jobseekers)
- Transitions Abroad has resources for people who want to work, live, volunteer, or study abroad (www.transitionsabroad.com)
- Expat.com and Expat Exchange are two websites containing information for expats written by expats (www.expat.com and www.expatexchange.com)
- Numbeo is a free online database reporting on worldwide cost of living indicators (www.numbeo.com/cost-of-living)
- Robert Walters Global Salary Survey 2016 (17th edition)
- *The World Factbook* is compiled by the CIA and includes information to help you assess the safety of various locations

Interviewing

Additional reading or resources related to interviewing:

- Paul Bailo, *The Essential Digital Interview Handbook: Lights, Camera, Interview: Tips for Skype, Google Hangout, GoToMeeting, and More* (Pompton Plains, NJ: Career Press, 2014).
- Robin Ryan, *60 Seconds and You're Hired* (New York: Penguin, 2016).
- Glassdoor provides common questions that are asked at interviews by specific companies (www.glassdoor.com/Interview/index.htm).

Job Listings

While you shouldn't spend all your time looking for jobs online, here are some of the better job search engines to check:

- Indeed and SimplyHired are two large aggregators of online postings from various job boards, including some large corporate websites. Be aware that many jobs posted to individual company sites may not be found here. (www.indeed .com and www.simplyhired.com).
- LinkUp is a job search engine that provides listings from many corporations that may not be found elsewhere (www.linkup.com).
- USAJOBS is the official employment website of the federal government (www .usajobs.gov).
- US.jobs is sponsored by the National Labor Exchange and allows employers to post jobs at reasonable rates. It also includes jobs from state sponsored employment sites (http://us.jobs).
- FlexJobs is niche job bank for part-time, virtual, freelance, and flexible jobs (www.flexjobs.com).
- Freelance.com, Guru, and Upwork are three places to look for freelance and contract work (www.freelance.com, www.guru.com, and www.upwork.com).
- ZipRecruiter will send Tweets and emails about jobs in various categories to those who sign up (www.ziprecruiter.com).

Military

Resources specific to ex-military job seekers and career changers:

- O*NET OnLine's Military Crosswalk Search provides a link between military and civilian skills (www.onetonline.org/crosswalk/MOC).
- The Veteran's Employment Center provides resources for veterans and their families (www.vets.gov/employment).
- LiveCareer has career, job, and entrepreneurial tools for veterans (www .livecareer.com/quintessential/former-military).

Networking

Additional reading and resources on networking:

- Dorie Clark, *Stand Out Networking: A Simple and Authentic Way to Meet People on Your Own Terms* (New York: Portfolio, 2015).
- Katherine Moody, *How to Have a Great Networking Conversation on the Phone* (2010).
- Devora Zack, *Networking for People Who Hate Networking: A Field Guide for Introverts, the Overwhelmed, and the Underconnected* (San Francisco, Berrett-Koehler, 2010).

Personality Type

If you are interested in reading more about how personality links with career issues, here are some books that explain it well:

- Paul D. Tieger and Barbara Barron-Tieger, *Do What You Are: Discover the Perfect Career for You Through the Secrets of Personality Type*, 2nd ed. (New York: Little, Brown, 2014).
- Shoya Zichy with Ann Bidou, *Career Match: Connecting Who You Are With What You Love to Do* (New York: AMACOM, 2007).
- Donna Dunning, *What's Your Type of Career? Find Your Perfect Career by Using Your Personality Type*, 2nd ed. (Boston: Nicholas Brealey, 2010).

Personality Type Websites:

- The Personality Page provides detailed information about the Myers-Briggs Type Indicator and a short survey that approximates your personality type (www.personalitypage.com).
- Visit the Myers-Briggs Type Indicator website to take an official assessment of your Myers-Briggs Type (www.mbtionline.com).
- The Self-Directed Search website uses Holland Codes to identify your theme code and links them to potential career fields (www.self-directed-search.com).
- You can get more information about the DiSC behavioral profile on its official website (www.discprofile.com/what-is-disc/overview).

Pre-Employment Assessments

These are good resources for information on pre-employment assessments and your rights:

- The U.S. Equal Employment Opportunity Commission has information about hiring procedures (www.eeoc.gov/policy/docs/factemployment_procedures.html).
- Visit the U.S. Citizenship and Immigration Services website to verify your eligibility to work in the United States (www.uscis.gov/mye-verify/self-check).
- The Work Number is an employment verification site used by many employers. You can check the accuracy of your information on the site (www.theworknumber.com/employees).

Productivity Tools

Some productivity tools that can help you in your job search:

- JibberJobber is a website that provides a complete system for managing your job search, resumes, and networking information (www.jibberjobber.com).
- Evernote is a free online tool you can use to store notes, articles, and links in a searchable format (www.evernote.com).
- Hootsuite is a social media dashboard you can use to efficiently manage your Twitter, LinkedIn, and Facebook posts (www.hootsuite.com).

Professional Development

Sites that provide courses you can take online at no or low cost:

- www.corsera.org
- www.edx.org
- www.lynda.com
- www.udemy.com
- www.udacity.com
- www.geteducated.com

For information on how to find good volunteer opportunities, visit:

- www.volunteermatch.org
- www.idealist.org
- Local volunteer sites

Resources for converting work experience into college credit:

- The Council for Adult and Experiential Learning (www.cael.org)
- College-Level Examination Program (https://clep.collegeboard.org).

Resumes

For more information on resume writing and identifying keywords for your resume:

- Wendy Enelow and Louise Kursmark, *Modernize Your Resume (Modernize Your Career)* (Coleman Falls, VA: Emerald Career Publishing, 2016).
- Susan Whitcomb, *Resume Magic: Trade Secrets of a Professional Resume Writer,* 4th ed. (Indianapolis: Jist Works, 2010).

Keyword Analyzers:

- Jobscan compares your resume to a job description to determine if you have the right keywords in your resume for that position (www.jobscan.co).
- Use Tagul and Wordle to help you identify keywords in your resume by creating a word cloud from its text (http://tagul.com and www.wordle.net).

Salary Negotiation

Additional resources on salary negotiation and good sources for salary information:

- Jack Chapman, *Negotiating Your Salary: How to Make $1000 a Minute* (2011).
- Bureau of Labor Statistics (www.bls.gov/audience/jobseekers.htm).
- Salary.com
- www.payscale.com
- www.glassdoor.com

Self-Employment

If you are considering self-employment, here are a few resources:

- The U.S. Small Business Administration is an independent agency of the federal government. It helps Americans start, build, and grow businesses through an extensive network of field offices and partnerships with public and private organizations (www.sba.gov).
- SCORE is a nonprofit association dedicated to helping small businesses get off the ground, grow, and achieve their goals through education and mentorship. SCORE helps volunteer businesspeople mentor aspiring business owners (www.score.org).
- Michael Masterson, *The Reluctant Entrepreneur: Turning Dreams Into Profits* (New York: John Wiley & Sons, 2012).

Skills and Strengths

For additional resources on identifying your skills and strengths:

- The O*NET Skills Search portal is a free tool that can help you understand what skills are best suited to which careers (www.onetonline.org/skills).
- *StrengthsFinder 2.0* is the new version of the book, *Now, Discover Your Strengths*. It is a comprehensive guide to hundreds of different strengths that an individual can possess (http://strengths.gallup.com).
- MindTools is a comprehensive career skills website that includes many resources about different skills, as well as a free career skills newsletter. Its comprehensive 15-question assessment evaluates your skill set in five different areas (www.mindtools.com).
- The MAPP career assessment is a 15-minute test that matches you with careers that fit your skills and strengths profile. In addition, the MAPP website also features a variety of resources to help get you started on your career planning journey (www.assessment.com).
- VIA Survey of Character Strengths is a 15-minute self-assessment that is based on Martin Seligman's research on happiness (www.viacharacter.org/www/Character-Strengths-Survey).
- The World of Work Map is an ACT resource that links interests with various career fields (www.act.org/content/act/en/education-and-career-planning.html).

Social Media and Branding

Additional resources and reading on social media and personal branding:

- Joshua Waldman. *Job Searching With Social Media For Dummies.* (Hoboken, NJ: John Wiley & Sons, 2013).

- Use Klout to measure the strength of your personal brand (http://klout.com).
- About.me allows you to create a personal website for free (http://about.me).

Target Companies

Some good resources for identifying target companies:

- The ReferenceUSA database is a listing of companies by SIC code. It is available through most public libraries with a library card (http://resource .referenceusa.com)
- ZoomInfo is a gold mine for job seekers, networkers, and those looking for information on companies in their region. You can sign up for the Community Edition for free, although you have to share your Outlook contacts to gain access to this site (www.zoominfo.com).

Workplace Culture

Good resources for helping you research the corporate culture of a potential employer:

- Visit Glassdoor to read reviews about company culture from current and former employees (www.glassdoor.com).
- Best Places to Work:
  - *Fortune*'s 100 Best Companies to Work For
  - www.greatplacetowork.net
  - Glassdoor's list of Best Places to Work
  - LinkedIn's North America's 100 Most InDemand Employers
- On SlideShare you can search by company name or use the culture code with the company name to find a presentation on the company (www.slideshare.net).
- The Muse is an online career website that offers a behind-the-scenes look at companies, including employee videos (www.themuse.com).
- CareerBliss is an online career community that offers data on job satisfaction, pay, and employee happiness, as well as a national job board. You can read company comments, reviews, and culture ratings (www.careerbliss.com).
- Vault is a career website that ranks companies, provides extensive information, and offers ratings and reviews (www.vault.com).
- DiversityInc lists the top 50 companies for diversity in a variety of categories (www.diversityinc.com).
- The Occupational Safety and Health Administration maintans a federal database of safety violations by company (www.osha.gov).

Publications by Our Contributors

- Vivian H. Blade, *FuelForward: Discover Proven Practices to Fuel Your Career Forward* (Parkerhouse Publishing, 2015).

- Vivian H. Blade, *FuelForward Mentoring Guide: Getting the Most From Your Mentor* (2015).
- Michelle Carroll and Alan De Back, "Marketing Your Career Brand," *TD at Work* (Alexandria, VA: ATD Press, 2014).
- Alan De Back, *Get Hired in a Tough Market* (New York: McGraw Hill. 2009).
- Marilyn Feldstein, "Defining and Leveraging Your Professional Value," *Infoline* (Alexandria, VA: ASTD Press, 2013).
- David Hosmer, "The Manager's Guide to Employee Development," *TD at Work* (Alexandria, VA: ATD Press, 2015).
- Susan Kaiden, "Keeping Your Career on Track," *TD at Work* (Alexandria, VA: ATD Press, 2015).
- Laura Labovich and Miriam Salpeter, *100 Conversations for Career Success: Learn to Network, Cold-Call and Tweet Your Way to Your Dream Job* (New York: LearningExpress, 2013).
- Sheila Margolis, *Job Seeker Manual: A Step-by-Step Guide for Using Culture Fit to Find the Right Workplace for You* (Atlanta: Workplace Culture Institute, 2016).
- Nicole Miller and Don Skipper, *Have Career . . . Will Travel: A Guide for Military Spouses Dealing With Relocations, Employment Interruptions and Job Search.*

References

AARP. 2016. "Get Paid and Stay Engaged in Retirement." Career Change—Recareering, May 11. www.aarp.org/work/working-after-retirement/info-2016/get-paid-working-in-retirement.html?.

About Careers. 2016. "Types of Pre-Employment Tests." About Careers, March 9. http://jobsearch.about.com/od/careertests/a/employmenttests.htm.

Adler, L. 2013. *The Essential Guide for Hiring & Getting Hired.* Workbench Media.

ASHA (American Speech-Language-Hearing Association). 2013. "Professional Certification vs. Certificate Program." ASHA, March 20. www.asha.org/CE/CEUs/Professional-Certification-vs-Certificate-Program.

Bailo, P.J. 2014. *The Essential Digital Interview Handbook: Lights, Camera, Interview: Tips for Skype, Google Hangout, GoToMeeting, and More.* Pompton Plains, NJ: Career Press.

Benko, C. 2010. "How the Corporate Ladder Became the Corporate Lattice." *Harvard Business Review,* November 4.

Bentley University. 2014. "The Millennial Mind Goes to Work: How Millennial Preferences Will Shape the Future of the Modern Workplace." A Bentley University-Commissioned Survey, October. www.bentley.edu/newsroom/latest-headlines/mind-of-millennial.

Berger, J. 1972. *Ways of Seeing.* New York: Penguin.

Bilazarian, L. 2015. "Employee Referrals: The 8 Most Important Studies." Teamable Blog, March 13. https://teamable.com/8-most-important-studies-on-employee-referals.

Blade, V.H. 2015a. *FuelForward Mentoring Guide: Getting the Most from Your Mentor.*

Blade, V.H. 2015b. *FuelForward: Discover Proven Practices to Fuel Your Career Forward.* Parkerhouse Publishing.

Bodell, L. 2014. "Soft Skills for the Future." TD.org, March 8. www.td.org/Publications/ Newsletters/Global-HRD-Newsletter-Middle-East/Soft-Skills-for-the-Future.

Bolles, R.N. 2016. *What Color Is Your Parachute? 2016*. New York: Ten Speed Press.

Buckingham, M., and D.O. Clifton. 2001. *Now, Discover Your Strengths*. New York: The Free Press.

Budden, R. 2014. "How Does Your Expat Package Stack Up?" BBC, May 8. www.bbc. com/capital/story/20140507-expat-smarts-get-a-good-package.

Bureau of Labor Statistics. 2015. "Employment Projections, 2014-24." U.S. Department of Labor, December 8. www.bls.gov/news.release/pdf/ecopro.pdf.

Byron, K., and S. Mitchell. 2002. *Loving What Is: Four Questions That Can Change Your Life*. New York: Harmony Books

C., V. 2014. "How to Get Your Foot in the Door of Any Company." Experience.com, November 12. www.experience.com/entry-level-jobs/news/how-to-get-your-foot-in-the-door-of-any-company.

Cajun, K. 2015. *Finding Your Niche: The World's Most Profitable Niches Exposed!*

Chamorro-Premuzic, T. 2015. "Ace the Assessment." *Harvard Business Review*, July-August.

Chapman, J. 2011. *Negotiating Your Salary: How to Make $1,000 a Minute*.

Chatterjee, C. 2015. "Interview Test Prep: 6 Common Personality Assessments—and How Employers Use Them." *Forbes*, May 28. www.forbes.com/sites/learnvest/2015/05/28/ interview-test-prep-6-common-personality-assessments-and-how-employers-use-them/#31e2e1356c21.

Clark, D. 2015a. *Stand Out Networking: A Simple and Authentic Way to Meet People on Your Own Terms*. New York: Portfolio.

Clark, D. 2015b. *Standout: How to Find Your Breakthrough Idea and Build a Following Around It*. New York: Portfolio.

Clarke, P. 2012. "Six Rules of Expat Pay Packages in the Middle East." eFinancial Careers, December 10. http://news.efinancialcareers.com/gulf-en/129366/six-things-to-push-for-in-expat-packages-in-the-middle-east.

Clifton, D.O., E. Anderson, and L. Screiner. 2002. *Strengths Quest*. New York: Gallup Press.

Covey, S.R. 2012. *The 4 Disciplines of Execution: The Secret to Getting Things Done, on Time, With Excellence*. Franklin Covey on Brilliance Audio.

Criteria Pre-Employment Testing. 2016. "What Job Candidates Should Know About Employment Tests." Criteria Pre-Employment Testing. www.criteriacorp.com/ resources/candidates.php.

Daum, K. 2014. "8 Things Really Great Problem Solvers Do." Inc.com, September 3.

DeZube, D. nd. "What's Inside an International Compensation Package?" Monster.com. www.monster.com/career-advice/article/international-compensation.

DiGiacomo, R. n.d. "Advancing Your Career with Social Network Sites." Monster.com, www.monster.com/career-advice/article/advancing-your-career-with-social-network-sites-hot-jobs.

Doyle, A. 2016. "How to Write a Value Proposition Letter." About Careers, March 31. http://jobsearch.about.com/od/valueproposition/fl/how-to-write-a-value-proposition-letter.htm.

Entrepreneur. 2016. "Home Based Business." Small Business Encyclopedia. www.entrepreneur.com/encyclopedia/home-based-business.

Feldman, J., and K. Mulle. 2007. *Put Emotional Intelligence to Work: Equip Yourself for Success.* Alexandria, VA: ASTD Press.

George. 2015. "2015 Social Media Demographics for Marketers." We Are Social Media, June 4. http://wersm.com/2015-social-media-demographics-for-marketers.

Gerber, M. 2004. *The eMyth Revisited: Why Most Small Businesses Don't Work and What to Do About It.* New York: HarperCollins.

Green, A. 2014. "How to Get a Job When You Don't Have Much Experience: Eight Job-Search Tips to Combat Your Professional Greenness." *U.S. News & World Report,* May 12.

Greenhaus, J., G. Callanan, and V.M. Godshalk. 2010. *Career Management,* 4th ed. Thousand Oaks, CA: Sage Publications.

Haden, J. 2013. "9 Habits of People Who Build Extraordinary Relationships." Inc.com, April 3.

Hansen, K. n.d. "Is the Hidden Job Market a Myth? A Quintessential Careers Investigative Report of the Unpublicized Job Market." Quintessential. www.livecareer.com/quintessential/hidden-job-market-myth.

Hansen, K. n.d. "Research Companies and Careers Through Job Shadowing." Quintessential. www.livecareer.com/quintessential/job-shadowing.

Hill, N. 2005. *Think and Grow Rich.* New York: Penguin.

Holland, J.L. 1973. *Making Vocational Choices: A Theory of Careers.* Englewood Cliffs, NJ: Prentice-Hall.

Hosmer, D. 2015a. "The Manager's Guide to Employee Development." *TD at Work.* Alexandria, VA: ATD Press.

Hosmer, D. 2015b. "Why Employee Development is a Necessity." Career Development Blog, April 25. www.td.org/Publications/Blogs/Career-Development-Blog/2015/08/Employee-Development-Is-a-Necessity-Not-An-Option.

Hovind, M. 2012. "Frequently Asked Questions (FAQ)." Job Bait. http://jobbait.com/a/faq.htm.

Hoyt, K.B. 2005. *Career Education: History and Future.* Broken Arrow, OK: National Career Development Association.

Institute of Psychometric Coaching (IPC). n.d. "Personality Test Guide." IPC. www.psychometricinstitute.com.au/Psychometric-Test-Guide/Personality-Test-guide.html.

Jeffers, S. 2006. *Feel the Fear and Do It Anyway: Dynamic Techniques for Turning Fear, Indecision, and Anger Into Power, Action, and Love.* New York: Random House.

Jobvite. 2012. "Ultimate Onboarding Guide." Jobvite.com. http://theundercoverrecruiter.com/infographic-employee-referrals-hire.

Jobvite. 2015a. *Job Seeker Nation Study: Inside the Mind of the Modern Job Seeker.* San Mateo, CA: Jobvite. www.careerthoughtleaders.com/resources/Pictures/CareerJam15/jobvite_jobseeker_nation_2015.pdf.

Jobvite. 2015b. "The Jobvite Recruiter Nation Survey 2015." Jobvite.com, September. www.jobvite.com/wp-content/uploads/2015/09/jobvite_recruiter_nation_2015.pdf.

Kaiden, S. 2015. "Keeping Your Career on Track." *TD at Work.* Alexandria, VA: ATD Press.

Kaye, B., and J.W. Giulioni. 2016. "Consider the Career Climbing Wall." ATD Career Development Blog, March 21. www.td.org/Publications/Blogs/Career-Development-Blog/2016/03/Consider-the-Career-Climbing-Wall.

Lees, J. 2011. "Crack the Hidden Job Market." *Harvard Business Review,* August 5. https://hbr.org/2011/08/crack-the-hidden-job-market.

Levinson, M. 2012. "5 Insider Secrets for Beating Applicant Tracking Systems." CIO, March 1. www.cio.com/article/2398753/careers-staffing/5-insider-secrets-for-beating-applicant-tracking-systems.html.

Lewis, K.R. 2014. "How to Advance When There Is No Career Ladder." Fortune.com, November 5.

Lipman, V. 2014. "Top Twitter Trends: What Countries Are Most Active? Who's Most Popular?" Forbes.com, May 24. www.forbes.com/sites/victorlipman/2014/05/24/top-twitter-trends-what-countries-are-most-active-whos-most-popular/#44544ecf76cb.

Margolis, S. n.d. "Organizational Priorities—Strategic and Universal." Core Culture and Five Ps. http://sheilamargolis.com/core-culture-and-five-ps/the-five-ps-and-organizational-alignment/priorities.

Margolis, S. 2010. *Building a Culture of Distinction: Facilitator Guide for Defining Organizational Culture and Managing Change.* Atlanta: Workplace Culture Institute.

Margolis, S. 2016. *Job Seeker Manual: A Step-by-Step Guide for Using Culture Fit to Find the Right Workplace for You.* Atlanta: Workplace Culture Institute.

Maslow, A. 1943. *A Theory of Human Motivation.* Public Domain.

McChesney, C., S. Covey, and J. Huling. 2012. T*he 4 Disciplines of Execution: Achieving Your Wildly Important Goals.* New York: Free Press.

Melecchi, T. 2015. "The Art of Building Relationships," TD.org, March 10.

Miller, H.R. 2016. "Starting a Business While Still in College." *Millennial Magazine,* January 20.

Monteiro, C. 2015. "Infographic: Who's Really Using Facebook, Twitter, Pinterest, Tumblr and Instagram in 2015." *Adweek,* January 12. www.adweek.com/news/advertising-branding/new-social-stratosphere-who-using-facebook-twitter-pinterest-tumblr-and-instagram-2015-and-beyond-1622.

Moody, K. 2010. *How to Have a Great Networking Conversation on the Phone.*

Morgan, D. 2009. "Five First Steps to Finding a Job Abroad." Forbes.com, September 25. www.forbes.com/2009/09/25/jobs-abroad-advice-leadership-careers-employment.html.

Morgan, H. 2015. "7 Things You Should Know About Employee Referrals." On Careers Blog, October 7. U.S. New & World Report. http://money.usnews.com/money/blogs/outside-voices-careers/2015/10/07/7-things-you-should-know-about-employee-referrals.

Oyer, P., and S. Schaefer. 2010. "Personnel Economics: Hiring and Incentives." Abstract. *The Handbook of Labor Economics,* vol. 4, April 20. https://faculty-gsb.stanford.edu/oyer/wp/hire.pdf.

Peggs, M. 2015. "Applicant Tracking Systems Solved." Peggs Blog, January 14. www.michaelpeggs.com/applicant-tracking-systems-solved.

Peters, T. 1997. "The Brand Called You." Fast Company, August 31. www.fastcompany.com/28905/brand-called-you.

Prueter, B. 2014. "Massive Open Online Courses (MOOCS)." Postsecondary National Policy Institute, June 1. www.newamerica.org/postsecondary-national-policy-institute/massive-open-online-courses-moocs.

Rad, M.R. 2014. "10 Characteristics of Good Problem Solvers." HuffingtonPost.com, January 24.

Rampton, J. 2014. "5 Personality Traits of an Entrepreneur." Forbes.com, April 14. www.forbes.com/sites/johnrampton/2014/04/14/5-personality-traits-of-an-entrepreneur.

Rampton, J. 2016. "10 Qualities of People With High Emotional Intelligence." *Inc.,* January 14. www.inc.com/john-rampton/10-qualities-of-people-with-high-emotional-intelligence.html.

Rath, T. 2007. *Strengths Finder 2.0.* Washington, DC: Gallup Press.

Resume Genius. 2014. "Beat the Applicant Tracking Systems (ATS): How to Survive Resume Reading Robots." ResumeGenius.com, September 29. https://resumegenius.com/blog/applicant-tracking-systems-resume-keyword-help.

Robbins, S., and T. Judge. 2016. *Essentials of Organizational Behavior.* Sage Publications.

Robert Walters. 2016. "Salary Survey 2016." Robert Walters. www.robertwalters.com.my/content/dam/salary-survey-2016.pdf.

Samuel, M. 2012. *Making Yourself Indispensable: The Power of Personal Accountability.* New York: Portfolio.

Sanger, D. 1980. "It Takes More Than a Resume." *New York Times,* October 12.

Santiago, J. 2015. "Why Studying Abroad Could Help You Get Hired." World Economic Forum, November 11. www.weforum.org/agenda/2015/11/study-abroad-get-hired?.

Scott, M. 2016. "15 Important Questions to Ask Before Accepting a Job Abroad." Transitions Abroad, June. www.transitionsabroad.com/listings/work/articles/ask-questions-when-taking-jobs-abroad.shtml.

Shannon, E. 2012. "Your Value Proposition Letter." Just Jobs Academy, May 30. http://academy.justjobs.com/the-value-proposition-letter.

SilkRoad Technology. 2015. *Top Sources of Hire 2015: The Definitive Report on Talent Acquisition Strategies.* SilkRoad Technologies, http://hr1.silkroad.com/top-sources-of-hire.

Smith, A. 2015. "Target Will Pay $2.8 Million Over Employment Tests." Legal Issues, August 25. Society for Human Resource Management. www.shrm.org/legalissues/federalresources/pages/target-employment-tests.aspx#sthash.Lui2lN9q.dpuf.

Smith, C. 2016. "How Many People Use 1000+ of the Top Social Media, Apps, and Digital Services?" DMR, June 11. http://expandedramblings.com/index.php/resource-how-many-people-use-the-top-social-media.

Sravani. 2015. "Best 17 Ways on How to Recruit Using Pinterest." WiseStep, February 22. http://content.wisestep.com/best-ways-on-how-to-recruit-using-pinterest.

Stack, L. 2015. "Triaging Time: Four Timewasters That May Not Occur to You," The Productivity Pro, February 23.

Statista. 2016. "Numbers of LinkedIn Members From 1st Quarter 2009 to 1st Quarter 2016 (in Millions)." Statista: The Statistics Portal. www.statista.com/statistics/274050/quarterly-numbers-of-linkedin-members.

Sullivan, J. 2012. "10 Compelling Numbers That Reveal the Power of Employee Referrals." ERE Media, May 7. www.eremedia.com/ere/10-compelling-numbers-that-reveal-the-power-of-employee-referrals.

Suttle, R. "Pros & Cons of Direct Mail Advertising." *Houston Chronicle*. http://smallbusiness.chron.com/pros-cons-direct-mail-advertising-1437.html.

Torpey, E., and D. Terrell. 2015. "Should I Get a Master's Degree?" Career Outlook, September. www.bls.gov/careeroutlook/2015/article/should-i-get-a-masters-degree.htm.

U.S. Department of State. n.d. "Learn About Your Destination." U.S. Passports & International Travel. http://travel.state.gov/content/passports/en/country.html.

U.S. Small Business Administration (SBA). n.d. "Self Employed & Independent Contractors." SBA. www.sba.gov/starting-business/how-start-business/business-types/self-employed-independent-contractors.

Wallace, W.T., and D. Creelman. 2015. "Leading People When They Know More Than You Do." *Harvard Business Review*, June 18.

Weber, L. 2015. "Today's Personality Tests Raise the Bar for Job Seekers." *The Wall Street Journal*, April 14.

Weiss, T. 2009. "When They Require Experience and You Have None." Forbes.com, June 10.

Zuckerberg, M. 2012. "Letter From Mark Zuckerberg." U.S. Securities and Exchange Commission, Form S-1 Registration Statement, Facebook, Inc. www.sec.gov/Archives/edgar/data/1326801/000119312512034517/d287954ds1.htm#toc287954_10.

About the Editor and Contributors

Sue Kaiden

Sue Kaiden is the manager for the Association for Talent Development's Career Development Community. Prior to joining ATD, Sue held executive and consulting roles in the healthcare, IT, and nonprofit sectors before founding her career coaching firm, CareerEdge. In addition, she started GetWorks, a job search support program for unemployed and underemployed people in suburban Philadelphia, which she ran as a volunteer for 11 years. Through this program and her coaching practice, Sue helped hundreds of people find meaningful work. Sue holds an MBA from Cornell University, a BS in business from Miami University (Ohio), and is a certified Myers-Briggs (MBTI) and Strong Interest Inventory practitioner.

Vivian Hairston Blade

As an executive coach, career coach, and leadership development trainer, Vivian Blade works with ambitious professionals and organizations to build leaders and develop excellence so they can achieve their vision of success. In 2009, Vivian founded Experts in Growth Leadership Consulting. Since then, she has worked with many global organizations, such as Johnson & Johnson, Proctor & Gamble, and GE, as well as individual professionals, to help them realize their full potential. She's seen professionals succeed as leaders—making a noticeable impact in their organizations and achieving their personal career goals. Vivian is the author of *FuelForward: Discover Proven Strategies to Fuel Your Career Forward*.

Alisa Cohn

Alisa Cohn is an executive coach who works with start-up founders, co-founders, CEOs, and executive teams. She is the executive coach for the "Runway" program at NYC Tech—an "accelerator" that focuses on supporting post-docs to commercialize their research and build companies. She is also on the Entrepreneurial Advisory Committee at Cornell University and is on the advisory boards of a number of startups. Alisa guest lectures at Harvard, Cornell, and Georgetown Universities, as well as in the Naval War College's accelerated leadership program. Alisa is a CPA and earned an MBA from Cornell University.

Alan De Back

Alan De Back is an independent career counselor and learning consultant located in the Metro D.C. area. He has more than 20 years' experience in career counseling and learning- and training-related functions. Alan also served as director of global learning for an Internet consulting firm and as manager of leadership development for a major aerospace corporation. Alan holds a bachelor's degree in psychology and history from the State University of New York at Geneseo, a master's degree in human resource development from Rochester Institute of Technology, and a graduate-level certificate in Industrial Labor Relations from Cornell University. He is the author of *Get Hired in a Tough Market* and the *TD at Work* issue "Marketing Your Career Brand."

Marilyn A. Feldstein

Marilyn Feldstein has more than 20 years' experience working in both corporate and nonprofit organizations, where she held management positions of increasing responsibility. She has contributed to the books *No-Nonsense Résumés*, *Expert Résumés for Baby Boomers*, *Directory of Professional Résumé Writers*, *Job Search Bloopers*, and *No-Nonsense Job Interviews*. Marilyn is a certified Job and Career Transition Coach and Professional in Human Resources, and has been certified in the Myers-Briggs Type Indicator. She has been a featured speaker on CBS and Clear Channel Radio, and is an adjunct professor in career management at Webster University Graduate School. She also has a master's degree from The Pennsylvania State University.

David Hosmer

David Hosmer has 26 years' experience in organization development, learning and development, and coaching as a manager, director, and consultant across a variety of industries. David is currently the director of talent management of the Specialty Diagnostics Group at Thermo Fisher Scientific. He is a graduate of the Harvard Graduate School of Education, MIT internal Leader to Leader, and the Harvard Kennedy School's Art and Practice of Leadership Development, and a lifetime associate member of the Career Thought Leaders Consortium. He has an EdM from Harvard University, and became a Certified Professional in Learning and Performance in 2011. David wrote the *TD at Work* issue "The Manager's Guide to Employee Development," as well as a number of other articles, including "Coaching With Questions" and "Mentoring Works," for the *Training Journal*.

Jean Juchnowicz

Jean Juchnowicz is the owner of Human Resources Simplified, a human resources consulting and training company. She also does career coaching, including resume writing services, bios, and profiles, as the owner of Career Advice Simplified. Jean received recognition as a Senior Professional in Human Resources, is a Certified Business Manager, a Senior Certified Professional, and a Certified Professional Resume Writer. She received a bachelor of arts degree from Rowan University and holds a master of business administration degree from Argosy University, with a concentration in human resources.

Thea Kelley

Thea Kelley is a certified coach and resume writer who has been facilitating career success for more than 10 years, first through larger agencies and since 2008 as Thea Kelley Career Services. A former training specialist, Thea understands the talent development field and enjoys working with learning and development professionals. She is skilled in interviewing individuals to discover their unique brand and helping them tell their story in a way that is both authentic and strategic. Her specialties include interview coaching and writing LinkedIn profiles for clients nationwide. Thea holds a degree in journalism and has 20 years of professional writing and editing experience. In addition, she is a Certified Professional Resume Writer, Global Career Development Facilitator, and a Certified Professional and Personal Coach.

Laura Labovich

As CEO of The Career Strategy Group, an outplacement firm in Bethesda, Maryland, Laura Labovich's contagious enthusiasm and powerful methodology make the perfect recipe for getting job seekers unstuck in their job search. She began her career with Walt Disney World, where she recruited nationwide for the Walt Disney World College Program, and America Online, where she launched the first company-wide internship program. Laura has contributed to the *Washington Post*, Sirius XM Radio, Fox News, NBC, *USA Today*, the *Chicago Tribune*, Yahoo, and Monster.com. She is the co-author of *100 Conversations for Career Success: Learn to Network, Cold-Call, and Tweet Your Way to Your Dream Job*, which was a 2013 Top Career Book Selection by *Forbes*. She is also author of the comprehensive job search course HIRED!

Sheila L. Margolis

Sheila Margolis holds a doctoral degree in human resource development, teaches part time at the J. Mack Robinson College of Business at Georgia State University, and is president of the Workplace Culture Institute. As an organizational culture expert, Sheila is quoted in newspapers and magazines including the *Wall Street Journal*, the *Washington Post*, and the *Atlanta Journal-Constitution*. Her expertise is in defining organizational culture, managing organizational change, and increasing employee engagement. Sheila is the author of the facilitator and participant guides for Building a Culture of Distinction, the organizational culture and change management program.

Lakeisha Mathews

Lakeisha Mathews is an independent career coach and director of the Career and Professional Development Center at the University of Baltimore. Committed to helping professionals find their passion, achieve their dreams, and refine their brand, Lakeisha is a dynamic career coach and higher education administrator who excels in collaboration, curriculum development, innovation, and project management. As a coach, she enjoys helping clients and students clarify goals and strategize action steps. She has worked with a broad range of clients in a variety of industries. Lakeisha holds several certifications, including Certified Professional Resume Writer, Certified Professional Career Coach, and Global Career Development Facilitator.

Nicole Miller

Nicole Miller has more than 20 years of experience in the career development field, including stints as a school support counselor helping guide students and as a vocational counselor helping injured employees re-enter the workforce. Her knowledge and experience served her well when she was appointed to be coordinator of a career center for military families. She is currently the assistant director of learning and professional development at the University of Ottawa in Canada. Nicole was the first person in Canada to receive the coveted Certified Resume Writer distinction; she is also a Certified Electronic Career Coach and an International Job and Career Transition Coach. Her work has appeared in many career publications, and she co-authored the e-book *Have Career . . . Will Travel.*

Michelle Riklan

Michelle Riklan has a combined 25 years of in-house corporate and targeted consulting experience. She services large corporations, small businesses, and individuals in all aspects of human resources and career management. Michelle is an internationally recognized, award-winning resume writer, and a member of several prestigious career, training, and resume writing organizations. As a Certified Professional Resume Writer and Certified Employment Interview Consultant, Michelle has written hundreds of resumes and coached clients through all phases of the job search. She holds a BA in theatre, English literature, and speech communications from Hofstra University, and an MA in speech and interpersonal communications from New York University.

Dan Schwartz

Dan Schwartz is the founder and chief education officer of the Ground Floor Leadership Institute (formerly College Coach Dan). He is a contributing author for the Association for Talent Development and a member of the coaching staff for Campus Career Coach.

He has published several articles in the areas of career development, leadership development, employee engagement, and learning and development. He is the author of *Winning Strategies: Achieving Success in the Classroom, Career, and Life,* and the *TD at Work* issue, "Managing as a Ground Floor Leader." Dan also works as a research and organizational development specialist for GEHA.

Barbara Seifert

Barbara Seifert is the founder and president of Committed to Your Success Coaching & Consulting. She has more than 25 years' experience in the workforce, holding various management positions in both corporate and nonprofit organizations. Barbara has mentored and trained employees and business leaders to become successful and achieve their personal, professional, and organizational goals. Barbara has a PhD in leadership and education, with a specialization in human resource development. She is a Certified Professional Coach and a Licensed Clinical Social Worker and Qualified Supervisor. Barbara is an adjunct professor at Webster University and is also on faculty at Florida Institute of Technology.

Lynne M. Williams

Lynne M. Williams is an on-site local and virtual assistant providing support to people in career transition, busy executives, solopreneurs, and small businesses. As the founder and owner of Around the Clock Executive Helper, Lynne provides executive assistance and operations management for sales, marketing, social media, and administrative work. Lynne is also an experienced trainer, researcher, and writer. She has a BS in business administration marketing from the University of Delaware, and an MA and doctoral work in educational leadership from Immaculata University. Lynne does training workshops on LinkedIn and other career transition topics, and has done extensive research and writing on web 2.0 social media applications.

Marie Zimenoff

As CEO of Career Thought Leaders and Resume Writing Academy, Marie Zimenoff is on a mission to change the world one career success story at a time. She develops content and training across multiple mediums to keep careerists and careers industry professionals ahead of trends. Using pioneering strengths-based coaching and marketing techniques, she consistently improves outcomes for job seekers, entrepreneurs, and organizations. Marie holds a master's degree in counseling and career development and the industry's top certifications in career coaching, leadership coaching, branding, and resume writing: Nationally Certified Counselor, Master Resume Writer, Certified Career Management Coach, and Certified Executive and Leadership Development Coach.

Index